M&E PROFESSIONAL STUDIES

Written by a team of practising lecturers and prepared under the General Editorship of a leading partnership of accountancy tutors, the *M & E Professional Studies* series has been specially designed to meet the course needs of professional students in virtually all the examined subjects at appropriate professional levels. The titles cover many of the subjects offered by the ACCA, the ICA, the ICMA, the AAT, the LCCI, the RSA and numerous other bodies.

With their carefully structured, thoroughly updated and revised texts, most titles include end-of-chapter progress tests (cross-referenced to the text, or, where worked answers are required, to an appendix), a large number of practice examination questions and suggested answers, a glossary of the more difficult key terms, and a very comprehensive index. An extensive programme of classroom testing, student surveys and independent assessment has been carefully completed in relation to this series prior to publication.

With twenty substantial texts in the series, *M & E Professional Studies* constitutes a major contribution to business education literature. They will enable students throughout the English-speaking world to gain the syllabus-related depth of knowledge and practice necessary to ensure a successful examination result.

GENERAL EDITORS

Emile Woolf

Emile Woolf first qualified in 1961 and joined the London Office of Deloitte Haskins & Sells. Since 1964 he has played a major part in pioneering accountancy education, first at Foulks Lynch and the London School of Accountancy, and then as founder and Chairman of the Emile Woolf Colleges in London and overseas. In 1984 he became a partner in Kingston Smith & Co. with special responsibility for technical standards and training. He is an established author, and a regular contributor to numerous professional and student journals and magazines in the UK and overseas. In 1980 he received the Distinguished Services Award for Authorship at Hartford University, Connecticut, USA. Recently he was commissioned by the ACCA to produce a series of audio cassettes and workbooks for students throughout the world. Between 1973 and 1979 he was also an Examiner for the ACCA in Advanced Auditing and Investigations. Emile Woolf lectures regularly on accountancy, financial and economic matters in Ireland, the UK, USA, Trinidad, Jamaica, Singapore, Hong Kong, Malaysia, Ghana and elsewhere. He also conducts seminars on financial management topics for industrial and commercial clients as well as for professional accountancy firms.

Suresh Tanna

Suresh Tanna graduated in 1971 in chemical engineering from Edinburgh University. Following a career in business management he qualified as a chartered accountant in 1978. In 1981 he joined Karam Singh in setting up the City Accountancy Centre, which merged with the Emile Woolf Schools in March 1983, and is now Director of Studies on ACCA courses, and Financial Director of the enlarged FACT Group. He specialises in accounting, advanced accounting practice and advanced financial accounting.

Karam Singh

After a period of project planning with Burmah Oil as a graduate chemical engineer, Karam Singh obtained his MBA from the Liverpool Business School whilst also engaged in part-time consultancy work for clothing manufacturers and retailers and research at a P & O subsidiary. In 1971 he joined the London accountancy firm of Harmood Banner and Company which later merged with Deloittes. He qualified as a chartered accountant in 1974, and lectured for several years at the London School of Accountancy and the North East London Polytechnic. In 1981 he joined Suresh Tanna in the formation of the City Accountancy Centre, where he began to develop study material geared for in-school and home studies students. At present he is Principal Lecturer for the FACT schools for Level 2 ACCA courses, specialising in quantitative analysis. He has contributed numerous articles to the various professional and students' journals.

Contributing authors

The titles in this series have been prepared under the General Editorship of Emile Woolf, Suresh Tanna and Karam Singh in conjunction with the staff and tutors of the FACT Organisation, 23 Hand Court, High Holborn, London WC1V 6JF. All contributors and authors are practising lecturers with many years' experience of teaching accountancy at all levels.

M&E PROFESSIONAL STUDIES

MANAGEMENT ACCOUNTING

by David Benjamin ACCA
Lecturer in Management Accounting and Costing
EW FACT Colleges

General Editors

Emile Woolf FCA FCCA FBIM
Suresh Tanna BSc(Hons) FCA
Karam Singh BTech MBA FCA

MACDONALD & EVANS

Pitman Publishing Ltd
128 Long Acre, London WC2E 9AN

A Longman Group Company

First published 1986

© Emile Woolf and Associates Ltd 1986

British Library Cataloguing in Publication Data
Benjamin, David
  Management accounting.—(M & E professional
  studies, ISSN 0266–8475)
  1. Managerial accounting—Great Britain
  I. Title
  658.1'511'0941   HF5635

  ISBN 0–7121–0493–3

Phototypesetting by
Anneset, Weston-super-Mare
and printed in Great Britain by
The Bath Press, Avon

Preface

Management accounting has in recent times become an ever more complex and challenging field for the practitioner and student alike, and this is increasingly reflected in the greater difficulties posed by the student syllabuses and examination papers set by the professional bodies. This book covers the new ACCA syllabus in particular, though it will also be invaluable for a large number of students of other professional bodies taking examinations in management accounting.

The text comprises short yet detailed chapters dealing with the basic principles of each aspect of the subject, plus relevant past examination questions with suggested worked answers provided as practice material in a series of appendixes. Each chapter has been logically and concisely written to facilitate study. Students should attempt to master both the topic under review and its associated examination questions in the appendixes before proceeding to the next chapter.

Chapters 2 to 6 include elements of costing, and will be of great use to those students with little basic knowledge of cost accounting, and those who wish to refresh their memories of this fundamental aspect of management accounting. A chapter on the application of quantitative analysis to management accounting has also been included to reflect recent trends in the setting of examination questions.

It should, however, be remembered that management accounting is not just a computational subject. It also involves the *interpretation* of the information provided for decision-making, planning and control purposes within a wide range of business and other enterprises. It is hoped therefore that an appropriate balance has been struck between the mathematical and the descriptive elements in the book, though the student should be reminded to attach equal importance to both of these areas.

The book concludes with a large number of examination-style questions accompanied by separate suggested answers. To achieve maximum benefit from this material students should attempt to answer these questions within a strict time limit under test conditions and without consulting the answers provided. In this way students will not only test the real extent of their knowledge and understanding, but also become familiar with the standard and type of question they will eventually encounter in their final examinations.

Contents

List of Illustrations

CHAPTER ONE

An Introduction to Management Accounting

1.0 DEFINITION

Management accounting is the application of accounting techniques to the provision of information designed to assist all levels of management in planning and controlling the activities of the firm, and in decision-making.

It involves producing and interpreting accounting and statistical information in order to assist management in its function of maximising efficiency, and achieving corporate goals.

1.1 Planning

Management is responsible for the organisation and implementation of resources in order to attain corporate plans at the least cost.

1.2 Controlling

This ensures that plans are carried out, by measuring actual performance, comparing it against plans so that any differences (variances) can be investigated, and control action taken where necessary.

1.3 Decision-making

Management decisions include those made when planning and controlling operations, and other "one-off" decisions which occasionally arise in the running of a business.

2.0 COST ACCOUNTING

Cost accounting provides information about costs, which the management accountant then uses in order to plan, control and make decisions. Cost accounting, therefore, provides the basis for management accounting.

Cost and management accounting formulate a management information system, which assists management in its task of planning, controlling and decision-making.

3.0 MAJOR DIFFERENCES BETWEEN MANAGEMENT AND FINANCIAL ACCOUNTING

Financial accounting involves the preparation of a set of final accounts, for each accounting period, in accordance with accounting standards and company legislation. It is basically a stewardship duty, to report to the owners of a business how their stewards (directors) have performed.

The main differences between the old branch of accounting, and the newer branch, management accounting, are as follows:

(a) Financial accounting is concerned with shareholders, the Inland Revenue, the law, and other parties "outside" the firm, whereas management accounting is an internal function, not governed by statute, and concerning management and employees. Management accounting will, of course, take into consideration customers' needs, and competitors' behaviour.

(b) Financial accounting is the recording of historic information. However, management accounting uses present and future information. The past only acts as a guide in predicting the future.

(c) Financial accounting takes a bird's eye view of a business by aggregating the performance of its divisions and departments into a single aggregate financial statement of income. Management accounting focuses attention on the microlevels of the organisation, that is, at the lowest levels of production or processing. This is crucial in the daily running of a business, and is an integral part of profit maximisation.

Both financial and management accounting have their own separate, yet important, purposes and uses.

4.0 CONCLUSION

It is important, even at this early stage, to recognise that management accounting takes a multidiscipline approach, and looks at: economics for supply and demand data; psychology for the behavioural aspects of a situation; and quantitative analysis for statistical and operational research analysis.

CHAPTER TWO

Cost Classification

1.0 INTRODUCTION

A cost can be defined as the value attributed to a resource. There are three elements of a cost — *material, labour* and *services* (expenses).

Students should be aware that different costs are used for different purposes; in other words, the classification of a cost depends on the purpose for which it is required.

2.0 TYPES OF CLASSIFICATION

(a) By time when computed:

  (i) *Historic (sunk) costs* have already been incurred and cannot, therefore, be affected by a decision. They are irrelevant for decision-making purposes. However, future cash flows (*incremental costs*) are affected by decisions, and are therefore relevant.

  (ii) *Standard (planned) costs* are important for budgeting purposes. *Historic costs* are used for comparison with budgeted performance in order to highlight areas where control action may be necessary.

(b) By financial costing:

  (i) *Revenue costs* — these are incurred when running the business and charged to the profit and loss account.

  (ii) *Capital costs* — these are incurred in acquiring long-term assets, which are not purchased for resale purposes. This expenditure is shown in the balance sheet.

(c) By responsibility:

  (i)   *Controllable costs* — all costs are controllable in the long run. Some fixed
        costs (*discretionary costs*), such as advertising, accounting, legal, and
        research and development, can be controlled in the short run.

  (ii) *Uncontrollable costs* — include those fixed costs which cannot be reduced
        without injuring the ability to meet long-range goals. They are called
        committed costs, such as rent, rates, depreciation and insurance.

(d) By identification with stock (or timing of charges against revenue):

  (i)   Those costs identified as part of stock are called *product costs*, and only
        become expenses in the form of cost of goods sold when the stock is sold.

  (ii) Those costs which are not identified with stock are called *period costs*, and
        are deducted as expenses during the period in which they are incurred.
        They are not carried forward in the closing stock to the next period.

(e) By tracing costs to end-products:

  (i)   All costs which are identifiable with the end-product are called *direct costs*
        and include the following: raw material used in manufacturing the
        product — *direct material*; machine operators who make the product —
        direct labour; royalties paid or special plant hired — *direct expenses*.

  (ii) Those costs not identifiable with the end product are called *indirect costs*
        and include the following: lubricants and scrap metal — *indirect material*;
        supervisors — *indirect labour*; rent, rates and depreciation — *indirect
        expenses*. Indirect costs are often called *overheads*.

It is important to know for what purpose a cost is being identified. For example, if
identification is with a sales area, then a salesman's salary is a direct cost, but indirect
if identified with the end product.

(f) By function (analysis of overheads):
     Factory or production overheads are those indirect costs incurred within the
     factory, for example, factory depreciation, power, rent and supervisors'
     salaries. Administration overheads include office rent, rates, power and
     salaries. Selling and distribution overheads include advertising,
     transportation, salesmen's salaries and depreciation and insurance on
     salesmen's vehicles.

(g) By behaviour (in relation to changes in activity):
     Each cost has some true cost behaviour pattern, called a *cost function*, which
     helps in the prediction of changes in costs (that is, cost estimation — *see*
     Chapter 3).
        The cost behaviour indicates the way in which costs vary with the level of
     activity. Level of activity may take the form of units of output, hours worked,
     sales, etc.

  (i)   A *fixed cost* is a cost which is unaffected by changes in the level of activity,
        such as salaries, rent and depreciation (Fig. 1).

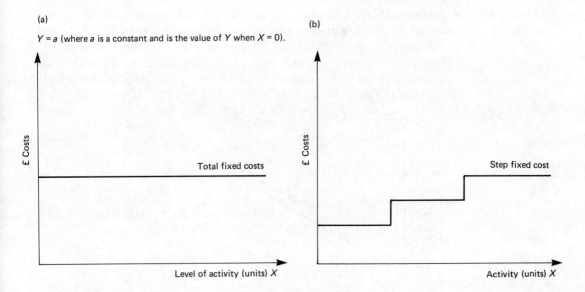

(a)

$Y = a$ (where a is a constant and is the value of Y when $X = 0$).

(b)

Fig. 1. *Fixed costs.*
(a) Although the total fixed cost is constant, the unit fixed cost decreases as output increases. (b) Fixed costs are subject to managerial decisions and will not therefore remain constant. In the long run as activity increases and more accommodation, plant and staff are required, fixed costs will increase in a step-like fashion.

      (ii)   A *variable cost* is a cost which is sensitive to changes in the firm's level of activity (Fig. 2). A variable cost will change immediately some alteration occurs to direct materials or direct labour or direct expenses.

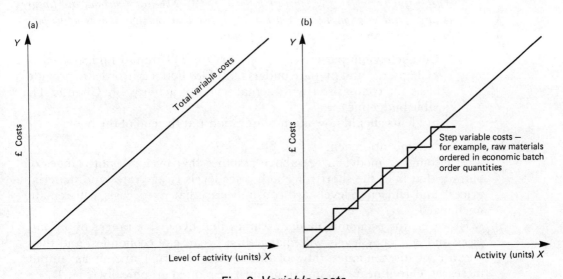

(a)

(b)

Fig. 2. *Variable costs.*
(a) Although total variable costs increase as activity increases, the unit variable cost is constant. (b) Most variable costs are also step costs, but the steps are too small to be significant and tend to be ignored.

(iii) *A semi-variable (mixed) cost* is a cost which comprises both fixed and variable elements, for example, a telephone cost consisting of a fixed rental charge, and variable costs associated with the calls made (Fig. 3).

Total costs for an organisation are the sum of its fixed and variable costs and therefore have the same cost behaviour pattern as semi-variable costs (*see* also Fig. 3).

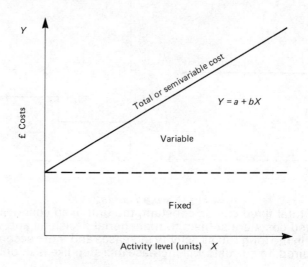

Fig. 3. *Relationship between semivariable and total costs.*

Note: The graphs in Figs 1–3 have assumed that: (1) The relationship between the dependent and independent variables is a credible one, and there is only one independent variable affecting cost behaviour. (2) The cost functions are linear (straight line relationships), which will suffice over relevant ranges of output, beyond which curvilinear functions are required.

Cost behaviour patterns are necessary to: (1) Estimate budgeted costs (*see* Chapter 3) and prepare budgets. (2) Flex budgets in order to provide a basis for comparison with actual levels of activity (*see* Chapter 11, flexible budgeting).

Students should now attempt question 1 at the end of the book.

(h) By an economic approach:

The accounting model in (g) above assumes that over relevant ranges of output, that is in the short run, both price levels (wage rates and material prices) and efficiency levels are constant and that fixed costs will remain unchanged.

However, the economic model assumes that over wide ranges of output, price and efficiency levels will change first because of economies, and then because of diseconomies (law of diminishing returns) arising as output increases. Curvilinear cost functions must be plotted graphically (Fig. 4).

From Fig. 4 it can be seen that over the relevant range both models provide similar cost estimates. Because of this similarity, and the fact that curvilinear cost functions are time-consuming and difficult to construct, the traditional accounting model is usually used.

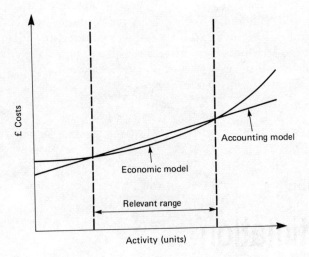

Fig. 4. *Total costs according to economic and accounting models.*

3.0 CONCLUSION

The above types of cost do not comprise an exhaustive list, and other ways of classification will be encountered in later chapters.

Students should not be obsessed with terminology, but rather with the basic principles which underlie the labels used to describe the costs.

It is important to identify the purpose for which the cost is required in order to classify it correctly.

CHAPTER THREE

Cost Estimation

1.0 INTRODUCTION

Cost estimation occurs when one attempts to measure historical costs in order to predict future costs. To achieve this measurement it is necessary to separate costs into their fixed and variable elements. Semivariable (mixed) costs can be separated, using the following techniques:

(a) The accounts classification method.

(b) The industrial engineering approach.

(c) The scattergraph.

(d) Regression analysis.

(e) High–low method.

2.0 ACCOUNTS CLASSIFICATION METHOD

This method entails the examination of the accounting records and the classification of each item of expenditure into one of three categories: variable, fixed, or semivariable costs.

Although it is a quick and inexpensive method, it has a considerable subjective element and can be inaccurate.

3.0 THE INDUSTRIAL ENGINEERING APPROACH

This method is suitable where no previous cost records exist or where circumstances have significantly changed. It involves quantifying in physical terms the level of input needed to sustain a particular level of output. Work study methods may be employed. These physical inputs are then transformed into standard or budgeted costs.

The engineering approach is expensive, and cannot be used in administration and other departments where the physical relationships between inputs and outputs may be difficult to establish. However, it can be an accurate method when used for the right purposes.

4.0 THE SCATTERGRAPH

In this graphical method historic costs from earlier periods and activity data are plotted, and a "line-of-best-fit" is then drawn (Fig. 5).

The dotted line drawn to show the intersection with the vertical axis estimates the fixed element of the cost. The slope of the line-of-best-fit represents the variable element.

This visual method is easy to use and understand, but is subjective and can be inaccurate.

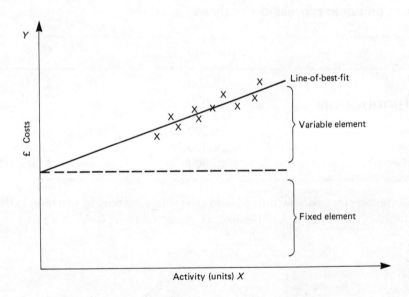

Fig. 5. *Example of a scattergraph.*

5.0 REGRESSION ANALYSIS

The graphical method of obtaining a line-of-best-fit is obviously inaccurate. Another approach to determining a regression line from a set of data is the *least squares method.*

Before linear regression analysis can be used it is necessary to make the following assumptions:

(a) There exists a cause and effect relationship between the variables.

(b) There is good evidence of correlation.

(c) Linearity in costs exists.

(d) The historic data used covers a large range of activity levels, otherwise a small error in the slope of the cost line, when extrapolated back to the Y axis, can give a large error in the fixed cost value.

(e) Where inflation exists historic costs have been adjusted by means of a price level index.

(f) Past circumstances will continue in the future.

(g) Only one independent variable (activity base) affects cost.

Multiple regression recognises that more than one factor can affect costs, for example, output, labour efficiency, time of year, political and economic circumstances. In order to calculate multiple regression coefficients and so derive estimates of a cost function, a computer package must be used.

Example 1: on linear regression analysis

1983	Service costs (£)	Hours
July	13,600	2,100
August	15,800	2,800
September	14,500	2,200
October	16,200	3,000
November	14,900	2,600
December	15,000	2,500

Analyse the service costs into fixed and variable elements in order to estimate the costs for January 1984 when 3,500 hours are expected to be used.

SOLUTION
$y = a + bx$

and

$$b = \frac{\Sigma (x - \bar{x}) (y - \bar{y})}{\Sigma (x - \bar{x})^2}$$

y = total cost; a = fixed cost; b = variable cost/hour; x = number of hours.
(Other formulae can be used.)

Costs y	Hours x	$(y - \bar{y})$	$(x - \bar{x})$	$(x - \bar{x})^2$	$(x - \bar{x})(y - \bar{y})$
£13,600	2,100	−1,400	− 433	+ 187,489	+ 606,200
15,800	2,800	+ 800	+ 266	+ 70,756	+ 212,800
14,500	2,200	− 500	− 333	+ 110,889	+ 166,500
16,200	3,000	+ 1,200	+ 466	+ 217,156	+ 559,200
14,900	2,600	− 100	+ 67	+ 4,489	− 6,700
15,000	2,500	—	− 33	+ 1,089	—
£90,000	15,200	—	—	591,868	1,538,000

Average of $y = \bar{y} = \dfrac{90,000}{6} = 15,000$

Average of $x = \bar{x} = \dfrac{15,200}{6} = 2,533 \cdot 3$

$\therefore$ Variable cost $= \dfrac{1,538,000}{591,868} = £2 \cdot 5985$ per hour

$\therefore$ Fixed cost $= £15,000 - (£2 \cdot 5985 \times 2,533 \text{ hours}) = £8,418$

$\therefore$ Estimated costs for January 1984:

Fixed costs	=	£8,418
Variable costs	=	£9,095
Total cost	=	£17,513

6.0   THE HIGH–LOW METHOD

In this method two previous accounting periods are chosen; the periods with the highest and lowest activity levels. The difference between the total costs of these activity levels will be the variable cost of the difference in activity levels.

Example 2

The costs of a service department for the last five periods are as follows:

Period	£ Costs	Activity level in hours
1	300,000	21,000
2	345,000	24,000
3	291,000	18,000
4	333,000	23,100
5	343,500	24,600

Estimate the costs for period 6 if the activity level is expected to be 23,000 hours.

SOLUTION

Highest activity level	24,600 hours	total cost	£343,500
Lowest activity level	18,000 hours	total cost	£291,000

Variable cost of the difference in activity levels	= 6,600 hours		£52,500

$$\therefore \text{ Variable cost per hour} = \frac{£52,500}{6,600} \text{ hours} = £7.95 \text{ per hour}$$

By using either the low or the high activity level the fixed costs can now be determined.

	Low level (18,000 hours) £		High level (24,600 hours) £
Total cost:	291,000		343,500
Variable costs (18,000 × £7·95)	143,100	(24,600 × £7·95)	195,570
∴ Fixed costs:	147,900		147,930
Fixed costs are approximately £147,900.			
Estimated costs for period 6:			
Variable costs (23,000 hours at £7·95)			£182,850
Fixed costs:			£147,900
∴ Total costs:			£330,750

Students should note the following:

(a) The highest and lowest activity periods may not be, as above, the periods with the highest and lowest cost.

(b) To allow for inflation, costs could be adjusted by a price level index.

(c) The high–low method is a simple and useful method to use in examination questions. However, it is unlikely to be very accurate as only two periods have been used in the computation and these periods may not be truly representative of all the past periods.

7.0 CONCLUSION

The choice of technique will depend on a cost/benefit analysis, and a trade-off between accuracy and simplicity. The learning curve (*see* Chapter 17) is another very important means of estimating costs.

CHAPTER FOUR

Overhead and Absorption Costing Principles

1.0 INTRODUCTION

Overheads were described in Chapter 2 as those costs which are not identifiable with the end-product, that is, indirect costs. However, these costs must be absorbed into the end-product in order to determine profit, value stock, and facilitate pricing. This chapter describes, in detail, the treatment of overheads in absorption costing.

Before students proceed they must be aware of two important points:

(a) Absorption costing only applies to production costs. Administration, selling and distribution overheads are charged to the profit and loss account as period costs, that is, they are not absorbed into the costs of goods sold;

(b) The production overheads absorbed are budgeted, not actual, costs. This is because:

   (i)   Actual overheads are often not known until the end of the year. This can cause considerable delays in the collection of data about actual costs;

   (ii) Fluctuations in costs between periods may arise owing to differing levels of efficiency or production. This, in turn, would result in variations in selling prices.

2.0 STAGES IN THE ANALYSIS AND ABSORPTION OF OVERHEADS

(a) Overheads are recorded and cost centres are established. A *cost centre* is any area of activity which attracts costs. It could be a machine, a salesman, or a department. The latter may comprise a number of cost centres.

Example 1

	Production overheads	Departments (Cost centres)				Total costs
		Production		Service		
		A (Machining)	B (Assembly)	1 (Maintenance)	2 (Stores)	
(i)	Managers' salaries	£1,000	£1,000	£1,000	£1,000	£4,000
(ii)	Depreciation of equipment	200	400	100	100	800
(iii)	Indirect labour	2,000	1,000	5,000	3,000	11,000
(iv)	Power					1,800
(v)	Rates					3,000
(vi)	Depreciation of buildings					600
(vii)	Heating, lighting					900
						£22,100

(b) In so far as one has failed to do so in the first stage, the second stage requires the allocation and apportioning of overheads to cost centres.

Overheads that can be specifically identified with a cost centre may be directly allocated to that centre, such as (i), (ii) and (iii) in the above example. Other overheads require apportionment using the following appropriate bases:

Overhead	Basis
Power	Horsepower or number of machines, or power points
Heat/light	Cubic capacity of space used, or number of radiators
Depreciation	Book value of machinery
Rent and rates	Area occupied
Canteen, wages and administration	Number of employees or labour hours

It will be evident in an examination question whether an overhead should be allocated or apportioned.

However, in the event of apportionment being required students will apply two basic rules when selecting an appropriate basis: (i) convenience of the base; (ii) the causal relationship between the base and the overhead, for example, area and rent.

Basis	Production		Service	
	A	B	1	2
Personnel (employees)	50	20	20	10
Number of machines	5 ($\frac{1}{3}$)	10 ($\frac{2}{3}$)	—	—
Floor area (sq. ft.)	1,000 ($\frac{1}{3}$)	1,000 ($\frac{1}{3}$)	500 ($\frac{1}{6}$)	500 ($\frac{1}{6}$)
Cubic volume (cu. ft.)	20,000 ($\frac{1}{3}$)	30,000 ($\frac{1}{2}$)	5,000 ($\frac{1}{12}$)	5,000 ($\frac{1}{12}$)

Overhead	Basis	Production		Service		Total
		A	B	1	2	
Power	Machines	£600	£1,200	—	—	£1,800
Rates	Floor area	1,000	1,000	£500	£500	3,000
Heating	Cubic volume	300	450	75	75	900
Depreciation of buildings	Cubic volume	200	300	50	50	600
Apportioned overheads		2,100	2,950	625	625	6,300
Allocated overheads:						
Managers' salaries		1,000	1,000	1,000	1,000	4,000
Depreciation of equipment		200	400	100	100	800
Indirect labour		2,000	1,000	5,000	3,000	11,000
Total overhead:		5,300	5,350	6,725	4,725	22,100

(c) The third stage is to reapportion or reallocate costs of the service departments to the production departments. This is necessary as units of output do not pass through service departments, and we are trying to charge all production overheads (including service departmental overheads) to these units of output.

Wherever possible service departments' overheads should be allocated to production departments, but when this is not possible, then apportionment, previously described, must be followed. However, a problem arises when service departments serve each other as well as the production departments; for example:

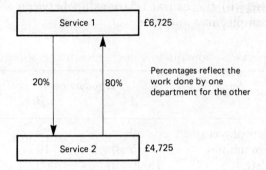

Service department 1 cannot apportion its costs until those of service department 2 have been received. But the same problem exists with service department 2. Two unknowns exist.

The following methods can be used to overcome this problem: (i) the direct method, and (ii) the repeated distribution or algebraic method.

Service department	to — 1	to — 2	Production Departments to — A	to — B	Total units
from — 1	. —	200	700	100	1,000
from — 2	1,600	—	400	—	2,000

The "units" referred to above reflect the benefit derived by each cost centre from each service department.

Direct method

This method ignores the reciprocal services between the service departments, and allocates their costs directly to the production departments.

Service department			Production department A		B
1	£6,725	$\frac{700}{800}$	£5,884	$\frac{100}{800}$	£841
2	4,725	$\frac{400}{400}$	£4,725	—	—
	£11,450		£10,609		£841

The direct method is simple to apply, but lacks accuracy.

Algebraic method

Let X = Service department 1 costs plus those apportioned from service
   department 2.
Let Y = Service department 2 costs plus those apportioned from service
   department 1.

Then $X = 6,725 + 0 \cdot 8Y$
      $Y = 4,725 + 0 \cdot 2X$

$\therefore X = 6,725 + 0 \cdot 8 \,(4,725 + 0 \cdot 2X)$ by substitution

$\therefore X = 6,725 + 3,780 + 0 \cdot 16X$

$\therefore 0.84X = 10,505$

$\therefore X = £12,506$

$Y = 4,725 + 0 \cdot 2 \,(12,506)$

$\therefore Y = £7,226$

Service department		Production department			
			A		B
1	£12,506	$\dfrac{700}{1,000}$	£8,754	$\dfrac{100}{1,000}$	£1,251
2	£7,226	$\dfrac{400}{2,000}$	£1,445	—	—
	£11,450	=	£10,199	+	£1,251

The repeated distribution method

Under this method each service department's costs are repeatedly apportioned by closing and reopening each department.

Service department		1 (20%)		2 (80%)	
		6,725		4,725	
	Closing	(6,725)	20% →	1,345	
		—		6,070	
	Reopening	4,856	← 80%	(6,070)	Closing
		(4,856)		971	Reopening
		777		(971)	

(777)	155
———	(155)
124	———
(124)	25
———	(25)
20	———
(20)	4
———	(4)
3	———
(3)	1
———	(1)
0	———

Total of distributions   £12,505   £7,226
i.e. sum of "closings".

Students will note that had department 2 been closed first, total distributions would be the same as the above.

Service department		Production department	
		A	B
1	£12,505	$\frac{700}{1,000}$ £ 8,754	$\frac{100}{1,000}$ £1,251
2	£7,226	$\frac{400}{2,000}$ £1,445	—
	£11,450 =	£10,199	£1,251

Both the repeated distribution and algebraic methods are accurate ways of apportioning service overheads.

Note: Further aspects of service departments:
Service departments' costs can be apportioned to other departments by using statistical cost allocation, that is, basing apportionment on a sample of jobs done.

Students also should consider the following points:

(i)   The managers of service departments will have no incentive, unless the charges made to other departments include an element of profit.

(ii) Unless other departments are charged according to the amount of service they use, (1) they will become greedy in their requirements; (2) it will not be known whether service departments are running efficiently; (3) there will be difficulty in deciding whether a service should be internally supplied, or acquired externally from a supplier.

(d) Now that all overheads have been allocated and/or apportioned they must be absorbed into the units of output. The fourth and final stage is therefore to determine overhead absorption (recovery) rates in order that this absorption may be achieved.

The general formula for an overhead absorption rate is:

$$\text{Rate} = \frac{\text{Budgeted overhead}}{\text{Level of activity}}$$

Let us apply this formula to Example 1.

	Production department	
	A (Machine)	B (Assembly)
Overheads	£5,300	£5,350
Service overheads	£10,199	£1,251
Total budgeted overheads	£15,499	£6,601
Level of activity	5,000 machine hours	6,600 labour hours
Rate =	£3·10 overhead per machine hour =	£1·00 overhead per labour hour

In the above example machine and labour hours have been chosen as the bases for overhead recovery as appropriate for their respective departments.

When determining overhead rates there are two things which must be carefully considered.

(i)   the choice of the basis of recovery;

(ii) the choice of activity level.

3.0   BASIS OF OVERHEAD ABSORPTION (RECOVERY)

Although machine hours and direct labour hours are frequently used for recovering overheads in machine and labour-intensive cost centres respectively, other possible choices are:

(a) Units of output where all units are homogeneous.

(b) A percentage of direct labour cost. This method can be dangerous as a job performed by a skilled and therefore more highly paid employee will be charged with more overhead than the same job being performed by a less skilled, lower-paid employee. Yet the latter may use a greater amount of overhead.

(c) A percentage of material cost where the value of materials has a significant relationship with the overhead, for example, the allocation of stores overheads.

(d) A percentage of prime cost.

In deciding on a suitable basis students should consider ease of application, and use as a base some measure which seems to be associated with the cause of the overheads. Direct labour hours and machine hours are most widely used.

Administration overheads are absorbed as a percentage of factory cost, and selling and distribution overheads as a percentage of sales or factory cost.

Example 2

Job XYZ requires five hours of direct labour (which include three hours of machine work) being 4 hours at £0·65/hour, and 1 hour at £0·40/hour. Direct material cost is £12. Administration overheads are to be absorbed on the basis of 10% of factory cost, and selling and distribution overheads on the basis of 20% of factory cost.

The following types of rates for absorbing production overhead are available:

Units of output	—	£2/unit
Direct labour hour	—	£0.50/hour
Machine hour	—	£0.625/hour
Wage %	—	100%
Material cost %	—	$33\frac{1}{3}$%

(a) Show the possible production overhead charges for this job;

(b) Arrive at a total cost using material cost % as a basis.

SOLUTION
Possible production overhead charges

(a) Units of output   =   £2/unit × 1 unit = £2
      Direct labour hour =   £0·50/hr × 5 hours = £2.50
      Machine hour   =   £0·625/hr × 3 hours = £1·875
      Wage %   =   100% of [4 × £0·65 + 1 × £0·40] = £3·00
      Material cost %   = $33\frac{1}{3}$ of £12 = £4

(b)		
Direct labour [4 × £0·65 + 1 × £0·40]	=	3·00
Direct material		12·00
Prime cost		15·00
Production overhead ($33\frac{1}{3}$% of £12)		4·00
Factory (production) cost		19·00
Administration overhead (10% of £19·0)		1·90
Selling and distribution overhead		
(20% of £19·0)		3·80
Total cost		£24·70

4.0   CHOICE OF ACTIVITY LEVEL

Activity levels can range from *actual activity* (that level of output experienced over the period in question) to *budgeted activity* anticipated for the period to *normal activity* (that level which represents a long-run average).

   Normal activity is usually used in preference to budgeted activity, since the latter can fluctuate and thereby cause absorbed overheads per unit to fluctuate, which in turn results in fluctuating gross profits.

Example 3

Years	Sales price/ unit	Variable cost/ unit	Units produced	Units sold	Budgeted costs fixed production
1	£10	£3	10,000	8,000	£30,000
2	£10	£3	8,000	8,000	£30,000
3	£10	£3	6,000	8,000	£30,000

There are no opening stocks.

Absorbing overheads on a budgeted activity level, the following results would occur:

	Year 1		Year 2		Year 3
Sales		£80,000		£80,000	£80,000
Opening stock	£0		£12,000		£13,500
Production costs					
Variable	30,000		24,000		18,000
Fixed	30,000		30,000		30,000
	60,000		66,000		61,500
Less: Closing stock	(12,000)*		(13,500)*		(0)
		(48,000)		(52,500)	(61,500)
Gross profit		£32,000		£27,500	£18,500
*Variable cost	£3		£3		
Absorption rate	£3 (£30,000 ÷ 10,000 units)		£3·75 (£30,000 ÷ 8,000 units)		
Closing stock	£6 × 2,000 units = £12,000		£6·75 × 2,000 units = £13,500		

Absorbing overheads on a normal level of activity (assuming an average of 8,000 units, and therefore an absorption rate of £30,000 ÷ 8,000 units = £3·75/unit), the following results would appear:

	Year 1		Year 2		Year 3	
Sales		£80,000		£80,000		£80,000
Opening stock	£0		£13,500		£13,500	
Production costs						
Variable	30,000		24,000		18,000	
Fixed	37,500		30,000		22,500	
	67,500		67,500		54,000	
Less: Closing stock	(13,500) *		(13,500) *			(0)
		54,000		54,000		54,000
Gross profit		£26,000		£26,000		£26,000
*Variable cost	£3		£3			
Fixed cost	£3·75		£3·75			

£6·75 × 2,000 units = £13,500   £6·75 × 2,000 units = £13,500

Students will note how a normal level of activity provides a better measure of performance each year than the budgeted activity level.

However, it may be difficult to set normal levels accurately over many years, because as a firm grows the notion of a normal level may be untrue, as output will be continually rising.

5.0 DEPARTMENTAL ABSORPTION RATES

Unless a firm manufactures a single product via one process, then a single (blanket) factory absorption rate should not be used.

Separate absorption rates should be used for each department in order to (a) associate the rate with the cause of the overheads and (b) ensure that overheads are equitably charged.

Example 4

	Using a plantwide rate		Using separate departmental rates	
	Machine	Finishing	Machine	Finishing
Overheads	£200,000	£16,000	£200,000	£16,000
Direct labour hours	20,000	20,000	20,000	20,000
Plant rate = $\frac{£216,000}{40,000}$ hours =		£5·40/hour	Departmental rates =	£10/hour	£0·80 hour

Job 1
Labour time required = 1 machine hour and 10 finishing hours.
Plant charge = 11 hours at £5·40/hour = £59·40 of overhead.

Departmental charges = 1 hour at £10/hour + 10 hours at £0·80/hour = £18 of overhead.

Job 2

Labour time required = 9 machine hours and 2 finishing hours.
Plant charge = 11 hours at £5·40/hour = £59·40 of overhead.
Departmental charges = 9 hours at £10/hour + 2 hours at £0·80/hour = £91·60.

From the above it can be seen that using a plantwide rate, each job receives the same overhead charge. This cannot be right as job 1 requires more labour hours than machine hours and therefore should be charged with less overhead than job 2, which demands mainly machine hours.

A plantwide rate will therefore undercost a department with high overheads (machine department), and overcost a department with low overheads (finishing department). The individual departmental rates ensure that the overheads are equitably charged, and that each department has a level of activity in its rate which is associated with the cause of its costs, that is, machine department — machine hour rate, finishing department — direct labour hour rate.

Example 5

In Cobalt Ltd one factory overhead recovery rate, which is a percentage of direct labour cost, is used. The current recovery rate is calculated on the basis of the following budget:

Department	Labour cost £000s	Direct labour hours 000 hours	Machine hours 000 hours	Factory overheads £000s
W	160	40	10	25
X	225	90	—	90
Y	90	30	60	45
Z	175	70	—	35

Job number 2160 has just been completed and is ready for final pricing. The details so far are:

Department	Direct material	Direct labour cost	Direct labour hours	Machine hours
W	£400	£1,520	400	50
X	570	1,200	500	—
Y	1,300	370	100	220
Z	320	1,740	600	—

20% of factory cost is added to cover administrative costs, and a further 40% of total cost is added as profit, to arrive at selling price.

Required

   (a) Calculate the current overhead recovery rate.
   (b) Show the selling price of job number 2160, using the rate calculated in (a).
   (c) Calculate individual departmental overhead recovery rates, using the most appropriate bases.
   (d) Show the selling price of job number 2160, using the rates calculated in (c).

SOLUTION

   (a)

Labour cost £000	*Factory overheads £000*
160	25
225	90
90	45
175	35
650	195

$$\therefore \text{Current overhead rate} = \frac{195}{650} \times 100$$
$$= 30\%$$

   (b) Direct material

W	£400	
X	570	
Y	1,300	
Z	320	
		£2,590

Direct labour

W	£1,520	
X	1,200	
Y	370	
Z	1,740	
		4,830

Prime cost:	7,420
Factory overhead	
(30% of £4,830)	1,449
Factory cost:	8,869
Administration costs (20%)	1,773·80
Total cost:	10,642·80
Profit (40%)	4,257·10
Selling price:	£14,899·90

(c) Department Y being more capital-intensive than the other departments has more machine hours than direct labour hours. Machine hours may therefore be a better measure of utilisation. For all other departments, direct labour hours appears to be the dominant feature.

Department	Direct labour hours (000)	Machine hours (000)	Factory overheads £000	Recovery rates
W	40		25	£0·625/labour hour
X	90		90	1·0/labour hour
Y		60	45	0.75/machine hour
Z	70		35	0.5/labour hour

(d) Direct material

	W	£400	
	X	570	
	Y	1,300	
	Z	320	
		———	
			£2,590

Direct labour

	W	1,520	
	X	1,200	
	Y	370	
	Z	1,740	
		———	
			4,830

Prime cost	7,420

Factory overhead:

$400 \times £0·625 = 250$
$500 \times £1·00 = 500$
$220 \times £0·75 = 165$
$600 \times £0·50 = 300$
———

	1,215
Factory cost:	8,635
Administration costs (20%)	1,727
	———
Total cost:	10,362
Profit (40%)	4,144·80
	———
Selling price:	£14,506·80

6.0 UNDERABSORBED/OVERABSORBED OVERHEADS

The overhead absorption rate is predetermined by the estimated level of activity and the budgeted cost. Under-recovery or over-recovery will occur if either actual costs or actual activity differ from budget.

Example 6

Jones Ltd has a budgeted activity level of 50,000 direct labour hours and budgeted production overheads of £100,000. You are required to calculate the underabsorbed and overabsorbed overheads, giving reasons, if:

(a) 50,000 direct labour hours are worked and the actual overheads were £94,000.

(b) 43,000 direct labour hours are worked and the actual overheads were £100,000.

(c) 43,000 direct labour hours are worked and the actual overheads were £94,000.

SOLUTION

$$\text{Recovery rate} = \frac{£100,000}{50,000} \text{ hours} = \underline{£2/\text{hour}}$$

(a) Recovered overheads (50,000 hours × £2)   £100,000
     Actual overheads incurred: £ 94,000
                                                 Overabsorbed £   6,000

The reason for this overabsorption is expenditure — that is, actual costs are less than anticipated.

(b) Recovered overheads (43,000 hours × £2):   £ 86,000
     Actual overheads incurred: £100,000
                                         Underabsorbed £ 14,000

The reason for this underabsorption is a production volume variance — that is, 7,000 less hours were worked than expected at £2/hour = £14,000.

(c) Recovered overheads (43,000 hours × £2):   £ 86,000
     Actual overheads incurred: £ 94,000
                                         Underabsorbed £   8,000

The reason for this underabsorption is twofold:

(i)   production volume variance of (50,000 hours − 43,000 hours) × £2/hour
                                                   = £14,000 adverse

(ii)   expenditure variance of (£100,000 − £94,000) = £6,000 favourable
                                                      ─────────
                                                      £8,000 adverse
                                                      ─────────

Overabsorbed and underabsorbed overheads are charged to the profit and loss account via an underabsorbed/overabsorbed overhead account. Overabsorbed overheads will be credited to the profit and loss account, and underabsorbed overheads will be debited to it.

Students will observe that *overheads incurred* remain the same; whereas *overheads absorbed* (the spreading of the overheads amongst the output) increases as output increases. The difference between them is the underabsorbed/overabsorbed overhead.

7.0 CONCLUSION

The advantages and disadvantages of absorption costing are fully described in the next chapter. However, before this is read, students must completely master the basic principles of overhead absorption which permeate the entire syllabus.

CHAPTER FIVE

Marginal and Absorption Costing

1.0   INTRODUCTION

There are basically two methods of reporting profits. These methods are absorption and marginal costing, which can be defined in the following way:

Absorption costing (full product costing)

Each unit of output is charged with both variable and fixed production costs. The fixed production costs are treated as part of actual production. Closing stock is therefore valued on a full production cost basis, and when sold in the next period these costs are released and matched with the revenue of that period.

Marginal costing (direct or period costing)

Each unit of output is charged with variable production costs. Fixed production costs are not considered as actual costs of production, but rather as those costs which provide the capacity for a period which allows production to take place. They are therefore treated as costs of the period and charged to the period. They are not carried forward in closing stock, which is valued on a variable production cost basis.

2.0 COMPARATIVE INCOME STATEMENTS

Example 1

The following information relates to Success Ltd and to a new product that has been produced at the commencement of the period just completed:

Sales   10,000 units sold at £5 each.

Production   15,000 units were produced at the following costs:

Direct materials	£15,000
Direct labour	30,000
Variable expenses	6,000
Fixed expenses	12,000

(a) Prepare income statements for the period under absorption and marginal bases.

(b) Reconcile the resulting profits/losses.

SOLUTION

(a)

	Absorption costing		Marginal costing	
Sales		£50,000		£50,000
Costs of production:				
Direct materials	£15,000		£15,000	
Direct labour	30,000		30,000	
Variable overhead	6,000		6,000	
Fixed overhead	12,000		—	
	────		────	
	63,000		51,000	
Less: Closing stock*	(21,000)		(17,000)*	
(5,000 units)	────	(42,000)	────	(34,000)
			Contribution	16,000
			Less:	
			Fixed overhead	(12,000)
				────
Net profit		8,000		4,000

*Closing stocks:

$$\frac{5,000 \text{ units}}{15,000 \text{ units}} \times £63,000 = \underline{£21,000}$$

$$\frac{5,000 \text{ units}}{15,000 \text{ units}} \times £51,000 = \underline{£17,000}$$

(b) The difference between the profits of (£8,000 − £4,000) = £4,000 is owing to
the difference in stock valuations of (£21,000 − £17,000) = £4,000.

Under the marginal basis all the fixed overhead has been charged to the
period, whereas under the absorption basis one-third of the fixed overhead —
£4,000 — has been carried forward in closing stock, thereby escaping from the
income statement, and thus rendering it higher than the marginal statement.

Example 2

W Ltd manufactures and markets a standard product and the following standard cost
data for 1983 have been supplied:

	Per unit		Total
Sales (120,000 units)	£1·00		£120,000
Production cost of sales:			
Variable cost	0·65	£78,000	
Fixed cost	0·20	£24,000	
	—— (0·85)	———	(102,000)
Gross profit	0·15		18,000
Selling and administration costs			
(fixed)			(8,400)
		Net profit =	£9,600

It was anticipated that production would be equal to sales. But actual production, sales
and stocks for the year were:

| | *Quarters (Units)* | | | | |
	1	*2*	*3*	*4*	*Total*
Opening stock		6,000	2,000	7,000	
Production	34,000	28,000	33,000	27,000	122,000
Sales	28,000	32,000	28,000	32,000	120,000
Closing stock	6,000	2,000	7,000	2,000	2,000

(a) Prepare quarterly statements of profitability on the basis of absorption and
marginal costing.

(b) Reconcile the resulting profits.

SOLUTION

(a) *Marginal costing*

		Quarters			Total
	1	*2*	*3*	*4*	
Sales	£28,000	£32,000	£28,000	£32,000	£120,000
Less: Variable production costs — £0·65/unit of sales	(18,200)	(20,800)	(18,200)	(20,800)	(78,000)
Contribution	9,800	11,200	9,800	11,200	42,000
Less: Fixed costs/quarter					
Production	(6,000)	(6,000)	(6,000)	(6,000)	(24,000)
Selling and administration	(2,100)	(2,100)	(2,100)	(2,100)	(8,400)
Net profit	£1,700	£3,100	£1,700	£3,100	£9,600

Absorption costing

		Quarters			Total
	1	*2*	*3*	*4*	
Sales	£28,000	£32,000	£28,000	£32,000	£120,000
Less: Full production costs — £0·85/unit of sales	(23,800)	(27,200)	(23,800)	(27,200)	(102,000)
Gross profit	4,200	4,800	4,200	4,800	18,000
Less: Selling and administration costs	(2,100)	(2,100)	(2,100)	(2,100)	(8,400)
	2,100	2,700	2,100	2,700	9,600
*(Underabsorbed)/ overabsorbed fixed overhead	800*	(400)*	600*	(600)*	400
Net profit	£2,900	£2,300	£2,700	£2,100	£10,000

	Quarters (units)				Total units
	1	2	3	4	
Budgeted production	30,000	30,000	30,000	30,000	£120,000
Actual production	34,000	28,000	33,000	27,000	122,000
	4,000	2,000	3,000	3,000	2,000
(× Budgeted fixed overhead rate of £0·20) = *(Underabsorbed)/ overabsorbed fixed overhead	£800*	(£400)*	£600*	(£600)*	£400

(b) *Reconciliation of profits*

	Quarters				Total
	1	2	3	4	
Absorption profit	£2,900	£2,300	£2,700	£2,100	£10,000
Marginal profit	1,700	3,100	1,700	3,100	9,600
Difference	£1,200	£800	£1,000	£1,000	£400

	Units				Units— total
	1	2	3	4	
Opening stock	—	6,000	2,000	7,000	—
Closing stock	6,000	2,000	7,000	2,000	2,000
Difference (× Fixed production cost/unit of £0·20) =	+ 6,000 £1,200	− 4,000 £800	+ 5,000 £1,000	− 5,000 £1,000	+ 2,000 £400

The following points should be noted about the difference between reported profits' underabsorption and marginal bases.

(i)   The difference is unaffected by the underabsorption/overabsorption of fixed overheads in the absorption-costing approach.

(ii) The difference is one of timing; the actual amount of expenses does not differ, only the periods in which they are charged against profits.

   (A)   Where stock levels are constant or nil there is no difference;

(B) Where stocks are increasing, that is, closing stock exceeds opening stock, higher profits are reported under absorption costing, as some fixed costs are carried forward in the stock valuation;

(C) Where stocks are decreasing, the converse applies and higher profits are reported under marginal costing.

(iii) Over the complete life of a product both methods will show the same total profits, as in the long run, production equals sales, that is, there will be no changes in the volume of stocks.

3.0 ADVANTAGES OF ABSORPTION AND MARGINAL COSTING

(a) Marginal costing

(i) Most fixed costs, such as rent, depreciation, and salaries, relate to time, and therefore should be charged to the period in which they are incurred, as in marginal costing.

(ii) It avoids the arbitrary apportionment of fixed costs, as in absorption costing.

(iii) Stock is valued on a variable cost basis, which accords with the argument that the additional cost of stock is limited to its variable cost.

(iv) The prudent principle of charging costs to the period in which they are incurred results in lower stock valuations, and therefore there is less chance of fictitious profits arising in the period should unsaleable stock be carried forward to the next period.

(v) The exclusion of fixed overheads in production costs allows pricing to be lower and therefore more competitive.

(vi) It eliminates volume variances, which cause underabsorbed or overabsorbed overheads, and can be confusing. This cannot arise in marginal costing as all fixed costs are charged to the period in which they are incurred.

(vii) Marginal costing facilitates control in the following ways: (1) costs are more easily controlled, when pooled into separate fixed and variable totals; (2) it enables flexible budgets to be prepared which provide a comparison for actual levels of activity (*see* flexible budgeting, p. 109.

(viii) The contribution approach aids profit planning (*see* cost–volume–profit (C-V-P) analysis in Chapter 6).

(ix) Marginal costing is a useful tool in short-run decision-making, as it shows the effects of such decisions on contribution.

(x) It avoids the problem of determining suitable overhead recovery bases.

(xi) Fixed costs may not be controllable at departmental level and therefore should not be included in product costs at cost centre level.

(xii) In absorption costing, profits can vary with production levels, even though sales levels are constant. In other words, profits can be raised when sales are low by simply increasing stock levels.

(b) Absorption costing

(i)   It avoids the separation of costs into fixed and variable elements, which is not easily and accurately achieved.

(ii) Fixed costs should be treated as actual costs of production as production cannot occur without them being incurred.

(iii) Stock valuation is in accordance with SSAP 9.

(iv) Absorption costing conforms with the accrual concept of SSAP 2 by matching costs with revenue as in the full costing of stocks.

(v)   Analysis of underabsorbed/overabsorbed overheads is useful to identify inefficient utilisation of production resources.

(vi) Full cost (cost plus) pricing (as is true of absorption costing) ensures that all costs are covered.

(vii) In the long run, decision-making based on a marginal costing approach may result in the contribution failing to cover fixed costs, and losses being incurred.

(viii) The apportionment and allocation of fixed costs make managers more aware of these costs and of services provided.

4.0 CONCLUSION

Both approaches are equally important. Any preference for one will depend upon the purpose for which the information is required. In practice some firms incorporate both costing techniques in their accounting systems.

CHAPTER SIX

Cost–Volume–Profit (C–V–P) Analysis

1.0 INTRODUCTION

Cost–volume–profit analysis studies the effects of changes in costs, volume and selling price on profits. It is a useful technique for planning profits (budgeting), pricing decisions, sales-mix decisions, and production capacity decisions.

One particular important aspect of C–V–P analysis is breakeven analysis.

2.0 BREAKEVEN CHARTS

(a) A breakeven chart is illustrated in Fig. 6. The breakeven point is where total costs equal sales, and there is no profit or loss.

(b) Unfortunately Fig. 6 does not show the contribution and therefore the chart given in Fig. 7 is more useful for breakeven analysis:

From Fig. 7 the following can be derived:

$$\text{Contribution} = \text{Fixed costs} + \text{Profit}$$

At breakeven point (B/E)

Contribution = Fixed costs

$\therefore$ $\text{Number of units at B/E} \times \text{Contribution per unit} = \text{Fixed costs}$

$\therefore$ $\text{Number of units at B/E} = \dfrac{\text{Fixed costs}}{\text{Contribution/unit}}$

$$\therefore \quad \text{B/E point in sales value } \pounds = \text{Fixed costs} \times \frac{\text{Selling price}}{\text{Contribution/unit}}$$

After the breakeven point has been reached any further contribution is equal to profit.

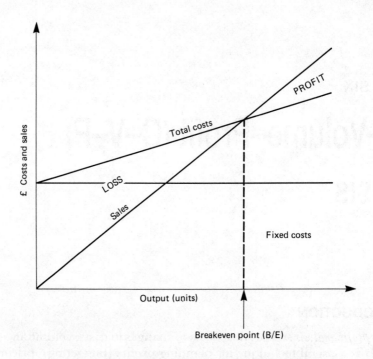

Fig. 6. Example of a breakeven chart.

Example 1

Classic Ltd manufactures a toy which has a variable cost of £10 per unit and a selling price of £15 per unit. Fixed costs are budgeted at £40,000.

   (a) Calculate the number of toys needed to be sold in order to break even.

   (b) What is the breakeven point in sales value?

   (c) How many toys must be sold to generate a profit of £15,000.

SOLUTION

   (a) Number of units at breakeven point $= \dfrac{\text{Fixed costs}}{\text{Contribution per unit}}$

$$= \frac{\pounds 40{,}000}{\pounds 15 - \pounds 10} = \underline{\underline{8{,}000 \text{ units}}}$$

   (b) Breakeven point in sales value $= 8{,}000 \text{ units} \times \pounds 15 = \underline{\underline{\pounds 120{,}000}}$

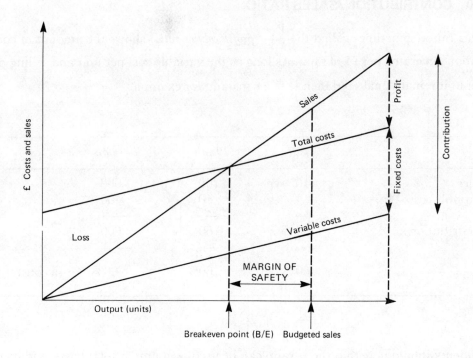

Fig. 7. *Breakeven chart showing contribution.*

(c) After the breakeven point profit and contribution are the same,

$$\therefore \frac{£15,000 \ (\text{Profit or contribution})}{£5 \quad (\text{Contribution per unit})} = 3,000 \text{ units (additional units)}$$

$$+$$

$$8,000 \text{ units (at breakeven point)}$$

∴ Number of units to make $= \underline{11,000 \text{ units}}$
   £15,000 profit

Alternatively students may just use the formula:

$$\begin{matrix}\text{Number of units to make} \\ \text{£15,000 profit}\end{matrix} = \frac{\text{Fixed costs} + \text{required profit}}{\text{Contribution per unit}}$$

$$= \frac{£40,000 + £15,000}{£5}$$

$$= 11,000 \text{ units}$$

3.0 CONTRIBUTION/SALES RATIO

This ratio (sometimes called the $\frac{P}{V}$ — *profit/volume ratio*) shows the amount of contribution generated per £1 of sales. As long as the variable cost per unit and selling price per unit remain unaltered then $\frac{C}{S}$ = a constant; for example:

	1 unit	*10 units*	*100 units*
Sales	10	100	1,000
Variable costs	4	40	400
Contribution	6	60	600
$\frac{C}{S} =$	60%	60%	60% (a constant)

Students should note that the $\frac{C}{S}$ ratio can be used on a unit or total basis, and its purposes include the following:

(a) It can act as a measure of performance;

(b) It helps in determining the breakeven point in sales value.
  If this B/E point = fixed costs $\times \dfrac{\text{selling price per unit}}{\text{contribution per unit}}$ *(See* 2.0(b).)

  then the B/E point = fixed costs $\times \dfrac{1}{\frac{C}{S}} = \dfrac{\text{fixed costs}}{\frac{C}{S}\ \text{ratio}}$

(c) If $\frac{C}{S}$ = a constant, then providing two of the three elements of the formula are known, the third can be determined; for example:

In Classic Ltd (*see* Example 1) if only 10,000 toys can be sold at £15 each, and thereafter the selling price is lowered to £12 per unit, what is the sales value needed to make the same profit as before?

$$\text{Contribution = fixed costs + profit}$$
$$\therefore \text{£55,000 = £40,000 + £15,000}$$

£55,000 of contribution is needed to make the same profit as before.

$\dfrac{C}{S}$ ratio		£ Contribution		£ Sales	
$\dfrac{5}{15}$	(contribution found)	50,000	←	150,000	up to 10,000 units × £15
$\dfrac{2}{12}$	(sales found)	5,000	→	30,000	after 10,000 units
		55,000		180,000	

£180,000 of sales will produce £55,000 of contribution and thereby make the same £15,000 profit as before.

Example 2

You have asked the accountant for four budgets based on different economic forecasts. He started work on these, but has fallen ill and cannot complete the figures in time. His secretary has found the work he has done to date which is as follows:

Economic forecast	Depressed	Average	Good	Excellent
Variable costs (£000s)	40	60	90	140

There are fixed costs of £72,000 and the $\dfrac{C}{S}$ ratio is 60%.

Calculate:

(a) the profit or loss at each of the four levels;

(b) the breakeven point in sales value;

(c) the sales value at which a profit of £15,000 would be made.

SOLUTION

(a) If the $\dfrac{C}{S}$ ratio is 60%, then $\dfrac{V}{S}$ must be 40%

	Depressed £000	Average £000	Good £000	Excellent £000
Sales	100	150	225	350
Variable costs	40	60	90	140
Contribution	60	90	135	210
Less: Fixed costs	72	72	72	72
Profit (loss)	(12)	18	63	138

(b) The breakeven point in sales value $= \dfrac{\text{fixed costs}}{\dfrac{C}{S}\text{ratio}}$

$$= £72{,}000 \times \frac{100}{60}$$

$$= £120{,}000$$

(c) Contribution = fixed costs + profit

∴ £87,000 = £72,000 + £15,000

$\dfrac{C}{S}$	*Contribution*	*Sales*
$\dfrac{60}{100}$ (Sales found) £87,000	$\longrightarrow$	£145,000

£145,000 of sales will generate £87,000 of contribution, and thereby make a profit of £15,000.

Contribution plays a part in pricing decisions where it is necessary to show by how much demand must respond to a change in price if extra profit is to be made.

Example 3

A company sells 15,000 units at £4 each, and incurs variable costs of £1·65 for each unit, and fixed costs of £32,000. What are the consequences of a price increase or decrease of 10%?

SOLUTION

Existing profit = contribution − fixed costs
£3,250   = (15,000 × £2·35) − £32,000

	Price increase (+ 10%) £	*Price reduction (− 10%)* £
Price	4·40	3·60
Variable costs	1·65	1·65
Contribution	2·75	1·95
$\dfrac{C}{S}$ ratio $=$	62·5%	54%

$$\begin{array}{c}\text{Number of units to be sold} \\ \text{to make existing profit}\end{array} = \dfrac{\text{Fixed costs + required profit}}{\text{Contribution per unit}}$$

$= \dfrac{£32{,}000 + £3{,}250}{£2\cdot75}$ $\qquad = \dfrac{£32{,}000 + £3{,}250}{£1\cdot95}$

$=$ 12,818 units $\qquad\quad =$ 18,077 units

∴ if prices are raised by 10% sales volume must not fall by more than	if prices are reduced by 10% then sales volume must increase by at least
$$\frac{(15,000 - 12,818)}{15,000} \times 100$$	$$\frac{(18,077 - 15,000)}{15,000} \times 100$$
= 14·5%, if profit is to be maintained	= 20·5%, if profit is to be maintained.

This is on the assumption that no pricing policy will be accepted if it provides a smaller profit than the existing one.

4.0   THE PROFIT/VOLUME (P/V) GRAPH

The P/V graph is another type of breakeven chart (Fig. 8) and shows the profit or loss at different levels of activity, usually sales.

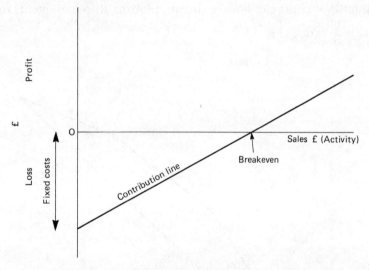

Fig. 8. *Example of a profit/volume graph.*

Example 4

A company, X Ltd, sells three components, A, B and C. Information provided is as follows:

	A	*B*	*C*
Variable cost per unit	£2	£3·50	£1·50
Selling price per unit	£3	£4	£3·50
Sales volume	3,000 units	3,000 units	3,800 units
Fixed costs are £5,000			

Construct a multiproduct P/V chart.

SOLUTION

	£ A	£ B	£ C	Total £
Contribution	3,000	1,500	7,600	12,100
		Less: Fixed costs		5,000
			Profit	7,100
Sales revenue	9,000	12,000	13,300	34,300
$\frac{C}{S}$ ratio	33·3%	12·5%	57·1%	

A multiproduct P/V chart can now be drawn, plotting the components in order of the highest ranking $\frac{C}{S}$ ratios (Fig. 9).

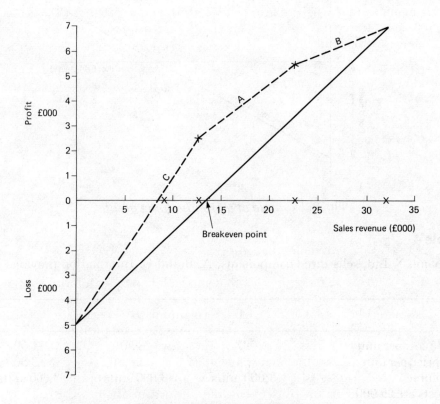

Fig. 9. *Multiproduct P/V graph.*

From Fig. 9 the breakeven point is approximately £14,000. This can be calculated as follows:

$$\text{Breakeven point in sales value } \pounds = \frac{\text{Fixed costs}}{\frac{C}{S}\text{ratio}}$$

$$= \pounds5{,}000 \times \frac{\pounds34{,}300}{\pounds12{,}100} = \underline{\pounds14{,}173}$$

5.0   LIMITATIONS OF THE ASSUMPTIONS IN C–V–P ANALYSIS

(a) It assumes that all costs can be easily and accurately separated into fixed and variable elements.

(b) It assumes that total fixed costs remain constant. However, they will increase in a steplike fashion as output increases beyond certain ranges of activity levels.

(c) There is the assumption that volume is the only factor affecting costs, but other factors also affect costs, for example, inflation, efficiency, economic and political factors.

(d) It assumes that where a firm sells more than one product the sales-mix is constant. Of course, the sales-mix will be continually changing owing to changes in demand.

This limitation can be overcome, to a certain extent, by feeding the following model into a computer, which can cope with the changing variables and determine the profit at any point of time.

$$P = (S_1 - V_1)\, X_1 + (S_2 - V_2)\, X_2 \ldots (S_N - V_N)\, X_N - FC$$

Where P = profit
   S = selling price
   V = variable cost
1, 2 ... N = type of product
   X = number of units sold
  FC = fixed cost

(e) C–V–P analysis assumes that costs and sales can be predicted with certainty. However, these variables are uncertain, and the management accountant must try to incorporate the effects of uncertainty into his information.

One way of achieving this is to employ sensitivity analysis. Under this technique each variable in the model is manipulated, in turn, keeping all other variables constant. The effects of these movements on the final result (profit) are measured. If a small variation in a particular variable gives rise to a significant effect on the final result, then that variable is said to be sensitive and will need to be closely observed. Any misforecasting of a sensitive variable could result in drastic consequences for the organisation.

Sensitivity analysis anticipates outcomes and acts as a means of feedforward control, unlike the traditional methods of control, for example, budgetary control, which initiate control after the event has actually occurred.

Sensitivity analysis can be combined with the probabilities (expected values) for each variable, in order to provide a useful method for assessing risk under conditions of uncertainty (*see* Chapter 8), and for estimating the probability of various profit levels.

(f) It assumes that sales volume and production volume are the same (that is, there are no stocks, or no changes in stock levels). Profit is therefore solely dependent on the sales level. However, when sales volume differs from production volume, and stocks are valued on an absorption costing basis, then profit will depend upon sales and production. For example, if sales are depressed, profit can be raised by increasing production and thereby increasing stock levels. In such a case profit is no longer a function of a single variable (sales) but of two independent variables (sales and production). This makes it impossible to use the conventional breakeven diagram (unless sales volume or production volume is held constant).

Students should note that if stocks are valued on a marginal basis then profit continues to be a function of sales volume and conventional C–V–P analysis applies.

(g) It assumes linearity of costs and revenue. However, in reality both the revenue and total cost functions will be curvilinear (Fig. 10) for the following reasons:

(i) the price elasticity of demand — as sales prices decrease in order to induce further demand, total revenue will not increase proportionately with output.

(ii) as output increases efficiencies are gained, and these economies of scale will reduce the marginal costs per unit, but eventually diseconomies of scale (diminishing returns), through inefficiency, will cause the marginal costs to rise.

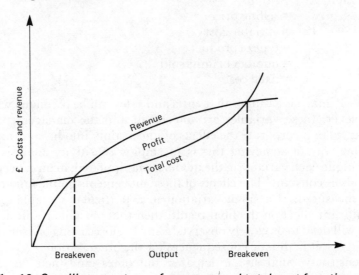

Fig. 10. *Curvilinear nature of revenue and total cost functions.*

The profit can be determined with the use of the mathematical technique called *calculus* and will be maximised when the slope or gradient of the revenue function equates with the slope or gradient of the total cost function.

Although the above economist's chart is theoretically valid, it is difficult to plot accurately mathematically complex curvilinear functions. Also over relevant ranges of output the difference between the economist's chart and the accountant's model is small, so that it is acceptable to use the latter.

6.0 CONCLUSION

C–V–P analysis provides important information for management decisions. However, a breakeven chart illustrates relationships that prevail under a particular set of assumptions. If these assumptions no longer operate then the cost–volume–profit relationships will alter.

CHAPTER SEVEN

Decision-making under Conditions of Certainty

1.0 INTRODUCTION

Decision-making is a fundamental aspect of management accounting, and may relate to:

(a) capacity;

(b) the shutdown of a division or department;

(c) the acceptance or rejection of contracts;

(d) the decision to make or buy products or components;

(e) the investment in capital equipment;

(f) the allocation of scarce resources;

(g) replacement of equipment;

(h) pricing products or jobs.

In this chapter two assumptions are made:

(a) information is known with certainty;

(b) the decision is of a short-term nature so that the time value of money is ignored. Money has a time value because cash flows received in earlier years are more valuable than those received in later years, as the former can be reinvested in the intervening period. Discounted cash flow techniques can be used to convert future values to present values.

2.0 RELEVANT INFORMATION

In decision-making it is necessary to distinguish between relevant and irrelevant information.

2.1 Relevant cost

A *relevant cost* can be described as a future cash cost which differs between alternatives. It is any cost which will be brought about by the decision at hand.

The main features of a relevant cost are as follows:

(a) It is a *future cost*. Any historic cost (sunk, past, committed costs) cannot be affected by the decision at hand and is therefore irrelevant.

(b) Relevant costs will be *cash costs*, which exclude depreciation, book values, and notional interest. Although net book values are irrelevant, net realisable values are relevant.

(c) Only incremental (additional) costs will be relevant, for example, additional (or avoidable) fixed costs, and variable overheads. However, absorbed fixed overheads will be irrelevant, as the spreading (allocating, apportioning) of these costs over different levels of activity does not result in any increase in these costs.

$$\frac{£50,000 \ \text{(overheads)}}{5,000 \ \text{units}} = £10/\text{unit (absorption rate)}$$

A change in the level of activity alters the absorption rate, but the fixed overheads remain unchanged.

$$\frac{£50,000 \ \text{unchanged}}{2,500 \ \text{units}} = £20/\text{unit (absorption rate)}$$

Example 1

The management of Smith Ltd want to replace an old machine with a more up-to-date one. Details are as follows:

	Old machine	New machine
Cost	£240,000	£120,000
Book value	80,000	—
Disposal value now	8,000	—
Disposal value at end of life	—	—
Variable costs	160,000	112,000
Annual revenue	200,000	200,000
Estimated life (remaining)	4 years (future)	4 years

Advise Smith on whether to replace the old machine.

SOLUTION
Relevant costs
(a)   Disposal value now — represents a future cash inflow.

(b)   Cost of new machine — represents a future cash outflow.

(c)   Variable costs — incremental costs.

Irrelevant costs
(a)   Cost of old machine — past (historical) cost.

(b)   Book value and gain or loss on disposal — both involve depreciation and original cost (that is, sunk cost).

(c)   Annual revenue — this would be relevant (as it represents a future cash inflow) if it differed between alternatives. But in this example it is common to both options.

On a four-year basis

	Keep		*Replace*
	£640,000	Variable costs	£448,000
		Cost	120,000
			568,000
		Disposal value	(8,000)
	640,000		560,000

∴ Replace and save £80,000

An alternative approach

		£	*Replace*
Savings in variable costs (160,000 − 112,000) 4		=	192,000
Costs	− 120,000		
Disposal value	− (8,000)		
			(112,000)
			£80,000 ∴ Replace

Example 2

Hub Ltd use a special component in the production of one of its consumer durables. Each year 100,000 of these components are purchased from an outside organisation for £1·00 each.

    Last year the management of Hub investigated the possibility of making these components themselves, and made calculations based upon the following information:

    (a) Materials to produce 100,000 components would have cost £30,000.

(b) Direct labour at the standard hourly rate of £1·00 would have cost £60,000.

(c) The company's overheads would have increased from £106,000 to £112,000.

Based on the increased figure for overheads, the standard recovery rate would have been £0·20 per direct labour hour.

The calculations made by Hub for the standard cost of manufacturing a component came out to £1·02 each. On the basis of this the management of the company decided to continue to purchase components from their outside supplier, as on their usage this meant a total saving of £2,000 per annum.

Hub have recently received a letter from the supplier of these special components that because of increased costs they will in future have to charge £1·17 per component. So Hub again decided to look into the costs of producing these components themselves. This time they found that the material costs had increased by 10%, wages by 20%, and overheads, which were now running at £134,000 per annum, would increase to £140,000 if the component was produced. New calculations showed that the cost of producing the components had increased by £0·18 per component against the £0·17 increase required by the outside manufacturer. Thus, it was concluded, if it had been preferable to purchase these components previously, it was even more desirable to do so now.

Required

(a) Demonstrate, with calculations, how you think that Hub arrived at the initial standard cost of £1·02 per component and at the revised standard cost of £1·20.

(b) Did the management of Hub use the relevant costs in coming to both decisions? If you do not think so, show the costs that you would have used and state whether you agree with their decisions.

(c) Assuming that the costs of purchasing or producing the special components were the same, or very similar, write a brief summary of seven major advantages of making the product.

SOLUTION
(a) *Standard cost of £1·02 per component*

Direct labour (60,000 hours at £1/hour)	£60,000
Direct materials	30,000
Overheads (60,000 hours at £0·20*/hour)	12,000

$$\text{£102,000} \div 100,000 \text{ units} = \text{£1·02/unit}$$

$$\frac{*0·2/\text{hour}}{(\text{given})} = \frac{\text{£112,000 (given)}}{560,000 \text{ hours (.·. found)}}$$

Standard cost of £1·20 per component

	£
Direct labour (+ 20%)	72,000
Direct materials (+ 10%)	33,000
Overheads (60,000 hours at £0·25*/hour)	15,000

$$£120,000 \div 100,000 \text{ units}$$
$$= £1·20/\text{units}$$

$$*\frac{£140,000}{560,000} \text{ hours} = £0·25/\text{hour}$$

Students should note that although the overheads incurred have increased (as has the overhead rate) the hours worked by the firm on the special component remain the same.

(b) *Relevant costs*

Original case		Revised case	
Direct labour	£60,000		£72,000
Direct material	30,000		33,000
Overheads		(140,000 − 134,000)	6,000
(112,000 − 106,000)	6,000		
			111,000 ÷ 100,000 units
96,000 ÷ 100,000 units			
= 96p/unit			= £1·11/ unit

These figures show that Hub Ltd should manufacture, rather than buy-in in the components.

(c) Major advantages would include the following:

(i)   To achieve the correct standard of quality.

(ii) To secure reliability of supply.

(iii) To secure reliability of delivery on time.

(iv) To improve labour relations by keeping the work force employed.

(v)   To maintain control over design.

(vi) To stimulate growth in the organisation.

(vii) To avoid outsiders knowing about your purchasing requirements, and product design plans.

Other qualitative factors which should be considered in decision-making are:

(i)   The availability of resources — cash, material, labour, equipment, etc., required to carry out the decisions.

(ii)   The effects on customer-demand and loyalty by the quality of output from new products, or decisions about product cessation.

(iii) The effects of any decision on competitors.

3.0   OPPORTUNITY COSTS

A relevant cost may be expressed as *an opportunity cost*, which is the greatest benefit foregone (or sacrifice made) by choosing a particular course of action or using a particular resource.

If the choice is between choosing alternatives A, B or C, then the opportunity cost of A is the benefit foregone from the more profitable of B and C. This is called *an internal opportunity cost*.

If the choice is between choosing alternative A or zero, then the opportunity cost of A is the incremental cost (the additional cash incurred). This is called *an external opportunity cost*.

Example 3

Z Ltd purchased some material for £1,000 some time ago which would realise £500 if sold now. If the material is not sold it could be used in making a product which would sell for £1,500 after incurring additional costs of £650. Advise Z Ltd.

TO MAKE PRODUCT

Revenue from product		£1,500
Costs		
External opportunity cost (incremental cost)	£650	
Internal opportunity cost	500	
	———	(1,150)
Net benefit		350

TO SELL MATERIAL

Revenue from material		500
Costs		
Internal opportunity cost (benefit foregone by not making product) (1,500 − 650)		(850)
Net loss		(350)

It is not always easy to identify all possible opportunities, and it can be even more difficult to impute values to these opportunities. Management often have difficulty in understanding the opportunity cost concept.

An alternative approach to the above example is to use incremental costing, where the difference between incremental revenues and *incremental* costs is computed.

	Make product	Sell material	Differential costs
Incremental revenue	£1,500	£500	£1,000
Incremental cost	(650)	—	(650)
	850	500	350

The same decision is made, resulting in the manufacture of the product to provide a £350 net benefit.

4.0   LIMITING KEY FACTORS (LKF)

A *limiting key factor* is one which limits the volume of output. Profit is maximised by allocating the scarce resources on the basis of contribution per unit of limiting factor.

Example 4

Products	A/unit		B/unit
Material 5 kg at £6/kg	30	10 kg at £6/kg	60
Labour 8 hours at £3/hour	24	4 hours at £3/hour	12
	54		72
Selling price	74		87
Contribution	20		15

If labour is in short supply	$\dfrac{£20}{8\,hours}$	$\dfrac{Contribution}{Labour\ hour}$	$\dfrac{£15}{4\,hours}$
	= £2·50/hour		= £3·75/hour

Product B would be preferable.

If material is in short supply	$\dfrac{£20}{5\,kg}$	$\dfrac{Contribution}{kg}$	$\dfrac{£15}{10\,kg}$
	= £4/kg		= £1·50/kg

Product A would be preferable.

Where more than one constraint exists the operational research technique called *linear programming* is used to arrive at an optimal product mix.

Opportunity costs are frequently involved in decisions affecting scarce resources.

Example 5

Thompson Ltd is offered £30,000 to undertake job X. The following costs would be incurred:

Labour — grade A: 2,000 hours are required at £4/hour.
This labour is working at full capacity.

— grade B: is currently idle but still paid £3/hour.
This job would require 1,000 hours.

Variable overheads are absorbed at £2/grade A labour hour.
Fixed overheads are absorbed at £3/grade A labour hour, and special equipment costing £3,000 is required.

Material — C: 1,000 units required which have been contracted for at £4/unit.
— D: 1,000 units required which are already in stock and have a book value of £2/unit, and a net realisable value of £1/unit. All of material D can be used on another job to replace material E of which there is no stock currently held. Material E currently costs £3/unit.

Labour grade A is in short supply and if the job is accepted people would have to be shifted from other work, currently earning contribution of £5/grade A labour hour.

SOLUTION

Revenue		£30,000
Relevant costs		
Labour A — (2,000 hours at £4)	£8,000	
Labour B — (not incremental; spare capacity)	—	
Material C — (sunk; committed cost)		
Material D — (1,000 units at £3) opportunity cost	3,000	
[Book value of £2 — historic cost. Realisable value of £1 is an opportunity cost, but not as great as £3 which could have replaced material E.]		
Variable overheads (2,000 hours at £2)	4,000	
Fixed overheads absorbed (not incremental)	—	
Additional fixed overheads (incremental costs)	3,000	
Opportunity cost of contribution forgone from other work (2,000 hours at £5)	10,000	
		(28,000)
	Net gain	£2,000

Job X should therefore be undertaken.

An alternative approach is as follows:

Revenue		£30,000
Relevant costs		
Labour A	£8,000	
Material D	3,000	
Variable overheads	4,000	
Fixed costs	3,000	
		(18,000)

$$\frac{\text{Contribution}}{\text{LKF (labour hours)}} = \frac{£12,000}{2,000 \text{ hours}} = \text{£6/hour which is preferable to £5/hour earned on other work}$$

∴ net gain by using men on job X is (£6–£5) × 2,000 hours
= £2,000

The labour cost of £8,000 and variable overheads of £4,000 will be incurred whether the men are used on job *X* or the other work. These costs are therefore not incremental and irrelevant. However, they have been included in the above computation. The reason for this is that the contribution of £5/hour on the other work has been arrived at after deducting all variable costs including the labour and variable overhead costs which are irrelevant, in other words,

Other work	—Revenue (assumed)	£11
per hour	Labour cost	4
	Variable overhead	2
		(6)
	Contribution of	£5

But because of the irrelevance of the labour and variable overhead costs the contribution should be £11/hour × 2,000 hours = £22,000. This £22,000 has been included in the above computation in the form of:

Lost contribution	£10,000
Labour A	8,000
Variable overheads	4,000
	£22,000

Students should note that, had the question stated that the contribution of £5/hour on the other work excluded the labour and variable overhead costs, then these costs would not have been included in the computation because of their irrelevancy. Only the lost contribution would have been shown, that is, £10,000.

5.0 ATTRIBUTABLE COSTS

Shillinglaw stated that an *attributable cost* is the cost per unit that could be avoided if a product or function were discontinued without changing the supporting organisation structure.

Attributable costs include (a) short-run variable costs, (b) fixed costs which are directly traceable to the product or function, and (c) other fixed costs which change if there are significant shifts in the volume of activity.

Example 6: Shutdown decision

V Ltd manufactures electric calculators at its factory in Ryde (Isle of Wight). This factory is the production centre and all sales occur at the two sales centres in Cowes and Ventnor.

For period 10, budgeted production is 80,000 units and the cost structure is as follows:

	£/Unit
Direct material and labour	9
Variable overheads (for example, power to operate plant)	1
Fixed overhead	2
	—
Production cost	12

Stock levels remain unchanged and can be ignored. Budgeted sales are: Cowes 50,000 units, Ventnor 30,000 units. Fixed selling price is £14 per unit and the sales depot costs are budgeted at:

	Cowes	*Ventnor*
Variable costs (sales, packaging, and sales commission)	£15,000	£9,000
Fixed costs (depot rent, administration etc)	£40,000	£54,000

Management is considering closure of the Ventnor depot. Ventnor's fixed costs include £6,000 for part of the costs of a central warehouse in Newport which is used by both sales depots, and if the Ventnor depot is closed the whole of the warehouse costs would have to be borne by Cowes.

The manager of the Ventnor depot would have to be offered a gratuitous pension of £3,000 per annum and has a long expectation of life (no funded pension scheme is in operation).

If the Ventnor branch is closed, factory production for period 10 will be cut to 50,000 units and it is not thought that there will be any immediate economies in factory fixed costs or alternative utilisation of spare factory capacity.

Required: Statement showing:

   (a) Why management is considering the closure of the depot.

   (b) What the effect will be on company profits.

SOLUTION

(a)

	Cowes	Ventnor	Total
Sales 50,000/30,000 units	£700,000	£420,000	
Production costs	600,000	360,000	
Gross profit	100,000	60,000	£160,000
Depot costs:			
Variable	15,000	9,000	24,000
Fixed	40,000	54,000	94,000
	55,000	63,000	118,000
Net profit/(loss)	45,000	(3,000)	42,000
(b) *Add:* Unavoidable costs	100,000*	69,000*	169,000
Contribution to unavoidable costs	£145,000	£66,000	£211,000

Notes

  (i)   The statement shows clearly that on the present budget, the Ventnor depot shows a loss of £3,000, and this is presumably why management is considering closure.

  (ii)

	Cowes	Ventnor	Total
Unavoidable costs are:			
Factory fixed overhead absorbed by 50,000/30,000 units at £2/unit	£100,000	£60,000	£160,000
Ventnor's costs which in future will have to be borne by Cowes or by the company as a whole:			
Warehouse costs		6,000	
Manager's pension		3,000	9,000
	£100,000*	£69,000*	£169,000*

(iii) The statement in part (b) also shows that if the Ventnor depot is closed, a valuable contribution of £66,000 towards unavoidable costs is lost, and that a budgeted profit totalling £42,000 will be turned into a loss of £42,000 from £66,000 = £24,000. In other words the whole of the factory fixed overhead, which on the evidence of the budget is 80,000 units at £2 = £160,000, together with the further unavoidable costs of £9,000, will have to be borne by Cowes. Cowes will therefore show a result of £145,000 from £169,000 (= £24,000) loss.

(iv) In this example the important distinction to be made is between avoidable and unavoidable costs, rather than just fixed and variable costs.

(v) There is an assumption that the Ventnor depot would be closed without any economies at the factory and without any alternative use of spare capacity. This is obviously unrealistic.

(vi) Students should pay particular attention to the presentation of the solution.

Example 7

B Ltd is an engineering company with six manufacturing departments but it has, unfortunately, a long history of poor labour relations. The most recent of a series of strikes involved the production workers in a department devoted solely to the manufacture of a single product exported under the name of "BIXIT". No stocks are held in the department.

By comparing budgeted and actual quantities for the period of the strike the company's accountant has prepared the following estimate of the cost of the strike.

Sales:	Number of units below budget		70,000
	Budget unit selling price		£2·50
	Total revenue lost as a result of strike		£175,000
Less:	Cost savings:		
	Materials not used (70,000 × budgeted unit material cost)	£35,000	
	Wages saved (70,000 × budgeted unit labour cost)	£70,000	
			£105,000
			£70,000
Add:	Wages paid during strike to:		
	Supervisory staff	£1,000	
	Production workers who did not strike	£2,000	
			£3,000
Fixed overhead not recovered (70,000 units × budgeted fixed overhead recovery rate)			£17,500
			£90,500

During the period of the strike there was a seasonal decline in the demand for the product and the marketing manager estimates that had the product been available actual sales would have been 20,000 units below budget. The sales manager has stated that in order to have achieved the reduced volume of sales the price of the last 30,000 units sold would have had to be reduced to £2.

The production workers who attended for work were utilised in maintenance work which was normally undertaken by an outside contractor who charged £6,000. Materials costing £2,000 had to be specially bought in for the maintenance work.

The budgeted fixed overhead rate is based solely on fixed costs that are unaffected by the activity in any department.

By the terms of the strike settlement, the production workers agreed to work exceptional overtime and produce 20,000 of the units lost so that orders for major customers could be met. For this work a special wage rate was negotiated amounting to a 25% increase in the budgeted unit labour costs.

You are required to prepare a statement, showing the cost of the strike.

SOLUTION

STATEMENT OF COST OF STRIKE

Loss of contribution

Sale units: lost in comparison to latest forecast			50,000
to be recouped at later date			20,000
actual forecast loss			30,000

Unit contribution
Variable cost per unit	£1·50		
Forecast selling price of 30,000 lost above	2·00		
	0·50		
Total contribution	30,000 × £0·50	= £15,000	

Additional costs incurred
25% increase in labour costs on 20,000
    units − budget £1,000   = £5,000

Saving on maintenance
Outlays avoided	£6,000	
Less: outlays incurred on production labour	2,000	
materials	2,000	
		£(2,000)
Total cost of strike =		£18,000

Assumptions made:
  (a) supervisory staff represent a fixed cost;

  (b) that the 30,000 units are totally irrecoverable.

6.0 CONCLUSION

In this chapter we have examined the basic principles of decision-making. Students must now practise their application, by attempting questions 14–24 (pp. 225–40).

CHAPTER EIGHT

Decision-making under Conditions of Uncertainty

1.0 INTRODUCTION

In the previous chapter it was assumed that information relevant to the decision was known with virtual certainty. However, in reality the preparer of information for decision-making purposes must incorporate the effects of uncertainty into his information without suffering an information overload and without straying from the relevant costing approach. His main objective is to provide management with information which illustrates most likely outcomes and the extent of their possible variations.

The methods used for assessing risk include:

(a) the conservative approach;

(b) the three-point estimate;

(c) minimax and maximin criteria;

(d) sensitivity analysis;

(e) probabilities and expected values as applied in

    (i) payoff matrices, and

    (ii) decision trees.

2.0 METHODS OF ASSESSING RISK

(a) *The conservative approach.* Under this approach cash flows are adjusted by a given percentage in order to be prudent. Outflows will be increased and inflows reduced. This is a crude method of assessing risk, as it ignores the use of probabilities, and the percentage used is arbitrary.

(b) *The three-point estimate.* Three sets of data are constructed showing most likely, best possible, and worst possible outcomes. Unless probabilities are applied to the data, then this method is as subjective as the conservative approach. Also three sets of information are not necessarily more acccurate than a single possible outcome.

(c) *The minimax/maximin criteria.* This is a conservative approach in the sense that the least worst outcome that could possibly occur is selected.

Example 1: The minimax applied to costs

Projects	Possible costs of outcomes A£	B£	C£	(Maximum costs) worst possible
X	(80)	(70)	(95)	(95)
Y	(90)	(75)	(80)	(90)*
Z	(100)	(87)	(78)	(100)

*(90) is the least worst possible outcome, and therefore project Y will be selected.

Example 2: The maximin applied to profits

Projects	Possible costs of outcomes A£	B£	C£	(Minimum profits) worst possible
L	50	70	90	50
M	60	55	80	55
N	75	65	85	65*

*65 is the best of the worst possible outcomes, and therefore project N will be selected.

It can be seen that the minimax criterion minimises maximum costs, and the maximin criterion maximises minimum profits.

(i) *The minimax regret criterion.* Under this criterion the difference between the outcome of a particular alternative and the best possible alternative is computed. This difference will represent an opportunity loss.
A regret table using the above example 2 is as follows:

Projects	A £	B £	C £	Maximum regret
L	25	0	0	25
M	15	15	10	15
N	0	5	5	5*

*5 represents the least opportunity loss (maximum regret) and therefore project N is chosen.

Students should note that the minimax regret criterion will not necessarily indicate the same choice as the maximin approach, as they are both entirely different methods.
   The above table was constructed by subtracting each figure in a column from the largest figure in that column; for example,

$$Column\ A$$
$$75-50 = £25$$
$$75-60 = £15$$
$$75-75 = \ £0$$

(ii) Limitations of the minimax/maximin criteria

   (1) They are too conservative, as a project which is slightly risky, yet reasonably profitable, may be rejected out of hand.

   (2) They ignore the use of probabilities.

   (3) They ignore the alternative of not selecting any project.

(d) *Sensitivity analysis.* This is a control technique, whereby all the variables in a given model are identified. Each variable is then manipulated in turn, keeping all other variables constant, and the effects on the final result are measured. If a small variation in a particular variable gives rise to a significant effect on the final result then that variable is said to be sensitive. Sensitive variables will need to be closely observed as there could be drastic consequences to the firm if they are wrongly forecasted.

Example 3

Roberts Ltd budgets for product *P* as follows:

Sales		£300,000
Less: Direct costs:		
Material	£100,000	
Labour	60,000	
Variable overhead	40,000	
Fixed overhead	50,000	
		250,000
Profit		£50,000

Test the sensitivity of the budget to 10% changes in all the variables.

SOLUTION

The effect on the final result, by manipulating a variable, can be expressed as

$$\frac{\text{the change in the profit}}{\text{original profit}} \times 100$$

The student must first identify all the variables in the model. They are material, labour, variable overhead, fixed overhead (though it is fixed it is still a variable, as it can be wrongly forecasted), sales volume, and sales price.

Material

10% of £100,000 = £10,000. This would cause the profit to be changed by £10,000.

$$\therefore \quad \frac{\text{change in profit}}{\text{original profit}} \times 100 = \frac{10,000}{50,000} \times 100$$
$$= \underline{20\%}$$

Labour

10% of £60,000 = £6,000. This would cause the profit to be changed by £6,000.

$$\therefore \quad \frac{\text{change in profit}}{\text{original profit}} \times 100 = \frac{6,000}{50,000} \times 100$$
$$= \underline{12\%}$$

Variable overhead

10% of £40,000 = £4,000. This would cause the profit to be changed by £4,000.

$$\therefore \quad \frac{\text{change in profit}}{\text{original profit}} \times 100 = \frac{4,000}{50,000} \times 100$$
$$= \underline{8\%}$$

Fixed overhead

10% of £50,000 = £5,000. This would cause the profit to be changed by £5,000.

$$\therefore \quad \frac{\text{change in profit}}{\text{original profit}} \times 100 = \frac{5,000}{50,000} \times 100$$
$$= \underline{10\%}$$

Sale price

10% of £300,000 = £30,000. This would cause the profit to be changed by £30,000.

$$\therefore \quad \frac{\text{change in profit}}{\text{original profit}} \times 100 = \frac{30,000}{50,000} \times 100$$
$$= \underline{60\%}$$

Sales volume

A change in this variable will *result in* the other variable costs being changed. The fixed overhead will remain fixed.

Sales		£330,000
Less: Direct costs:		
Material	£110,000	
Labour	66,000	
Variable overhead	44,000	
Fixed overhead	50,000	
		270,000
Profit		£60,000

$$\therefore \quad \frac{\text{change in profit}}{\text{original profit}} \times 100 = \frac{60,000 - 50,000}{50,000} \times 100$$

$$= \underline{\underline{20\%}}$$

From this example we can see that the selling price and, to a lesser extent, the sales volume and material are sensitive variables and will need to be carefully forecasted and monitored.

Sensitivity analysis can be coupled with probabilities to provide a powerful feedforward control technique which, unlike traditional control techniques in management accounting such as budgetary control, anticipates events rather than initiating control action after they have occurred.

The EBQ (stock control), cash flow, and C–V–P models lend themselves easily to sensitivity analysis.

(e) *The use of probabilities*
A *probability* expresses the likelihood of an event occurring. It can range from 0 ———→ 1. The closer to 1 the greater the likelihood that the event will occur.

Probabilities can be assigned from historical data (past frequencies).

Example 4

K Ltd has recorded its weekly output in units for the previous 100 weeks as follows:

Sales (units)	Frequency		Probability	Probability × Sales
100	10	10/100 =	0·1	£10
200	20	20/100 =	0·2	40
300	35	35/100 =	0·35	105
400	30	30/100 =	0·3	120
500	5	5/100 =	0·05	25
	100 weeks		1·0	EV 300

The EV (expected value) of £300 is a weighted average, and represents the most likely future average weekly sales, on the assumption that the activity is repeated a large number of times.

The main purpose of calculating expected values is to assist in the decision-making process. In the above example, for instance, the expected value of 300 units per week provides the management with an indication of the average amount of productive resources (labour, material and capital) required each week, together with the required stock levels to ensure that in weeks where sales output is greater than expected, demand can still be satisfied.

Limitations of expected values

(a) Unless there is an adequate amount of historical data, probabilities may be merely subjective estimates.

(b) Past frequencies are of less use if there are any changes in the underlying circumstances surrounding the firm.

(c) If it is assumed that the data as in example 4 are discrete (in other words, sales will be 100, 200, 300, 400, 500 with no other "in-between" result possible), then an expected value of, say, 285 would not be achievable.

This is a very important point which is particularly relevant in the case of one-off decisions. A company may be considering accepting a major new capital project and has estimated that the cash inflow will be either £5,000 or £45,000 with equal probability. The expected cash inflow is therefore £25,000, but the probability of the cash flow being £25,000 is nil — it is not an achievable value. This illustrates the point that the concept of expected value is only really applicable in the case of long-run, or frequently reoccurring events.

(d) An expected value alone does allow for uncertainty, but does not reflect the risks involved.

Example 5

M Ltd is considering accepting one of two mutually exclusive projects, X and Y. The cash flows and probabilities are estimated as follows:

Project X		Project Y	
Probability	Cash flow	Probability	Cash flow
0·10	£12,000	0·10	£ 8,000
0·20	14,000	0·25	12,000
0·40	16,000	0·30	16,000
0·20	18,000	0·25	20,000
0·10	20,000	0·10	24,000

Advise M Ltd.

SOLUTION

	PROJECT X	
Probability	*Cash flow*	
0·10	£12,000	£1,200
0·20	14,000	2,800
0·40	16,000	6,400
0·20	18,000	3,600
0·10	20,000	2,000
		EV = 16,000

	PROJECT Y	
Probability	*Cash flow*	
0·10	£8,000	£800
0·25	12,000	3,000
0·30	16,000	4,800
0·25	20,000	5,000
0·10	24,000	2,400
		EV = 16,000

On the basis of expected value, the company would be indifferent between the two. A measure of risk is therefore required, which shows the degree of dispersion about the expected value. This measure of dispersion is the standard deviation.

$$\sigma = \sqrt{\Sigma p \, (x - \bar{x})^2} \qquad \text{Where } \bar{x} = \text{EV}$$

$\uparrow$
(Standard deviation)

x = cash flows
p = probability

Project X		$p\,(x - \bar{x})^2$	*(£000s)*	*Project Y*		$p\,(x - \bar{x})^2$
$0{\cdot}10\,(12{-}16)^2$	=	1·6		$0{\cdot}10\,(\,8{-}16)^2$	=	6·4
$0{\cdot}20\,(14{-}16)^2$	=	0·8		$0{\cdot}25\,(12{-}16)^2$	=	4·0
$0{\cdot}40\,(16{-}16)^2$	=	nil		$0{\cdot}30\,(16{-}16)^2$	=	nil
$0{\cdot}20\,(18{-}16)^2$	=	0·8		$0{\cdot}25\,(20{-}16)^2$	=	4·0
$0{\cdot}10\,(20{-}16)^2$	=	1·6		$0{\cdot}10\,(24{-}16)^2$	=	6·4
	Σ =	4·8			Σ =	20·8
$\therefore \sigma = \sqrt{4{\cdot}8}$	=	2·19		$\therefore \sigma = \sqrt{20{\cdot}8}$ =		4·56
	=	£2,190			=	£4,560

The coefficient of variation $= \dfrac{\sigma}{\text{EV}} \times 100$, represents the degree of variation around the most likely outcome.

	Project X	Project Y
$\dfrac{\sigma}{\text{EV}} \times 100$	$\dfrac{2 \cdot 19}{16} \times 100 = 13 \cdot 68\%$	$\dfrac{4 \cdot 56}{16} \times 100 = 28 \cdot 5\%$

This result confirms that project Y is more risky as it is more susceptible to wider degrees of variation around the most likely outcome than project X. Project X should therefore be accepted.

(e) Expected values ignore the utility theory. *Utility value* is that value placed on the outcome of a project by a particular decision-maker. It may not be the same as the expected monetary value.

Event	Probability	Cash flow	
Win	0·7	£90,000	£63,000
Lose	0·3	(£170,000)	(£51,000)
			EV = 12,000

Although the positive expected value indicates acceptance of this project, the decision-maker is aware of the fact that a heavy loss can be incurred. His acceptance or rejection will depend on the utility value he places on this project, which in turn depends on his personal attitude towards risk, in other words, whether he is risk-averse or risk-seeking.

Risk profiles of decision-makers can be constructed by plotting *utility values* (measured in *utiles* and found by logarithms) against expected gains/losses (Fig. 11).

From Fig. 11 it can be seen that the risk-averse manager places high utility value on losses, but little value on gains. However, the risk-seeking manager's utility value is relatively unaffected by losses, yet significantly affected by gains.

3.0 APPLICATION OF EXPECTED VALUES

(a) *Pay-off matrices (decision tables)*. These should contain the following elements:

   (i)   Events — possible states of being; for example, demand could be high or low.

   (ii) Probabilities — likelihood of the events occurring.

   (iii) Actions — alternative courses of action available to the firm.

(iv) Objective function — assumed to be the maximisation of profitability.

(v)   Outcomes — the consequences of the various possible combinations of events and actions, and expressed in terms of expected values.

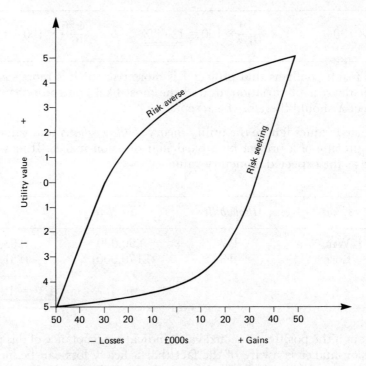

Fig. 11. *Example of a risk profile.*

Example 6

S Ltd has a choice between three projects X, Y and Z. The following information has been estimated:

| | *Market demand (profits) £000s* | | |
	A	*B*	*C*
Projects X	190	50	15
Y	110	200	160
Z	150	140	110

Probabilities are: A = 0·6, B = 0·2, C = 0·2

Which project should be undertaken?

SOLUTION

The elements of the matrix should be identified — profits, events (demand), probabilities, actions (projects X, Y or Z), outcomes (EVs).

		Profit £000	Probability	£000
Project X	A	190	0·6	114
	B	50	0·2	10
	C	15	0·2	3
			EV =	127
Project Y	A	110	0·6	66
	B	200	0·2	40
	C	160	0·2	32
			EV =	138
Project Z	A	150	0·6	90
	B	140	0·2	28
	C	110	0·2	22
			EV =	140

Project Z should be chosen because it has the highest EV of £140,000.

(b) *Perfect information.* Sometimes a firm may consider obtaining so-called perfect information from market researchers about future states of demand.

The maximum value of this perfect information will be equal to the EV with the information, less the EV without the information.

Using example 6

Demand	Choose	Profit £000s	Probability	EV £000s
A	X	190	0·6	114
B	Y	200	0·2	40
C	Z	160	0·2	32
		EV with perfect information =		186

Therefore the value of the perfect information = 186,000 − 140,000
= £46,000

This sum of £46,000 represents a maximum value and S Ltd would pay a proportion of this figure that reflects the degree of confidence which they have in the market researchers.

    (c) *Decision-tree analysis. A decision tree* is a way of applying the expected value criterion to situations where a number of decisions are made sequentially.

Example 7

A company is considering whether to expand its plant or to stay as it is. Demand over the next five years is uncertain, and may be generally high or low.

    This information may be represented in a tree diagram as shown in Fig 12.

    The object is to select that action (expand or no change) that maximises the expected value. [The lines coming out of a chance point represent uncertain events, and *not* actions.]

    Suppose further information is now available.

Probability of high demand   = 0·7
Probability of low demand   = 0·3

    Total revenue over the five-year period associated with each outcome is:

Outcome	Revenue
A	£500,000
B	200,000
C	300,000
D	200,000

The expansion costs amount to £100,000 (*Note: The time value of money may be ignored.*)

    The situation may now be analysed as shown in Fig. 13.

Expected value at chance point S $= (0·7 \times 500,000) + (0·3 \times 200,000) = (£410,000)$

Expected value at chance point T $= (0·7 \times 300,000) + (0·3 \times 200,000) = (£270,000)$

    The approach adopted is generally referred to as "*roll back*", whereby one starts over on the right hand side of the diagram, and by progressively calculating expected values from right to left, a final set of expected values can be calculated for each action at any decision point. The action with the greatest expected value is then selected.

    To "roll back" from chance point S to decision point R, the expansion costs of £100,000 have to be deducted from £410,000. Obviously no costs are associated with the other action so that has an expected value of £270,000. Therefore, on the basis of expected value only, the company would choose to expand, although it would be taking a 30% chance that demand would be low.

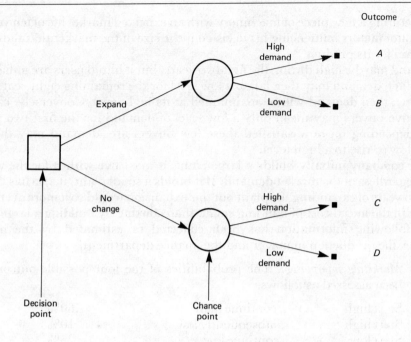

Fig. 12. *Example of a decision tree.*

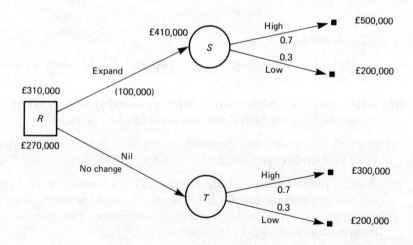

Fig. 13. *Analysis of a decision tree.*

Example 8

The manager of Sprout Ltd, a newly formed specialist machinery manufacturing subsidiary, has to decide whether to build a small plant or a large plant for manufacturing a new piece of machinery with an expected market life of ten years. One of the major factors influencing his decision is the size of the market that the company can obtain for its product.

Demand may be high during the first two years, but if initial users are unhappy with the product, demand may then fall to a low level for the remaining eight years. If users are happy, then demand will be maintained at its high level. Conversely, caution by prospective buyers may mean only a low level of demand for the first two years but again, depending on how satisfied these few buyers are, demand may then either remain low or rise to a high level.

If the company initially builds a large plant, it must live with it for the whole ten years, regardless of the market demand. If it builds a small plant, it also has the option after two years of expanding the plant but this expansion would cost more overall, when taken with the initial cost of building small, than starting by building a large plant.

The following information has been collected or estimated by the marketing manager, the production manager and the finance department.

(a) *Marketing information*. The probabilities of the four possible outcomes have been assessed as follows:

Start high	continue high	60%
Start high	subsequently low	10%
Start low	continue low	25%
Start low	subsequently high	5%
		100%

(b) *Annual income estimate*

(i) A large plant with high market demand would yield £1 million per annum, for each of ten years.

(ii) A large plant with low market demand would yield only £0·1 million per annum because of high fixed costs and inefficiencies.

(iii) A small plant with low demand throughout the ten-year period would yield £0·4 million per annum.

(iv) A small plant during an initial period of high demand would yield £0·45 million per annum for the first two years but this would drop to £0·25 million per annum if high demand continued, because of increasing competition from other manufacturers.

(v) If the initially small plant were expanded after two years and demand was high in the last eight years, it would yield £0.7 million per annum, in other words, being less efficient than one that was initially large.

(vi) If the small plant were expanded after two years but demand was low for the eight-year period, then it would yield £0·05 million per annum.

(c) *Capital costs*

(i) Initial cost of building a large plant   £3 million

(ii)   Initial cost of building a small plant   £1·3 million

(iii) Additional cost of expanding a small plant   £2·2 million

Using expected value as the decision criterion, advise the manager on what choice of plant to make. Ignore the time value of money and taxation.

SOLUTION

(a) The first stage in solving a problem of this nature, which involves more than one decision being made over a period of time, is to construct a decision tree to demonstrate the relationship between the decisions which have to be made, and the uncertain events surrounding them.

DECISION TREE: SPROUT LTD (*Diagram 1*)

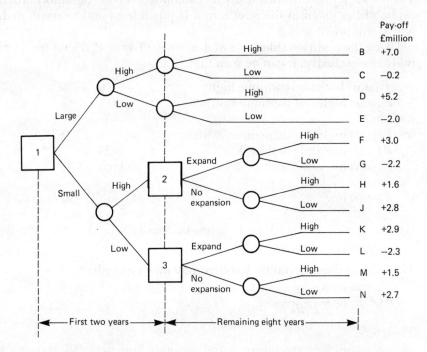

(b) Each path represents a different series of events and outcomes; for example path AG represents an initial decision to build a small plant, demand for the first two years turns out to be high, whereupon a further decision is taken to expand the plant, but unfortunately demand for the next eight years falls to a low level.

(c) It is now necessary to evaluate each path along the decision tree. If the decision to build a small plant is taken, the initial cost will be £1·3 million. If demand in the first two years is high, net income will be £0·45 million per annum and a second decision after two years is required. If it is decided to expand, then a further cost of £2·2 million will be incurred. Finally, demand in the last eight years could be high or low; if it is low, then the net annual income for these last eight years will be only £0·05 million. Thus, in total, the net result of this series of events will be:

Path	Build small	2-year demand high	Expansion	8-year demand low	=	Outcome
AG	− 1·3	+ 2 × 0·45	− 2·2	+ 8 × 0·05	=	− 2·2

If the same is done for each path, the results obtained are shown in Diagram 1 above.

Each of the twelve possible monetary outcomes has a certain chance of occurring, depending on which decisions are made, and since expected value is the criterion to be used in making the decisions, the expected value of building the large plant must be compared with the expected value of building the small plant (whichever gives the higher value being chosen).

(d) The various probabilities must be calculated. From the information about probabilities given in the question, it is possible to make certain deductions which will prove useful.

Using the addition rules that $P(A + B) = P(A) + P(B)$, where A and B are mutually exclusive, it can be seen that:

$$
\begin{array}{lll}
P\,(\text{start high and continue high}) & : & 0\text{·}6 \\
P\,(\text{start high and continue low}) & : & 0\text{·}1 \\
\hline
\text{so}\quad P\,(\text{start high}) & : & \phantom{0\text{·}6}\quad 0\text{·}7 \\
P\,(\text{start low and continue low}) & : & 0\text{·}25 \\
P\,(\text{start low and continue high}) & : & 0\text{·}05 \\
\hline
\text{so}\quad P\,(\text{start low}) & : & \phantom{0\text{·}6}\quad 0\text{·}3 \\
\hline
& & \phantom{0\text{·}6}\quad 1\text{·}0 \\
\hline
\end{array}
$$

The rules of conditional probability may now be applied:

$$ P\,(A/B) = \frac{P(A + B)}{P(B)} $$

Therefore:

$$
\left.
\begin{aligned}
P\,(\text{Continuing high/started low}) &= \frac{0\text{·}6}{0\text{·}6 + 0\text{·}1} = \frac{0\text{·}6}{0\text{·}7} = \frac{6}{7} \\[2ex]
P\,(\text{Continuing low/started high}) &= \frac{0\text{·}1}{0\text{·}6 + 0\text{·}1} = \frac{0\text{·}1}{0\text{·}7} = \frac{1}{7}
\end{aligned}
\right\} \Sigma = 1
$$

$$
\left.
\begin{aligned}
P\,(\text{Continuing low/started high}) &= \frac{0\text{·}25}{0\text{·}25 + 0\text{·}05} = \frac{0\text{·}25}{0\text{·}30} = \frac{5}{6} \\[2ex]
P\,(\text{Continuing high/started low}) &= \frac{0\text{·}05}{0\text{·}25 + 0\text{·}05} = \frac{0\text{·}05}{0\text{·}30} = \frac{1}{6}
\end{aligned}
\right\} \Sigma = 1
$$

(e) The probabilities are now included in the decision tree (Diagram 2) and the payoffs are rolled back along the arms to calculate the expected values. The following steps are taken:

Step 1

Calculate the expected value at point A (Diagram 2), that is, the expected value given that a large factory was built and demand for the first two years was high.

Expected value at $A = (\frac{6}{7} \times 7 \cdot 0) + (\frac{1}{7} \times - 0 \cdot 2) = 5 \cdot 97$

Step 2

Calculate similarly the expected value at point B, where a large factory was built and demand for the first two years was low.

Expected value at $B = (\frac{1}{6} \times 5 \cdot 2) + (\frac{5}{6} \times - 2 \cdot 0) = - 0 \cdot 8$

Step 3

Work back a further step, calculating the expected value at C, where a large factory has been built, but resulting demand is not yet known.

Expected value at $C = (0 \cdot 7 \times 5 \cdot 97) + (0 \cdot 3 \times - 0 \cdot 8) = 3 \cdot 94$

Step 4

Similarly, calculate the expected values at points, D, E, F and G (the student should do these calculations for himself). Points 2 and 3 are decision points, and by the expected value criterion the action that will be taken will be that with the greatest expected value. Thus, at 2 the decision to expand will be taken (expected value of 2·26 compared with 1·77) and at 3 the decision not to expand would be taken (expected value at 2·5 compared with − 1·43).

Step 5

Then work back one further step to point H.

Expected value at $H = (0 \cdot 7 \times 2 \cdot 26) + (0 \cdot 3 \times 2 \cdot 5) = 2 \cdot 33$

Step 6

The first decision point has now been reached. The criterion of taking the path with the highest expected value is applied.

Conclusion

The decision should be to build big initially, as this has an expected value of £3·94 million compared with £2·3 million for building small.

DECISION TREE: SPROUT LTD (*Diagram 2*)

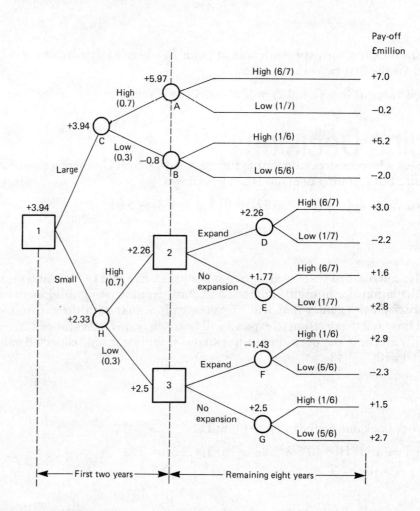

4.0 CONCLUSION

In this chapter we have adopted a broad approach to uncertainty analysis, which must be integrated into any management information system.

CHAPTER NINE

Pricing Decisions

1.0 INTRODUCTION

When making pricing decisions a firm will have to answer the following questions:

(a) What type of competition exists for the product or service?

(b) What are the firm's objectives?

(c) Is the pricing decision a long-run decision or a one-off spare capacity decision?

(d) What is the existing state of the economic and political climate, and is this likely to change in the near future?

(e) What is the likely demand for the product or service?

(f) Which departments are concerned with the pricing decision? These will normally be the marketing, production and accounts departments.

The points above will be amplified as we now consider the different methods of pricing, which are the cost-plus approach, the contribution approach, the economic approach, and "other approaches".

2.0 THE COST-PLUS METHOD

This method is consistent with absorption costing in that all costs are absorbed into the product and a profit margin is added in order to arrive at a selling price.

	£
Direct costs	x
Absorption of overheads	x
Total cost	x
Add: Profit mark-up	x
Selling price	x

Example 1

G Ltd manufactures a single product and has produced its master budget for 19X3 as follows:

	£000	£000
Sales		6,600
Direct materials	1,600	
Direct labour	800	
Variable overheads	600	
Total direct costs	3,000	
Factory overheads	1,000	
Factory cost	4,000	
Administration overheads	400	
Total cost		4,400
Profit		2,200

From this budget the following is determined:

(a) Factory overheads are recovered on the basis of $33\frac{1}{3}$% on total direct cost.

(b) Administrative overheads are recovered on the basis of 10% on factory cost.

(c) The profit mark-up is 50% on total cost.

Towards the end of 19X3 an enquiry is received from a potential customer. Direct costs have been estimated as follows:

Direct material	£26,000
Direct labour	14,000
Variable overheads	8,000

What price should it quote to the customer?

SOLUTION: *Cost-plus approach*

Direct costs	£48,000
Factory overheads	
($33\frac{1}{3}$% of 48,000)	16,000
	———
Factory cost	64,000
Administration overheads	
(10% of 64, 000)	6,400
	———
Total cost	70,400
Mark-up	
(50% on 70,400)	35,200
	———
Selling price	£105,600

(a) *Advantages of the cost-plus approach:*

(i)   It is cheap and simple to operate.

(ii) It standardises pricing decisions, thereby enabling such decisions to be delegated to lower management.

(iii) It ensures that all costs are covered, and a reasonable rate of return is earned.

(iv) It avoids the hazards of estimating demand (although this can be claimed as a disadvantage).

(v)   It enables a firm to justify its price, which is particularly important when pricing government contracts.

(vi) It is consistent with absorption costing principles.

(b) *Limitations of the cost-plus approach*

(i)   It ignores competition.

(ii) The arbitrary nature of absorption costing can generate differing rates of overhead absorption, which in turn result in different selling prices.

(iii) It fails to distinguish between those costs which are affected by the decision, and therefore relevant (such as variable costs and incremental fixed costs), and those costs which are irrelevant to the decision (such as committed fixed costs, not incremental costs).

(iv) It ignores demand and therefore fails to recognise the impact of price elasticity of demand in its pricing policy. This may lead to either the underpricing/overpricing of products. The following example illustrates this criticism.

Example 2

X Ltd budgets to make 100,000 units of product P. The variable cost/unit is £10. Fixed costs are £600,000.

The finance director has suggested that the cost-plus approach should be used with a profit mark-up of 25%. However, the marketing director disagrees and has supplied the following information:

£ Price/unit	Demand (units)
18	84,000
20	76,000
22	70,000
24	64,000
26	54,000

SOLUTION: *Finance director's cost-plus approach*

	£/Unit
Variable cost	10
Fixed cost	6
Total cost	16
Profit	4
Selling price	20

At this price the above table shows that 76,000 will be demanded, leaving closing stock of $(100,000 - 76,000) = 24,000$ units.

At a contribution of $(£20 - £10) = £10$/unit, total contribution = 76,000 units × £10 = £760,000. After subtracting fixed costs of £600,000, the net profit = £760,000 − £600,000 = £160,000.

Let us calculate the net profit for the other selling prices.

£ Price/ unit	£ Contribution/ unit	Units demand	£ Total contribution	£ Fixed costs	£ Net profit
18	8	84,000	672,000	(600,000)	72,000
20	10	76,000	760,000	(600,000)	160,000
22	12	70,000	840,000	(600,000)	240,000
24	14	64,000	896,000	(600,000)	296,000
26	16	54,000	864,000	(600,000)	264,000

It can be seen that the marketing director was correct, as £20/unit is not the best price, because £24/unit maximises profitability.

This underpricing by the finance director is a result of his failure to recognise the price elasticity of demand.

(v)   Another limitation of the cost-plus approach is that levels of activity used in the absorption rates are based on budgeted volumes of activity. However, the volume of activity may itself be based on product prices. In other words a price has already been assumed in arriving at the cost-plus selling price.

The cost-plus approach is frequently used in practice, and the above limitations are overcome, to a certain extent, by adjusting the size of the mark-up to take into account differing degrees of competition, demand, the size of the order, and the particular stage of the product's life cycle (Fig. 14).

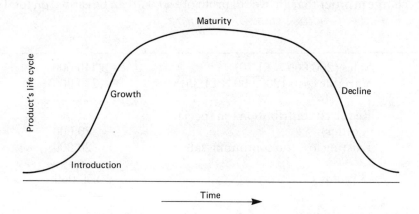

Fig. 14. *The cost-plus approach.*

Introduction stage — low mark-up in order to penetrate market;
— high mark-up to skim the profits in the market where the product is unique.
Growth and maturity — high mark-up (although it may be lowered if competition is strong).
Decline — low mark-up awaiting entry of new products to replace declining ones.

3.0   THE CONTRIBUTION APPROACH

This approach is of particular importance in spare capacity pricing situations where it is vital to distinguish between the relevant (incremental) costs and the irrelevant costs in the decision at hand.

Example 3

W Ltd: Profit and Loss Account (abridged) for 19X6

Sales (1,000,000 units) at £2·50	£2,500,000
Less: Variable costs	(1,600,000)
Contribution	900,000
Less: Fixed costs	(920,000)
Loss	£(20,000)

S Ltd approaches W Ltd, which has spare capacity, and offers to purchase 200,000 units from W Ltd. If W Ltd accepts this order it will save 25p/unit in sales commission. Existing sales will continue as above. What is the price/unit on this special order that W Ltd must charge in order that an overall profit of £50,000 can be earned on total sales?

SOLUTION

Sales (200,000 × £1·70)	£340,000
Variable costs (200,000 × £1·35)*	(270,000)
Required contribution (on special order)	70,000
Existing loss (on continuing sales)	(20,000)
Profit	£50,000

Selling price for special order is £1·70

Existing variable costs = £1,600,000 ÷ 1,000,000 units = £1·60
New variable costs = £1·60 − £0·25 = £1·35*

In this example the fixed costs are irrelevant as they are unaffected by the decision. They are represented by the £20,000 loss. The selling price is determined by the contribution from the special order, which is needed to cover the loss and result in a £50,000 profit.

(a) *Advantages of the contribution approach*

(i)   It is ideal for spare capacity pricing decisions.

(ii) It enables an organisation to penetrate new markets more easily.

(iii) The firm can be more competitive in existing markets.

(iv) It enables a firm to survive in trade depressions.

(v)   Surplus or obsolete stock can be disposed of.

(b) *Limitations of the contribution approach*

   (i)   "Cut-throat" pricing can lead to price wars.

   (ii) In the long run fixed costs may not be covered.

   (iii) Once charged a low price, a customer may expect further low prices.

   (iv) If the price set is too low a customer could resell products to existing customers, thereby affecting customer goodwill.

4.0   THE ECONOMIC APPROACH

Under this approach a manufacturer will continue to produce as long as his marginal revenue exceeds his marginal costs. The optimal level of output is where marginal revenue equals marginal cost. At this level a selling price can be determined from the demand curve.

Example 4

P Ltd sells a single product, and for the coming year has estimated the following information relating to market demand:

(1) Price	(2) Quantity demanded units	(3) Total revenue	(4) Marginal revenue total	(5) Marginal revenue per unit
£24	12,000	£288,000	£ + 288,000	£24
20	20,000	400,000	+ 112,000	14
16	28,000	448,000	+ 48,000	6
12	36,000	432,000	− 16,000	− 2
8	44,000	352,000	− 80,000	− 10
4	52,000	208,000	− 144,000	− 18

The data in columns (1) and (2) constitute the demand curve (or average revenue curve) for the product. They show the price or average revenue per unit necessary to sell the associated number of units. The marginal revenue shown in column (4) is derived from the total revenue figures in column (3). So, for instance, if the firm reduced its selling price per unit from £24 to £20, the marginal revenue produced from selling the additional 8,000 units would be £112,000 and the marginal revenue per unit would therefore be £112,000 ÷ 8,000 = £14.

The marginal and average revenue curves may therefore be plotted as in Fig. 15.

Note: For the first unit the marginal revenue per unit will be the same as the average revenue per unit. For the next 12,000 units the marginal revenue is £14 per unit.

It is interesting to note that when the price is approximately £16.50 per unit, with a volume of about 26,000 units, the marginal revenue per unit is zero, and with a lower price the marginal revenue becomes negative. This is where the total revenue starts to fall, and with zero costs this price constitutes the minimum price that the firm could charge without losing money on the next unit sold.

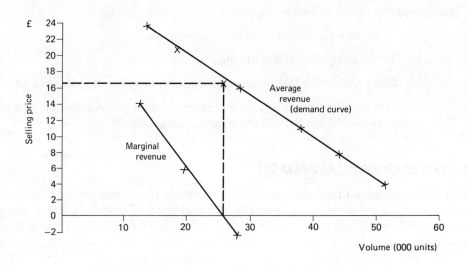

Fig. 15. *Marginal and average revenue curves.*

Example 5

Facts are as in Example 1, with the additional information given below relating to costs.

Quantity units	Total cost	Marginal cost total	per unit	Profit/(loss)
0	£144,000	—	—	£(144,000)
12,000	288,000	£144,000	£12	nil
20,000	300,000	12,000	1·50	100,000
28,000	314,000	14,000	1·55	134,000
36,000	330,000	16,000	2·00	102,000
44,000	352,000	22,000	2·55	nil
52,000	384,000	32,000	4·00	(176,000)

The marginal cost has been derived from the total cost figures, such that an increase in output from 12,000 to 20,000 units has caused costs to rise by £12,000 or £1·50 per unit. Therefore, to produce one more unit (12,001 units) will cost £1·50 and derive a marginal revenue of £14, making it clearly worthwhile.

The final column highlights the profit at discrete levels of output, and shows that profit is maximised at an output level of 28,000 units. If the data are assumed to be continuous, we can show that profit is maximised somewhere between 20,000 and 28,000 units, that is, a selling price of between £16 and £20. This true optimal point may be determined by finding the level of output where marginal revenue equals marginal cost (*see* appendix to this chapter).

The marginal cost and marginal and *average* revenue data can be plotted as in Fig. 16.

The marginal cost and marginal revenue are seen to equate at a level of output of

24,000 units (approximately). If a vertical line is extended to the average revenue curve this then provides the optimal price of £18 per unit (approximately) where profit is maximised. If production is increased beyond this point the additional cost is greater than the additional revenue and there is thus no profit incentive to increase output.

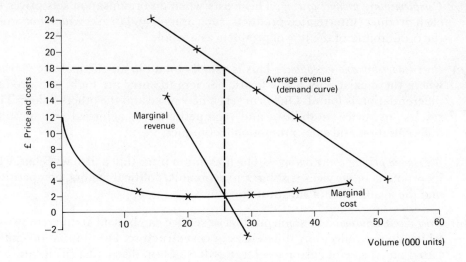

Fig. 16. *Marginal cost and marginal and average revenue data.*

(a) *Limitations of the economic approach*

  (i) Government price controls may impinge on the freedom of firms to control pricing policy.

  (ii) It is implicit in the model that profit maximisation is the only objective.

  (iii) It is unlikely that firms know accurately the relevant marginal cost and revenue data.

  (iv) The demand curve (average revenue) is very difficult to estimate as it is a function of many variables which are continually changing, for example, the price of the product itself, consumer tastes, competition, availability of substitute products, consumers' incomes, sales promotion, and the economic and political climate.

  The demand curve may be estimated using either:

  (1) market research: interviewing and sampling techniques;

  (2) historical data: analysis of past price and quantity data;

  (3) derived demand: where demand for the firm's product depends on the primary demand for another product;

  (4) pilot scheme: where a carefully selected area of the market is directly tested by offering the product at a chosen price to consumers.

5.0 "OTHER" METHODS OF PRICING

(a) *Loss leaders*. These are products or services priced at a loss in order to entice customers who may buy other goods or services at normal prices. It is a form of sales promotion frequently employed by supermarkets.

(b) *Complementary product pricing*. This exists when an organisation sets prices for each product (interrelated products, such as food and drink) which maximise the profitability of the line of products as a whole.

(c) *Price leadership and acceptance*. This is usually found in an oligopolistic market; where there exist only a few firms, barriers to entry are high, and product differentiation is found. One firm sets a new price and the others follow. This results in price stability, and competition is achieved by product differentiation and sales promotion techniques.

(d) *Maximum pricing (price ceilings)*. The maximum price that a firm will charge for its products or services is subject to economic/political factors, competition, and the availability of substitute products.

(e) *Price discrimination*. The same product or service can be sold at different prices, which do not reflect any differences in cost structure. Discrimination can be based on (i) size of custom — large orders obtain discounts; (ii) location — centrally positioned theatre tickets are more expensive than others; (iii) time — travelling in high-peak season is more costly than travelling in the low-peak season.

(f) *Price bidding*. When tenders are submitted by firms in order to secure contracts, a bid must be put forth which is low enough to compete, yet high enough to reap satisfactory profits.

(g) *Minimum pricing (price floors)*. The minimum price will depend on whether the goods have been, or are to be, made and if there are any scarce resources used in their manufacture.

  (i) *When the goods have been made*. The minimum price will be whatever is recoverable subject to covering any disposal costs. All costs incurred in producing the goods are sunk costs and therefore irrelevant to the pricing decision.

  (ii) *When the goods are to be made and there are no scarce resources*. The minimum price will be one which covers the incremental costs of making the goods.

  (iii) *When the goods are to be made and there are scarce resources:*

    The minimum price =

    incremental costs of making   the opportunity costs of the
    the goods (external   +   scarce resources (internal
    opportunity costs)   opportunity costs)

Example 6

V Ltd manufactures desks. The following information is provided:

	£/Unit
Labour	5
Material (3 kg at £2/kg)	6
Variable overheads	4
Allocated fixed overheads	2

Material is currently used to make chairs which provide contribution of £5/unit; 2 kg of material are required for each chair.

What is the minimum price per desk if (a) material is plentiful, (b) material is scarce?

SOLUTION

(a) Minimum price = Incremental cost of making desks
£5 + £6 + £4 = £15/desk

(b) Minimum price = Incremental costs + internal opportunity costs of scarce resource.

$$= £15 + \left[\frac{\text{contribution}}{\text{kg of material}} = \frac{£5}{2 \text{ kg}} \times 3 \text{ kg} \right]$$

$$= £15 + £7·50 = £22·50/\text{desk}$$

6.0   CONCLUSION

A firm's pricing policy is a vital part of its survival and success in a competitive world. Students must think broadly when making pricing decisions, and remember the effects of pricing policies when evaluating performance.

APPENDIX TO CHAPTER 9: MATHEMATICAL APPROACH TO OPTIMAL PRICING (USING CALCULUS)

If the average revenue (demand curve), marginal revenue and marginal cost functions are assumed to be linear over the range of output considered, it is possible to determine the optimal price and output mathematically.

(Note: It is also possible if these functions are non-linear, but the analysis is rather more complicated.)

Using the data in examples 4 and 5, and assuming a marginal cost per unit of £4, the analysis would be as follows:

(a) The demand curve $P = a + bq$, where
P = price, q = quantity, a = point of intersection with y axis, b = gradient of line.

For example 4, $a = £30$, $b = -4/8,000 = -0·0005$
∴ $P = 30 - 0·0005q$.

(b) The total revenue TR is Pq, therefore
$TR = 30q - 0.0005q^2$

and marginal revenue $MR = \dfrac{\mathrm{d}TR}{\mathrm{d}q}$

$\therefore \dfrac{\mathrm{d}TR}{\mathrm{d}q} = MR = 30 - 0.001q$

(c) The total cost TC function is $TC = FC + VCq$, where FC = fixed costs, VC = variable cost per unit.

For example 5, FC = £144,000 and VC = £4 (approximately).

$\therefore TC = 144,000 + 4q$

and marginal cost $MC = \dfrac{\mathrm{d}TC}{\mathrm{d}q}$

$\therefore \dfrac{\mathrm{d}TC}{\mathrm{d}q} = MC = 4$

(d) Profit is maximised $MR = MC$

$\therefore 30 - 0.001q = 4$

$\therefore q = 26,000$ units

(e) Substituting for q in the original demand curve,

$P = 30 - (0.0005 \times 26,000)$
$\ = £17$

Therefore, profit is maximised at a price of £17 per unit through selling 26,000 units.

(f) Maximum profit $\ =\ \ TR - TC$
$=\ \ Pq - (144,000 + 4q)$
$=\ \ (17 \times 26,000) - (144,000 + 4 \times 26,000)$
$=\ \ £194,000$

(Note: This is different from the solution provided earlier due to the assumption made in this appendix relating to a constant variable cost per unit of £4.)

CHAPTER TEN

Joint Product and Byproduct Costing

1.0 INTRODUCTION

When two or more products are simultaneously produced from a common set of inputs by a single process they are called *joint products*. Joint products are frequently found in the chemical and meat industries; for example, crude oil is refined into fuel oil, gasoline, lubricating oil and other products. A *byproduct* is incidental to the main joint products and of much lower sales value. Waste or residue is considered to have no value attaching to it.

The point at which joint products become separately identifiable is called *the split-off point*.

Production costs incurred prior to the split-off point are called *joint production costs*, and after this point are called *separable (additional) costs*. This may all be illustrated diagrammatically as in Fig. 17.

2.0 METHODS OF ALLOCATING JOINT PRODUCTION COSTS TO FINAL PRODUCTS

Joint costs need to be allocated to the final units of output in order to (1) value stock, (2) facilitate pricing decisions and (3) determine profit.

The main methods available are: (a) physical quantity basis, (b) sales value basis, and (c) net realisable value basis.

  (a) *Physical quantity basis.* Under this method joint costs are allocated on the basis of each product's relative portion of the total quantity.

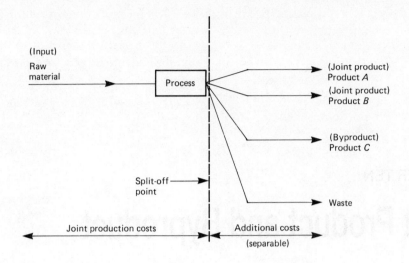

Fig. 17. *Joint and byproduct costing.*

Example 1

K Ltd processed chemical A (10,000 litres) into two joint products: B (8,000 litres) and C (2,000 litres). Joint production costs were £190,000. All output was sold, B at £22·50 per litre and C at £10 per litre.

Joint products	Physical quantity (litres)	Allocation of joint costs	£	Unit cost £	Net* income £
B	8,000	80% × 190,000 =	152,000 ÷ 8,000 = 19/litre		28,000
C	2,000	20% × 190,000 =	38,000 ÷ 2,000 = 19/litre		(18,000)
	10,000		190,000		£10,000

Net income*	£ B	£ C	£ Total
Sales	180,000	20,000	200,000
Allocated joint costs	152,000	38,000	190,000
	£28,000	£(18,000)	£10,000

When there is a close relationship between the physical measure and the selling price of individual products, this procedure is satisfactory. If this is not the case then this method of allocation will not result in an equitable apportionment of profitability between the joint products. Also it may be difficult to apply this method to heterogeneous products, such as a gas and a liquid.

    (b) *Sales value basis.* This method allocates joint costs on the basis of each product's relative portion of the total sales value.

Example 2

(facts as in example 1)

Joint products	Sales value	Allocation of joint costs £		Unit costs £	Net* income £
B	180,000	90% × 190,000 =	171,000	÷ 8,000 = 21.375/litre	9,000
C	20,000	10% × 190,000 =	19,000	÷ 2,000 = 9.50/litre	1,000
	£200,000		£190,000		£10,000

Net income*	£ B	Gross margin	£ C	Gross margin	£ Total
Sales	180,000		20,000		200,000
Allocated joint costs	171,000		19,000		190,000
	£9,000	5%	£1,000	5%	£10,000

This method provides a more equitable apportionment of profitability between the joint products (5% gross margins each).

    However, because this method is based on selling prices, allocated costs cannot be used as an input to pricing decisions. Standard selling prices can be used to overcome this problem.

    (c) *Net realisable value basis (NRV).* To make a product saleable, additional processing beyond the split-off point may be necessary. The associated costs incurred are easily identifiable with the product, but it is necessary to modify the sales value method. The additional costs must be deducted from the sales values to arrive at the NRV at the split-off point. These relative NRVs form the basis of joint cost allocation.

Example 3

(Facts as in examples 1 and 2 except that product C does not have a market. It must first be converted into product D, which sells for £40 per litre, and additional processing costs of £10 per litre are incurred.)

Joint products	Sales value	Additional costs	NRV	Allocation of joint costs		Unit Costs joint additional	Net* income
	£	£	£	£	£	£/litre	£
B	180,000	—	180,000	75% × 190,000 =	142,500 ÷8,000= 17·81—		37,500
D	80,000	20,000	60,000	25% × 190,000 =	47,500 ÷2,000= 23·75+10 = 33·75		12,500
			£240,000		£190,000		£50,000

Net income	£ B	Gross margin	£ D	Gross margin	£ Total
Sales	180,000		80,000		260,000
Allocated joint costs (including additional costs)	142,500		67,500		210,000
	£37,500	20·8%	£12,500	15·6%	£50,000

This method also provides an equitable apportionment of profitability. However, a change in the NRV of one joint product affects the joint costs allocated to another; for example, the change in C's NRV affects the cost of sales (allocated joint costs) and the gross profit of B. This fact is sometimes cited as an argument against the sales value method.

3.0 MULTIPLE SPLIT-OFF POINTS

Example 4

Facts as in examples 1, 2 and 3, except instead of converting product C into product D, management converts C into products E and F. This process requires mixing 3 litres of W with each litre of C to obtain 1 litre of E, 1 litre of waste, and 2 litres of F. The joint processing costs of E and F are £20 per litre of F. The joint processing costs of E and F are £20 per litre of C processed. After the second split-off point, E requires additional processing costs of £10 per litre. E is then sold for £50 per litre and F is sold for £20 per litre.

A diagram of the flow of products is shown below:

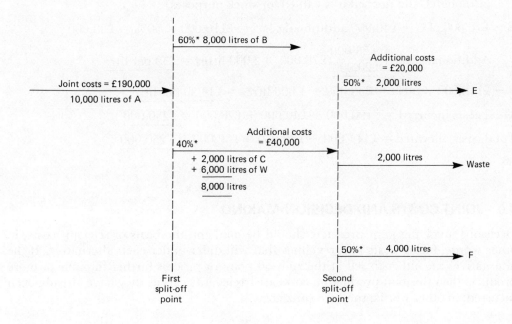

When multiple split-off points exist it is necessary to work backwards, commencing with the last split-off point in order to find a NRV basis for allocation of joint costs.

Product	Sales value	*Second split-off point* Additional costs	NRV	Basis for allocation
E	£100,000	£20,000	£80,000	50%*
F	80,000	—	80,000	50%*
			£160,000	

Product	Sales value	*First split-off point* Additional costs	NRV	Basis for allocation
B	£180,000	—	£180,000	60%*
C	160,000	£40,000	120,000	40%*
[from E and F]			£300,000	

The above percentages are now applied, working forward through the split-off points, to allocate joint costs to the units of output:

B — 60% of £190,000 = £114,000 ÷ 8,000 litres = <u>£14·25 per litre</u>

C $-$ 40% of £190,000 $=$ £76,000 $\div$ 2,000 litres $=$ <u>£38 per litre</u>
(although C did not sell it is valued for stock purposes)

E $-$ £76,000 of C + £40,000 additional costs $=$ £116,000 $\times$ 50% $=$ £58,000

Additional costs $+ \dfrac{£58,000}{£20,000}$ £78,000 $\div$ 2,000 litres $=$ <u>£39 per litre</u>

F $-$ £116,000 $\times$ 50% $=$ £58,000 $\div$ 4,000 litres $=$ <u>£14·50 per litre</u>

Total costs incurred $=$ £190,000 + £40,000 + £20,000 $=$ <u>£250,000</u>

Total costs allocated $=$ £114,000 + £78,000 + £58,000 $=$ <u>£250,000</u>

4.0   JOINT COSTS AND DECISION-MAKING

Decisions involving joint products should be made on the basis of relevant costs, in other words, future costs and revenues that will differ under each alternative. If the alternatives are either to sell at the split-off point or process further into one or more products then the joint production costs are irrelevant costs as they have already been incurred; in other words, they are sunk costs.

Example 5

Q Ltd produces two joint products — A (200,000 units) and B (100,000 units). Selling prices at the split-off are A $-$ £2·50, B $-$ £4. Joint production costs are £300,000.

A could be processed further to produce 120,000 units of C, but extra fixed costs of £40,000 and variable costs of 30p/unit of A processed would be incurred. C would sell for £6·50/unit.

Should Q Ltd process further?

SOLUTION
The joint production costs of £300,000 are sunk costs and therefore irrelevant to this decision. It is necessary to consider only relevant costs and revenue, which are the incremental revenue and the incremental costs of further processing.

Incremental revenue	= revenue from further processing − revenue from sales at the split-off.	
	= (120,000 of C × £6·50) − (200,000 of A × £2·50)	
	= £780,000 − £500,000	= £280,000
Incremental costs	= extra fixed costs + extra variable costs	
	= £40,000 + (200,000 × 30p)	= £100,000
	Net benefit from processing further	= £180,000

5.0 BYPRODUCT COSTING

Because byproducts tend to have a much lower sales value, costs are seldom assigned to them.

The basic accounting treatments of byproducts are:

(a) The net realisable value of the byproduct (not actual sales) is deducted from the cost of production;

(b) The net realisable value of the byproduct is deducted from the cost of sales.

Example 6

		Units	
Major product sales		800	£17,600
	production	1,000	16,000
Byproduct	sales	400 at £1 per unit	
	production	500	
	costs of disposal	20p per unit	

Calculate the profit using both methods above.

SOLUTION

(a) *NRV of byproduct deducted from cost of production*

	Units	
Sales of major product	800	£17,600
Cost of production:		
Production costs (500 × 80p) NRV of byproduct	1,000	16,000 (400)
Production costs		15,600
Less: Closing stock of major product	200	(3,120)
Cost of sales	800	12,480
Gross profit		£5,120

(b) *NRV of byproduct deducted from cost of sales*

	Units	
Sale of major product	800	£17,600
Cost of sales		
Production costs	1,000	16,000
Less: Closing stock of major product	200	3,200
	800	12,800
NRV of byproduct		(400)
Cost of sales		£12,400
Gross profit		£5,200

Students should note the following:

(i)   no costs are assigned to the byproduct;

(ii) the NRV is used in the calculations, not the actual sales and closing stock of the byproduct;

(iii) other accounting treatments of byproducts can be used; for example, byproduct income is shown as an addition to the sales of the main product, or as a separate source of income.

6.0 CONCLUSION

This topic has been frequently examined in recent examination papers, therefore students must master the basic principles as outlined above.

CHAPTER ELEVEN

Budgeting and Budgetary Control

1.0   INTRODUCTION

This chapter, in the main, deals with the mechanical aspects of budgeting, whereas the behavioural aspects are considered in Chapter 12. Students should note that a significant proportion of the written questions contained in section B of the paper examine topics that are covered in both these chapters.

Definition of a *budget*

A financial and/or quantitative plan for a defined period of time (usually one year, though it can be of shorter periods for control purposes).

Definition of *budgetary control*

A control technique whereby actual results are compared with budgets, and any differences (variances) arising are made the responsibility of key individuals who can either exercise control action or revise the original budgets.

Budgeting and budgetary control are therefore concerned with the preparation of budgets, establishing areas of responsibility and the comparison of actual results with budget. In other words we are considering the planning and control functions of the management accountant, which ensure that corporate objectives are achieved.

Planning involves estimating costs, determining priorities and allocating resources, in order to achieve corporate goals.

Budgeting is the detailed decision-making which determines how the resources are to be used.

Both are integrated as a unified system of control.

2.0 ADVANTAGES OF BUDGETING AND BUDGETARY CONTROL

(a) Planning is compelled: formal budget procedures compel management at all levels to think about the future, and to ensure that the long-term corporate plan is achieved.

(a) They promote coordination and communication: information about proposed activities of the firm is dispersed throughout the organisation to all levels of management, and departmental activities are brought in line with each other.

(c) Areas of responsibility are clearly defined so that costs and revenue can be assigned to those persons deemed responsible for them.

(d) A basis for performance evaluation is provided. Once the budget has been prepared then it provides a yardstick against which to measure the performance of the firm both in total and for each of its subcomponents. It is better to compare actual results with the budget than with the past, which may no longer be appropriate to current and future circumstances.

(e) Efficient and inefficient areas of the organisation are highlighted in the form of favourable and adverse variances, thereby prompting remedial action where necessary.

(f) Motivation is increased as the budgetary control system encourages participation in the setting of budgets, gives people more responsibility, and endeavours to align individual goals with the corporate goals.

(g) They should improve the allocation of scarce resources, and control spending.

(h) They economise on managerial time by using the management-by-exception principle.

The above list of advantages is not exhaustive and students must explore this topic through further reading.

3.0 PROBLEMS IN BUDGETING

(a) Apathy can exist amongst the work force; motivation becomes a difficult task.

(b) Budgets are seen as pressure devices imposed by management; this can lead to bad labour relations and inaccurate record keeping.

(c) Departmental conflict arises over resource allocation, and because departments blame each other if targets are not attained.

(d) It is difficult to reconcile personal and corporate goals, as the former continually change and may be considerably lower than the latter.

(e) Waste is found in budgets when managers adopt the view "we had better spend it or we will lose it". This problem, coupled with "empire building" in order to enhance the prestige of a department, can be overcome by using the technique called *zero base budgeting* (*see* 8.0 below).

(f) Inflation and other uncertainties can cause problems in the system (*see* 9.0 below).

(g) There is the problem of linking responsibility with controllability; in other words, costs are only controllable by a manager within a certain time span, and some costs are under the influence of more than one person.

(h) Dysfunctional decisions may arise when a manager aims to improve his short-run performance at the expense of the organisation as a whole; for example, delaying maintenance expenditure which needs to be carried out but would have the effect of increasing the charge to the department concerned.

(i) Managers may overestimate costs in order that they will not be blamed in the future should they overspend.

4.0   BUDGETS FOR PLANNING AND BUDGETS FOR CONTROL

Budgets for planning are based on what management believes will happen. However, budgets for control may exclude some items which are not thought likely to happen and may be based, for motivational purposes, on standards which are unlikely to reflect actual levels of achievement; for example, in planning for the effects of a possible strike, the potential effects will not usually be formalised into the monthly budget allowances of each department.

The main points of similarity and difference between the two types include:

(a) *Participation.* This is encouraged for control purposes, but not for the planning process.

(b) *Comprehensiveness.* Planning must embrace the whole firm whereas budgetary control may embrace only part of it.

(c) *Standards.* Planning budgets are based on standards of performance which management believe will exist. Control budgets have a motivational impact and therefore are based on standards which are likely to influence managerial behaviour in a way which is beneficial to the firm.

(d) *Flexibility.* Planning budgets must be flexible to changes in circumstances, and control budgets to changes in activity levels (*see* flexible budgets, 7.0 below).

(e) *Feedback.* This is essential for both types of budgets in order to ensure that standards are relevant, budgets are feasible and performance is constantly monitored.

(f) *Analysis of costs and revenue.* Budgets for planning frequently base cost estimates on an analysis of costs along product lines; budgets for control will analyse the cost into departments or cost centres irrespective of product lines dealt with.

5.0   BUDGET ORGANISATION AND ADMINISTRATION

The following prerequisites are necessary before a system of budgetary control can be implemented.

(a) *Budget centres.* These are clearly defined areas of the organisation where responsibility lies for the preparation of budgets; a budget centre may encompass several cost centres.

(b) *Budget committee:* this is comprised of senior members of the organisation (departmental heads and executives), and has the following purposes:

   (i)   gives support to the budgetary control system;

   (ii)   reviews budgets;

   (iii)   authorises the master budget;

   (iv)   establishes long-term plans;

   (v)   reviews actual results compared with budgets.

(c) *Budget officer.* He or she controls the budget administration; the job involves liaising between the budget committee and managers responsible for budget preparation, dealing with budgetary control problems, ensuring that deadlines are met, and educating people about budgetary control.

(d) *Budget manual.* This charts the organisation, and details the budget procedures; it contains account codes for items of expenditure and revenue, and timetables, and takes the form of a documented rule book, clearly defining the responsibilities of persons involved in the budgeting system.

6.0   BUDGET PREPARATION

The first thing to determine when preparing budgets is the limiting or principal budget factor, that is, the factor that limits output. It is usually sales, though material or labour can easily be a limiting factor.

6.1   Sales budget

This budget is expressed in quantitative and financial terms and will involve a realistic sales forecast.

Methods of sales forecasting include a combination of all or some of the following: salesforce opinions; market research; statistical methods (correlation analysis and examination of trends); mathematical models.

When using these methods several factors that influence consumer demand must be considered: company's pricing policy; general economic and political conditions; changes in the population; competition; consumers' tastes and incomes; advertising and other sales promotion techniques; strength of salesforce; aftersales service; credit terms offered, etc.

6.2   Production budget

The production budget is expressed in quantitative terms only, and is geared to the sales budget. The production manager's responsibilities involve plant utilisation and work-in-progress budgets.

If requirements exceed capacity, he may subcontract, plan for overtime or shift work, or hire or buy additional machinery. If requirements are less than capacity then any spare capacity may be used for other profitable purposes by management.

6.3   Raw materials and purchasing budget

The materials usage budget is in quantities, whereas the materials purchases budget is quantitative and financial. Factors influencing these budgets include production requirements; planning stock levels; storage space; trends of material prices.

6.4   Labour budget

This budget is quantitative and financial, and influenced by production requirements, man-hours available, grades of labour required, wage rates (union agreements), and the need for incentives.

6.5   Cash budget

The cash budget is a cash plan for a defined period of time. It summarises monthly cash receipts and payments, thus highlighting monthly surpluses and deficits.

Its main purposes are:

(a) to maintain control over a firm's cash requirements, particularly with respect to stock and debtor levels;

(b) to enable a company to take precautionary measures and arrange in advance for investment and loan facilities where budgeted surpluses and deficits arise;

(c) to show the feasibility of management's plans in cash terms;

(d) to illustrate the financial impact of changes in management policy, such as a change of the credit terms offered to customers.

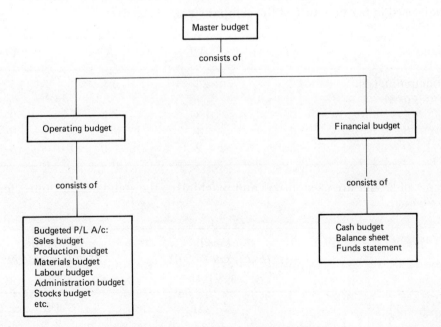

Fig. 18. *Composition of master budget.*

6.6 "Other" budgets

These include budgets for administration, research and development, selling and distribution expenses, capital expenditure (usually covering a period of five to ten years), and working capital (showing changes in debtors and creditors).

The master budget encompasses all of the above budgets, once they have been authorised by the budget committee. The following diagram illustrates a simplified sub-classification of the master budget.

In preparing this comprehensive plan, many subsidiary budget schedules are necessary (Fig. 18).

In the example that follows try and prepare the required budgets before working at the solution. The solution illustrates a mechanical step-by-step approach to formulating a master budget.

Example 1

B Ltd manufactures three types of product for the building industry. Budgeted sales of the products *A, B* and *C* are as follows:

Product	Quantity	Price
A	3,000	£60
B	7,000	70
C	5,000	80

Materials used in manufacture of the company's products are:

Components	X1	X2	X3	X4
Component unit cost	£2	£3	£4	£5
Quantities used:				
A	5	3	1	2
B	4	4	2	3
C	3	2	1	5

Two types of labour are used, fitters and machinists, the standard unit times for each product being:

	Fitters (hourly rate £0.50) hours	Machinists (hourly rate £0.60) hours
A	3	1·5
B	4	2
C	5	2·5

Production overheads which are absorbed into product costs on a direct basis are budgeted as follows:

Building occupancy	£30,050
Equipment utilisation	16,100
Personal services	12,150
Materials handling	9,310
Production planning and control	9,790

Selling and distribution costs budgeted are:

Representation	£101,300
Sales office	30,100
Advertising and publicity	29,100

and are charged to products in proportion to the sales income of the period.

Stocks at the beginning of the budget period are expected to be:

Finished goods	Quantity	£ Unit cost
A	1,000	39
B	3,000	51
C	2,000	51

Components	Quantity	£ Unit cost
X1	40,000	2
X2	20,000	3
X3	10,000	4
X4	30,000	5

The company plans an increase of 10% in the quantities of finished stocks held at the end of the budget period, and a reduction of 20% in the quantities of component stocks.

(a) Prepare budgets for:

   (i) sales;

   (ii) production;

   (iii) material usage;

   (iv) material purchases;

   (v) direct labour.

(b) Prepare a statement showing the valuation of finished stocks at the end of the budget period.

(c) Prepare a budget profit statement for the period, showing the amount of profit contributed by each product.

SOLUTION

(a) (i) *Sales budget*

Product	Quantity	Selling price	Sales volume
A	3,000	£60	£180,000
B	7,000	70	490,000
C	5,000	80	400,000
			£1,070,000

(ii) *Production budget*

Product	Sales budget	Stock increase	Production
A	3,000	100	3,100
B	7,000	300	7,300
C	5,000	200	5,200

(iii) *Materials usage budget*

Product	Components X1	X2	X3	X4
A	15,500	9,300	3,100	6,200
B	29,200	29,200	14,600	21,900
C	15,600	10,400	5,200	26,000
	60,300	48,900	22,900	54,100

(iv) *Materials purchases budget*

	X1	Components X2	X3	X4	Total
Budgeted usage	60,300	48,900	22,900	54,100	
Stock decrease	8,000	4,000	2,000	6,000	
Purchased quantities	52,300	44,900	20,900	48,100	
Cost prices	£2	£3	£4	£5	
Purchase values	£104,600	£134,700	£83,600	£240,500	£563,400

(v) Direct labour utilisation and cost budget

Product	Production budget	Fitters	Machinists	Total
A	3,100	9,300	4,650	
B	7,300	29,200	14,600	
C	5,200	26,000	13,000	
Total direct labour hours		64,500	32,250	

	Fitters	Machinists	
Budgeted labour rates/hour	£0·50	£0·60	
Total direct labour costs	£32,250	£19,350	£51,600

(b) Finished stock valuation

Product	Quantity	Unit cost	Stock value
A	1,100	£39	£42,900
B	3,300	51	168,300
C	2,200	51	112,200
			£323,400

(c) Budgeted profit statement

	A		B		C		Total
Sales units	3,000		7,000		5,000		15,000
		per unit		per unit		per unit	
Sales revenue	£180,000	£60·00	£490,000	£70·00	£400,000	£80·00	£1,070,000
Production costs	117,000	39·00	357,000	51·00	255,000	51·00	729,000
Selling and distribution costs	27,000	9·00	73,500	10·50	60,000	12·00	160,500
Profit	£36,000	£12·00	£59,500	£8·50	£85,000	£17·00	£180,500

Workings

Calculation of unit product costs

		A £	B £	C £
(i)	Components (usage and costs per materials budget)			
	X1	10	8	6
	X2	9	12	6
	X3	4	8	4
	X4	10	15	25
		— 33	— 43	— 41

(ii) Direct labour hours (hours and rates per direct labour budgets)

	A	B	C
Fitter	1·5	2·0	2·5
Machinist	0·9	1·2	1·5
	— 2·4	— 3·2	— 4·0

(iii) Production overheads:

Total overheads £30,050 + 16,100 + 12,150 + 9,310 + 9,790)

= £77,400

Total direct labour hours (64,500 + 32,250) = 96,750

∴ Rate per hour (£77,400 ÷ 96,750) = £0·80

hours	£	hours	£	hours	£
4·5	3·60	6·0	4·80	7·5	6·00

(iv) *Unit cost of production*

	A £	B £	C £
Components	33·00	43·00	41·00
Labour	2·40	3·20	4·00
Overheads	3·60	4·80	6·00
	£39·00	£51·00	£51·00

(v) *Apportionment of selling and distribution costs:*

$$\frac{\text{Total costs}}{\text{Sales value}} = \frac{£160,500}{£1,070,000} = 15\%$$

	A £	B £	C £
Selling price	60	70	80
Selling and distribution costs apportionment 15%	9	10·5	12

Examination example 2

Textiles Ltd operates a subsidiary, the Sunny Textile Company Ltd, which manufactures ladies swimwear. Following the success of this subsidiary it has been decided to expand it by diversifying into the production of swimwear for all the family. An extension to the Sunny Textile Company Ltd's factory is now being built for this purpose. The contract for this extension is for £100,000; 10% of the contract price had to be paid on signing the contract in December 19X5. Another £50,000 has to be paid on 30 March 19X6 with the balance due on the later of 30 May 19X6 or completion.

The financial year of the Sunny Textile Company Ltd runs from the 1 April and budgeted figures for the 19X6 calendar year have been produced as follows:

Month	Sales (before discounts allowed)	Purchase of raw materials (before discounts received)	Wages	Fixed overheads (including depreciation of £1,000 per month)
January	£6,000	£10,000	£5,000	£2,000
February	6,000	10,000	5,000	2,000
March	24,000	10,000	5,000	2,000
April	48,000	10,000	5,000	2,000
May	48,000	10,000	5,000	2,000
June	48,000	10,000	5,000	7,000
July	24,000	10,000	5,000	2,000
August	12,000	—	4,000	2,000
September	2,000	10,000	5,000	2,000
October	4,000	10,000	5,000	2,000
November	4,000	10,000	5,000	2,000
December	2,000	10,000	6,000	7,000
Total	£228,000	£110,000	£60,000	£34,000

In budgeting cash at bank on 1 April 19X6 at £50,000 the company has overlooked the contract payment for the factory extension due on 30 March 19X6.

Although the Sunny Textile Company Ltd requires payment for its sales in the month following that in which the sale is made, and offers a settlement discount of 5% for accounts settled within this period, experience has taught it to expect only half the payments when due. One-quarter of the payments follow during the second month after sale and the balance comes in the third month. Bad debts average $2\frac{1}{2}$% of sales.

It is the company's policy to pay for supplies during the month in which they are delivered in order to take advantage of a 10% prompt settlement discount offered by all its suppliers.

The level of stocks at the end of December 19X6 are expected to remain unchanged from those prevailing in January. These are valued on a variable cost basis. The architect issued a final certificate for the factory extension on 19 April.

Required:
Prepare for the Sunny Textile Company Ltd:

(a) a budgeted profit and loss account,

(b) a cash budget on a monthly basis,

both for the six months commencing 1 April 19X6, stating clearly any assumptions that you need to make.

SOLUTION
Budgeted profit and loss account for the six months commencing 1/4/X6

Sales		£182,000	
Less: Discounts (5% of £91,000)	£4,550		
Bad debts ($2\frac{1}{2}$% of £182,000)	4,550		
	———	9,100	
			£172,900
Less: Expenses and costs:			
Discounts received (10% of £50,000)		(5,000)	
*Material cost of sales (48·25% of revenue)		87,800	
*Wages (26·3% of revenue)		47,900	
Fixed overheads		11,000	
Depreciation		6,000	
		———	147,700
		Budgeted net profit	£25,200

Workings

To ascertain the material and labour costs of sales for the six-month period a decrease in the volume of stocks over the period must be recognised. A percentage cost of materials and labour to sales for the year is taken as applicable to the six-month period, as a basis for cost of sales (and conversely stock valuation).

$$*\text{Materials} \quad = \frac{£110,000}{£228,000} \times 100 = 48 \cdot 25\%$$

$$*\text{Labour} \quad = \frac{£60,000}{£228,000} \times 100 = 26 \cdot 3\%$$

Fixed overheads are treated as period expenses, and therefore problems of stock valuation do not arise.

Discounts received have been treated as financial items in the period in which the discount is taken (Table 1).

7.0   FLEXIBLE BUDGETS

All budgets discussed so far have been fixed (inflexible), that is, tailored to a single level of activity.

In contrast, flexible budgets are prepared for a range of activity levels in order to provide a basis for comparison with actual.

Example 3

The planned level of activity for a machining department is 5,000 finished units for the next month, with the following budgeted variable overhead:

Indirect labour	£2,100
Material	500
Maintenance	400
	£3,000

Actual output was only 4,700 units and the actual variable overhead was:

Indirect labour	£2,080
Material	480
Maintenance	400
	£2,960

Table 1: *Cash budget for the six months commencing 1/4/X6 in £s*

Month	April	May	June	July	August	September	Total
Balance of cash (brought down)	nil	(750)	(25,600)	(5,400)	25,200	54,400	nil
Cash from sales							
January	1,350						1,350
February	1,500	1,350					2,850
March	11,400	6,000	5,400				22,800
April		22,800	12,000	10,800			45,600
May			22,800	12,000	10,800		45,600
June				22,800	12,000	10,800	45,600
July					11,400	6,000	17,400
August						5,700	5,700
Total cash Received from debtors	14,250	30,150	40,200	45,600	34,200	22,500	186,900
Payments							
Suppliers	9,000	9,000	9,000	9,000	nil	9,000	45,000
Wages	5,000	5,000	5,000	5,000	4,000	5,000	29,000
Fixed overheads	1,000	1,000	6,000	1,000	1,000	1,000	11,000
Building		40,000					40,000
Total cash paid	15,000	55,000	20,000	15,000	5,000	15,000	125,000
Balance of cash (carried forward)	(750)	(25,600)	(5,400)	25,200	54,400	61,900	61,900

7.1 Performance report: variable overhead

	Actual	Budget	Variance
Units	4,700	5,000	300 adverse
Indirect labour	£2,080	£2,100	£20 favourable
Material	480	500	20 favourable
Maintenance	400	400	—
	£2,960	£3,000	£40 favourable

The above report illustrates that comparing performance at one activity level with a plan developed at some other activity level is nonsense from the viewpoint of judging how efficiently a manager has produced a given output.

7.2 The flexible budget: variable overhead

Units produced	per unit	4,600	4,700	4,800	5,000	5,200
Indirect labour	£0·42	£1,932	£1,974	£2,016	£2,100	£2,184
Materials	0·10	460	470	480	500	520
Maintenance	0·08	368	376	384	400	416
	£0·60	2,760	2,820	2,880	3,000	3,120

The actual output was 4,700 units, and a better indication of true performance would be as follows:

	Actual	Budget	Variance
Units	4,700	4,700	—
Indirect labour	£2,080	£1,974	£106 adverse
Materials	480	470	10 adverse
Maintenance	400	376	24 adverse
	£2,960	£2,820	£140 adverse

The flexible budget presents a more meaningful comparison of the manager's day-to-day overhead cost control, because the level of activity underlying the comparison is the same.

The problem of measuring and reporting the resulting variances is dealt with in Chapters 13, 14 and 15 on standard costing and variance analysis.

The flexible budget approach is based on an adequate knowledge of cost behaviour patterns. Cost behaviour and methods of cost classification have been discussed in earlier chapters.

Example 4

Thomas Ltd is a small firm which manufactures cleaning fluid. Its management realise that, as a small company, it must constantly strive to control and reduce costs in order to be competitive. The accounting department provided the following information to aid the planning process.

Plant capacity — 2,250,000 litres of cleaning fluid per year.
Selling price will average an expected 52p per litre next year.

	Worst			*Best*	*Actual 19X6*
Litres of product sold (000s)	1,200	1,400	1,750	2,000	1,800
Revenue from sales	£600,000	£650,000	£750,000	£900,000	£850,000
Cost of goods sold:					
Materials	£300,000	£340,000	£375,000	£500,000	£495,000
Labour	120,000	154,000	200,000	250,000	240,000
Factory overhead	17,000	19,000	22,500	25,000	23,000
Total	437,000	513,000	597,500	775,000	758,000
Gross profit	£163,000	137,000	152,500	125,000	92,000
Marketing expenses	16,000	16,000	18,000	20,000	20,000
Administration expenses	30,000	30,000	30,000	30,000	30,000
Total	£46,000	46,000	48,000	50,000	50,000
Net profit before tax	£117,000	91,000	104,500	75,000	42,000

Prior to his resignation, the former chief accountant had devised a standard labour cost for 19X6 at 10·909p per litre for the entire process. An examination of the figures indicates that they are quite adequate except for an expected rise of 10% in wage rates since 19X6 prices. The average cost of the mix of materials was 26p per litre of fluid. Materials usage seldom varies. Overhead expenses are anticipated to remain at 19X6 price levels.

Prepare a flexible budget in profit statement form for the year 19X7, to cover a range from 1,250,000 to 2,500,000 litres, with increments of 250,000 litres. Use the high and low method in segregating the fixed and variable elements of any semivariable expenses. You may assume that only administrative expenses are fixed costs.

SOLUTION

Profit statement for the year 19X7

Sales (litres)	1,250,000	1,500,000	1,750,000	2,000,000	2,250,000
Revenue (£)					
52p/litre	650,000	780,000	910,000	1,040,000	1,170,000
Cost of goods sold					
Materials					
(26p/litre)	325,000	390,000	455,000	520,000	585,000
Labour (12p/litre)	150,000	180,000	210,000	240,000	270,000
Factory overhead:*					
Fixed	5,000	5,000	5,000	5,000	5,000
Variable	12,500	15,000	17,500	20,000	22,500
Total	£492,500	590,000	687,500	785,000	882,500
Gross profit	£157,500	190,000	222,500	255,000	287,500
Marketing expenses:					
Fixed	10,000	10,000	10,000	10,000	10,000
Variable	6,250	7,500	8,750	10,000	11,250
Administration					
expenses	30,000	30,000	30,000	30,000	30,000
Total	£46,250	47,500	48,750	50,000	51,250
Net profit	£111,250	142,500	173,750	205,000	236,250

Workings*

	Factory overhead Litres (000s)	Total cost
High	2,000	£25,000
Low	1,200	17,000
Difference	800	£8,000

$$\frac{£8,000}{800 \text{ litres}} = £10 \text{ per thousand litres variable cost per litre}$$

$$2,000 \times £10 = £20,000 \text{ variable factory overhead}$$

£25,000 Total factory cost

£5,000 Fixed factory overhead

Marketing expenses are segregated into fixed and variable elements in the same way.

8.0   ZERO BASE BUDGETING (ZBB)

Zero base budgeting is a technique whereby every item of expenditure in the budget is fully justified, i.e. we start from scratch or zero.

In production departments planned input to sustain budgeted output can easily be costed. However, in other departments (e.g. accounts, personnel, research and development, etc.) it is very difficult to even identify output, let alone cost the input to sustain the output. Instead last year's budgets tend to be subjectively increased, to allow for the next year's budgeted expenditure. However, last year's budgets may be inefficient and mere adjustments to these budgets lead to increased wastage. Zero base budgeting should, to a certain extent, overcome this problem.

8.1   The application of ZBB

The basic approach can be described in the following stages:

(a) Each separate activity of the organisation is identified and called *a decision package*.

(b) The existence of every decision package must be justified.

(c) If justified, then the minimum effort required to sustain each package is costed.

(d) Alternatives for each package are considered in order to select the best options for packages.

(e) *Incremental packages* (for additional work) are justified and costed as above.

(f) Managers rank their decision packages in order of priority for resource allocation.

(g) Resources are allocated.

8.2   Advantages of ZBB

(a) It identifies and eliminates wastage.

(b) It ensures that the best possible methods of performing jobs are used, and that new ideas are generated.

(c) It should result in more efficient allocation of resources.

(d) It increases communication within the organisation.

(e) It involves participation of management and should therefore motivate.

(f) The documentation of decision packages provides management with a deep, coordinated knowledge of all the firm's activities.

(g) It makes managers more aware of the costs of inputs, and helps them to identify priorities.

8.3   Disadvantages of ZBB

(a) The costs of preparing a vast number of decision packages in a large firm are very high.

(b) A large volume of additional paper work is created.

(c) Managers feel threatened by it.

(d) The ranking of decision packages and allocation of resources is subjective to a certain degree and can give rise to departmental conflict.

(e) Despite increased participation, a large volume of information travels one-way — downwards.

9.0 UNCERTAINTY IN BUDGETING

Uncertainty exists in budgeting because of problems with inflation, weather, technological change, competition and the expense of forecasting techniques.

Management must be made aware of the consequences of unexpected results and the following methods of analysing uncertainty are used:

(a) *The use of probabilities:* to show the likelihood of events arising and to ascertain expected values. *Standard deviation* can then be applied as a measurement of risk.

(b) *The three-point estimate:* three levels of budgets are projected showing most likely, worst possible, and best possible conditions. Probabilities can be applied to these possible outcomes.

(c) *Simulation:* a simulated model can be developed with the aid of a computer. This model is representative of a real life situation as it possesses all the variables and the interrelationships between them, such as *the economic batch order quantity model* for stock control, and a cash flow model.

(d) *Sensitivity analysis:* tests how sensitive profit or cash flow, etc., is to changes in the variables in the budget, e.g. what effect would a 10 per cent increase in labour costs, or a 15 per cent drop in sales volume have on profit or cash flow.

Students should note that the above methods are explained in more detail in Chapter 8.

Uncertainty can be reduced by using certain techniques which include:

(a) market research;

(b) delphi technique — consensus of expert opinions for sales forecasting;

(c) government indices to allow for inflation;

(d) shorter budget periods.

(e) continuous budgeting *(rolling budgets):* this involves extending the current budget by an extra period as the current period ends; budgets can then be prepared on a monthly basis; for example,

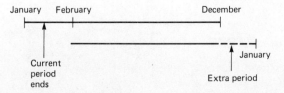

Although continuous budgeting is more expensive it reduces uncertainty, particularly when there is rapid inflation.

10.0 COSTS FOR BUDGETARY CONTROL PURPOSES

These costs can be classified into three types of costs — committed, engineered, and discretionary costs.

10.1 Committed costs

These are the least responsive of the fixed costs, and cannot be reduced without injuring the ability to meet long-range goals. They are difficult to influence by short-run decisions. Examples include depreciation, insurance, and construction costs, that is, costs that arise from having property, plant, and equipment. They are controlled through capital expenditure budgets.

10.2 Discretionary costs

Also called managed or programmed costs, these are fixed costs that (a) arise from periodic appropriation decisions (annual budgets), and (b) do not have a demonstrable relationship between input (costs) and output. Examples include advertising, public relations, research and development, accounting and legal costs. They are more easily reduced than committed costs, and are best controlled through zero base budgeting. There tends to be uncertainty about the correct amount to be spent.

10.3 Engineered costs

These are any costs which have an explicit specified relationship with a selected measure of activity, for example, physical and human resources such as direct material, direct labour and fuel costs. They are repetitive, and their quality and value are easily determined. There is no uncertainty about these costs as they can be physically observed and controlled through flexible budgets. Engineered costs are usually variable costs.

Students should note that management policy can transform a fixed cost into a variable cost, such as the replacement of equipment with labour (and vice versa).

11.0 CONCLUSION

Budgeting and budgetary control are integral parts of management accounting, without which the firm's long-term goals could not be achieved.

Students must attach equal importance to the next chapter which considers the "human" side of budgeting, that is, the behavioural aspects of budgeting, and motivation.

CHAPTER TWELVE

Behavioural Aspects of Budgeting

1.0 INTRODUCTION

One of the main purposes of management accounting is to influence the behaviour of managers and employees so that their resulting actions yield maximum efficiency. This influence can be exercised either by establishing administrative procedures (a budgetary control system), with its inherent rigidity and "red tape", or by the motivation of individuals. It is the latter which is examined in this chapter.

2.0 THEORIES OF MOTIVATION

Human behaviour cannot be motivated on the basis of economic factors alone, and theories of leading writers on this subject are summarised below.

2.1 Maslow

Maslow believed that the individual is striving to satisfy a hierarchy of basic needs represented in Fig. 19.

Maslow suggested that individuals' needs should be identified and then satisfied. However, there are two problems with this theory — (a) some people are willing to forego a lower need in order to achieve a higher need, and (b) different people behave in different ways towards the same need.

2.2 Herzberg

Herzberg's research identified the following factors, which he calls *real motivators:* achievement, recognition, the nature of the work, responsibility, and advancement.

Other factors which do not motivate, but prevent dissatisfaction, he called *hygiene factors* and include: company policy and administration, supervision, salary, interpersonal relations, and working conditions.

Herzberg prescribed job enrichment as an employee motivator. *Job enrichment* involves challenging work, in which responsibility can be assumed.

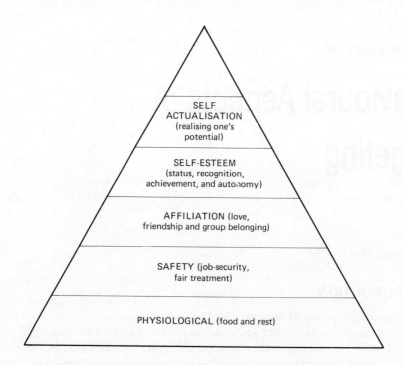

Fig. 19. *Maslow's hierarchy of needs.*

2.3 McClelland

McClelland suggested that there are two major needs; these are: the need for achievement, and the need for power (power over oneself and others). The drive for these needs varies in individuals according to their personality and background.

He classified people as *"high achievers"* and *"low achievers"*. The high achiever relishes responsibility, thrives on challenges, and sets himself high standards. He is less concerned with money because satisfaction flows from accomplishment, and he makes a more successful manager than the low achiever.

If the best is to be got out of people it is important to identify the personal characteristics of the high achiever and low achiever, in the context of the budget and general management.

2.4 Christopher Argyris

Argyris identified four problems with budgeting:

(a) The budget is seen by employees as a pressure device imposed by management because it considers employees to be lazy. Management use pressure to improve performance. This is resented and causes bad labour relations.

(b) Budgets are used by managers to express their leadership style. Subordinates who dislike their leader's presentation blame the budget rather than the leader.

(c) Departmental conflict arises as a result of managers being preoccupied with their own departments instead of cooperating together to achieve overall company goals. Failure is blamed on other departments.

(d) There is a feeling of "them" and "us" between the accounting department (who enforce the budgetary control system) and the other departments, as the success of the former (in finding an adverse variance) is the failure of the latter. This feeling of failure demotivates the workforce and lowers performance.

Argyris advocated that participation (real not pseudo) by employees in budget-setting would encourage responsibility, boost morale and thereby increase motivation. Also he stated that training in communication and labour relations should be present in order to alleviate the above problems.

2.5 Charles Horngren

Horngren suggests that there are two aspects to motivation:

(a) *Goal congruence:* the alignment of individual managerial goals with the goals of the organisation as a whole.

(b) *Incentive:* the driving force that influences action towards a goal.

Horngren states that an accounting system should be designed so as to motivate its users, as long as such a system is cost-effective.

2.6 McGregor

McGregor identified two types of leadership style which affect motivation:

(a) *Theory X:* an authoritarian approach with communication one way, from the top downwards, and no participation. Discipline is strict and pay rewards are good.

(b) *Theory Y:* which adopts the view that employees are not innately lazy, and can be motivated towards work, provided management knows how to motivate them. Responsibility and participation should be encouraged.

Rensis Lickert agreed with the theory Y view, and observed that the best managers cared about their subordinates, as well as expecting a high level of performance both from them and themselves.

2.7 Becker and Green

Becker and Green suggested that budgets should be linked with a group's level of aspiration instead of fixed calendar time periods. If performance exceeds the level of aspiration the budget is revised upwards, but if performance falls short of aspirations the budget is revised downwards. A good feedback system is necessary in order to inform groups regularly about their actual performance.

The main problem with this idea is that levels of aspiration of different groups continually change, and may not be congruent with the goals of the organisation as a whole.

2.8 Anthony Hopwood

Hopwood observed the following problems with budgets:

(a) Budgets are arrived at after a bargaining process in which managers compete for resources. They therefore represent a "watered-down" version of original goals, in order to satisfy all interested parties.

(b) Budgets should represent all the objectives of the organisation, but tend to be too profit-orientated.

(c) Employee aspirations may not be congruent with management expectations.

Hopwood also criticised the arguments in favour of participation, and stated that successful participation will depend upon (i) whether individuals want to participate; (ii) if the social climate at work lends itself to participation; (iii) if the work is unpredictable.

Hopwood concluded that although participation does boost employee morale, its effect on productivity is unknown. Furthermore, both authoritarian and participative styles of management are necessary, depending on the circumstances.

3.0 INFERENCES FROM THE ABOVE WRITERS

The following series of guidelines can perhaps be listed as being indicative of good budgeting given the implications of behavioural science.

(a) Budgets should be prepared on a participatory basis, and participation must be real not pseudo.

(b) Budgets should not be used to pressurise employees.

(c) Responsibilities must be clearly defined.

(d) Information should flow downwards and upwards.

(e) There should be frequent communication (meetings) between manager and subordinates.

(f) Good performance should be well rewarded, and may take the form of increased salary, promotion, etc.

(g) Budget accountants must avoid technical jargon when communicating with non-financial staff, and be sensitive to the reactions of employees outside of their domain — the accounts department.

(h) The budgetary control system must be supportive rather than punitive.

(i) Budgets which are attainable but not too tight are the best motivators.

(j) The needs of individuals should be identified and where possible satisfied.

(k) The nature of the work is important and management must try to make it as interesting as possible.

(l) Budgets should be linked to aspiration levels in order that an individual's objectives are congruent with those of the organisation, thereby increasing his or her motivation.

4.0 CONCLUSION

Management accounting is inextricably bound up with human behaviour. The above list of writers on this topic is not exhaustive, and students should supplement this chapter with further reading. The subject of motivation is referred to again in the chapter on the setting of standards (*see* Chapter 13).

CHAPTER THIRTEEN

An Introduction to Standard Costing and Basic Variance Analysis

1.0 INTRODUCTION

Standard costing is the setting of predetermined cost estimates in order to provide a basis for comparison with actual. The term "standard cost" is a unit concept, in other words, the standard cost of material is £1 per unit. However, the term "budgeted cost" is a total concept, in other words, the budgeted cost of material is £10,000 if 10,000 units are to be produced.

2.0 ADVANTAGES OF STANDARD COSTING

(a) Standards are the building blocks which are used to compile budgets.

(b) Actual costs can be compared with standard cost in order to measure performance.

(c) The setting of standards should result in the best resources and methods being used, which will increase efficiency.

(d) It highlights areas of strength and weakness.

(e) Standard costs can be used to value stock, and as a basis for setting wage incentive schemes.

(f) It operates through the management by exception principle, where only those variances which are outside certain tolerance limits are investigated, thereby economising on managerial time.

(g) Standard costing simplifies bookkeeping, as information is recorded at standard, instead of a number of historic, figures.

(h) Control action is immediate; for example, as soon as material is issued from stores in order to make a product it can be compared with the standard material which should have been used for the actual production.

(i) Managers are made responsible for standards.

3.0 TECHNICAL AND COST STANDARDS

Technical standards determine standard quantities for material and labour. Work study and the learning curve are useful techniques for this purpose. Students should note that *a standard hour* is not just a measure of time, but a measure of work content; for example, 100 chairs at three hours per chair and 200 desks at six hours per desk can be expressed as 1,500 hours of output.

Cost standards determine standard prices and rates for material and labour. Suppliers' prices, discounts, inflation, union negotiations, etc. are some of the variables that must be considered when these standards are set.

4.0 PROBLEMS IN STANDARD COSTING

(a) A heavy load of input data is required which is expensive.

(b) Standard costing is only applicable in organisations where processes or jobs are of a repetitive nature.

(c) Unless standards are set which are accurate with respect to labour efficiency, quality and price of material, any comparison with actual will be meaningless.

(d) Because of uncertainty, especially that related to inflation, standards need to be continually updated and revised.

5.0 TYPES OF STANDARDS

There are three main types of performance standards:

(a) *Basic standards:* these are unchanging standards relating to past circumstances and are therefore seldom used. They do have an advantage of identifying trends of efficiency and price changes over the years.

(b) *Ideal standards:* these assume perfect conditions; in other words, material and labour can be acquired at the cheapest cost, and there is no inefficiency, wastage, nor machine breakdowns. These standards are unrealistic and tend to have an adverse motivational effect on the workforce.

(c) *Expected (currently attainable) standards:* these are realistic and do allow for some normal loss, machine breakdowns, and inefficiency. However, an expected standard is still high enough to have a motivational effect on employees, and tends to be commonly used.

Standards which are too loose will have no motivational impact on labour, therefore tight standards should be set so that operators of the system will consider the achievement of standard performance to be worthwhile.

However, it is important that standards are not too tight as they become unrealistic (that is, unattainable) and therefore not worth the challenge.

6.0   VARIANCE ANALYSIS

Variances explain the differences between expected and actual results, so that operating statements can be prepared which reconcile actual profit with budgeted profit or contribution.

Figure 20 is a summary of the main variances to be calculated. Some of these variances are dealt with in this chapter, and others in the next chapter.

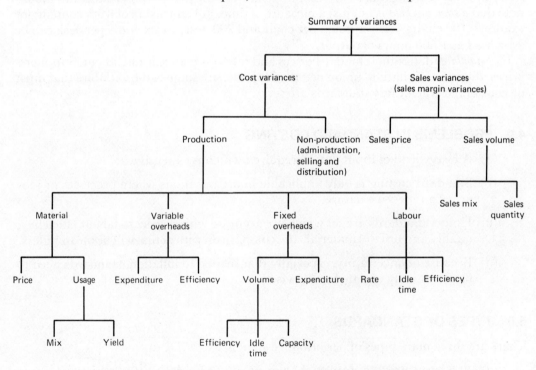

Fig. 20. *Summary of main variances.*

7.0   REASONS FOR VARIANCES

Labour rate   use of higher/lower grade of skilled workers, and wage
                       inflation.

Labour efficiency   use of higher/lower grade of skilled workers, and quality of
                       material used.

Idle time	illness, machine breakdown, and hold-ups because of lack of material.
Material price	good/bad purchasing, and material price inflation.
Material usage	high/low quality of material, quality control, efficiency of workforce.
Overhead expenditure	inflation, and greater/less economical use of services.
Overhead capacity	underutilisation/overutilisation of plant capacity.
Overhead efficiency	a different recovery of overhead from that of standard, as expected and actual output differed.

Students will note the interdependence between variances; for example, an adverse material price variance may be a result of buying a superior quality of material, which in turn has caused a favourable material usage variance. Another example is where favourable efficiency variances may be a result of using more highly paid and skilled workers, which causes an adverse labour rate variance.

8.0   COMPREHENSIVE EXAMPLE

Before attempting this example students must master the general approach to the analysis of variances.

A total variance (cost variance) can be subdivided into two (or more) component variances, namely:

    (a) price, rate or expenditure variance; and

    (b) usage, efficiency or volume variance.

8.1   Price or rate variance

Actual cost	is compared with	*what it should cost.*
∴ Actual quantity × actual price	is compared with	actual quantity × standard price.

This can be simplified to the formula of:

$$\text{(Actual price} - \text{standard price) actual quantity}$$

8.2   Usage or efficiency variance

Actual quantity used	is compared with	*what should be used*
∴ Actual quantity × standard price	is compared with	standard quantity × standard price.

This can be simplified to the formula of

$$\text{(Actual quantity} - \text{standard quantity) standard price}$$

In order to find the standard quantity for actual production it will be necessary to flex the budget.

Example 1

(a) *Standard data per unit*

Standard price	£	£6	
Direct labour	0.64		(budget for 2,400 direct labour hours (12,000 units))
Material	3·00		(standard labour cost £3·20/hour)
Variable overheads	0·16		
		(3·80)	(5 units/hour to be made)
Contribution		2·20	
Fixed overheads		(0.20)	(standard material cost £1·50/kg and each unit
Profit		£2·00	requires 2 kg)

(Budget fixed over-heads £2,400 based on direct labour hours)

(budget variable overheads/direct labour hour = £0·80)

(b) *Actual data*

11,500 units manufactured — 2,320 direct labour hours, paid for at £3·25/hour.

25,000 kg of material were purchased for £1·48/kg, 23,400 kg were consumed. Stocks are valued at standard cost.

Actual variable overheads	£1,750
Actual fixed overheads	£2,462

10,000 units were sold for £7 each.

Prepare opening statements using absorption and marginal costing principles.

SOLUTION

(a) *Calculation of variances*

Labour variances

Rate variance = (actual rate − standard rate) actual hours *paid*
= (£3·25 − £3·20) 2,320 hours   = £116 *adverse*

Efficiency variance = (actual hours worked − standard hours) standard rate.
= (2,320 hours − 2,300 hours) £3.20   = £64 *adverse*

↑ 11,500 units   ↑ 11,500 units should use − 5 units/hour (flex to actual production).

Material variances

Rate variance = (actual price − standard price) actual quantity *purchased*
= (1·48 − £1·50) 25,000 kg = <u>£500</u> *favourable*

Usage variance = (actual quantity *used* − standard quantity) standard price
= £23,400 kg − 23,000 kg) £1·50 = <u>£600</u> *adverse*

11,500 units   11,500 units should use 2 kg/unit
(flex to actual production).

Variable overheads

Expenditure variance = (actual rate − standard rate) actual hours *worked*.

= (£1,750 − £0·80 × 2,320 hours) (variable overheads are
not incurred during idle
(Actual hours − Standard × Actual time).
× actual rate)   rate   hours

= £106 *favourable*

Efficiency variance = (actual hours *worked* − standard hours) standard rate
= (2,320 hours − 2,300 hours) £0·80 = <u>£16</u> *adverse*

11,500 units   11,500 units should use 5 units/hour
(flex to actual production).

Fixed overheads

The analysis of fixed overhead variances differs from the general approach towards variable costs. At the outset, a budgeted fixed overhead absorption (recovery) rate is calculated by dividing the budgeted cost by the normal activity level (in this case selecting direct labour hours as the basis of activity)

= £2,400 ÷ 2,400 hours = £1/hour.

This is the basis of the charge to production for fixed overheads.

Overheads recovered by production may differ from actual overheads incurred for reasons of expenditure and/or volume.

Expenditure variance = (actual fixed overheads − budgeted fixed
overheads)
= (£2,462 − £2,400) = <u>£62</u> *adverse*

Volume variance = (budgeted hours − standard hours) standard fixed
overhead rate
= (2,400 hours − 2,300 hours) £1 = <u>£100</u> *adverse*

This variance (volume) is adverse because the fixed overheads are *underrecovered*. This may have arisen from one or both of two causes — a capacity effect and an efficiency effect.

Capacity variance
= (budgeted hours − actual hours worked) standard fixed overhead rate
= (2,400 hours − 2,320 hours) £1   =   £80 *adverse*

This is adverse as capacity was underutilised resulting in an underrecovery of overheads.

Efficiency variance
= (actual hours worked − standard hours) standard fixed overhead rate
= (2,320 hours − 2,300 hours) £1   =   £20 *adverse*

This is adverse as more units should have been made in the hours actually worked.

The volume variance   = capacity + efficiency variances
£100 adverse   = £80 adverse + £20 adverse

Students will note that it is impossible to have volume variances associated with variable costs because, by definition, the amount of the cost is expected to vary with activity.

Sales margin variances
These variances calculate the effect that sales price differences or sales volume differences between budget and actual have on the profit or contribution margin.

Price variance   = (actual price − standard price) actual quantity sold
                   = (£7 − £6) 10,000 units   =   £10,000 *favourable*

Volume variance
= (actual quantity sold − budgeted quantity sold) standard profit or
   contribution per unit

        = (10,000 units − 12,000 units) £2   = £4,000 *adverse*

underabsorption costing, using standard profit.

$$or \quad = (10{,}000 \text{ units} - 12{,}000 \text{ units}) \; £2{·}20 \qquad\qquad = \underline{£4{,}400} \; adverse$$

undermarginal costing, using standard contribution.

For simple sales variances showing budgeted sales revenue, actual sales revenue should not be used as it ignores changes in costs, that is, the net effect of a volume change.

(b) *Calculation of actual profit*

Sales			£70,000
Less: Cost of goods sold			
Materials (25,000 kg × £1·48)	£37,000		
Less: Closing stock valued at standard			
(1,600 kg × £1·50)	(2,400)		
		£34,600	
Labour		7,540	
Fixed overheads		2,462	
Variable overheads		1,750	
		46,352	
Less: Closing stock finished units valued at			
standard (1,500 units × £4)		(6,000)	
			(40,352)
		Actual profit =	£29,648

The difference of £300 between the profits in the standard absorption and standard marginal operating statements is due to the valuation of finished goods stock.

Stock   *Stock valuation*
1,500 units   (Absorption = £4·00 unit − marginal = £3·80 unit)
                    = £300 profit difference

(c) *Operating statements*
The operating statement is a simple list of variances, in a particular format, reconciling budgeted profit or contribution to actual profit.

Standard absorption costing operating statement

Budgeted profit	£24,000	
Less: volume variance*	(4,000)	*adverse*
Flexed budget profit	20,000	
Add: Sales price variance	10,000	*favourable*
Profit subject to cost variances	30,000	

Cost variances	Adverse	Favourable		
Material price		£500		
usage	£600			
Labour rate	116			
efficiency	64			
Variable overheads:				
efficiency	16			
expenditure		106		
Fixed overheads*				
expenditure	62			
capacity	80			
efficiency	20			
	(958)	606	(352)	*adverse*
		Actual profit =	£29,648	

*See notes in (d) below

(d)   *Standard marginal costing operating statement*

Budgeted contribution	£26,400	
Less: Volume variance*	(4,400)	*adverse*
Flexed budget contribution	22,000	
Add: Sales price variance	10,000	*favourable*
Contribution subject to cost variances	32,000	

Cost variances (only variable variances)	Adverse	Favourable		
Material price		£500		
usage	£600			
Labour rate	116			
efficiency	64			
Variable overheads:				
efficiency	16			
expenditure		106		
	(796)	606		
			(190)	adverse
Actual contribution			31,810	
Less: Budgeted fixed overheads*		2,400		
Plus expenditure variance		62 adverse		
			(2,462)	
		Actual profit =	£29,348	

*Notes: Students should observe the following points concerning the above operating statements:

(i) Volume variance — In the absorption operating statement standard profit/unit is used, whereas in the marginal operating statement standard contribution/unit is used.

(ii) Fixed overhead variances — The fixed overhead expenditure is the same in both statements, but there cannot be a fixed overhead volume variance in a marginal operating statement due to the actual volume of activity differing from the budget, because fixed overheads are not absorbed into products. They are charged to the period.

Sales variances will not appear in the books of account as sales are recorded at the actual amount.

(e) Further points to be noted

(i) Idle time variance = (hours paid − hours worked) standard rate
= (2,320 hours − 2,320 hours) £3·20 = nil

In this question hours paid and worked are the same, but that will not always be the case.

(ii) Material price variances are calculated on quantities purchased for the following reasons: (1) material stocks can be valued at standard price instead of FIFO etc.; (2) price variances are calculated when material is purchased rather than later when material is used. This facilitates responsibility accounting. At the end of the period it will be necessary to pro-rate the material price variances between cost of sales and stocks in order to comply with the accrual concept. Thus, stocks are revalued to actual cost, and the price variances relating to materials in goods sold are charged to the profit and loss account.

In the above example (the £500 favourable price variance) 1,600 kg of stock

$$\therefore \quad \frac{1,600}{25,000} \times £500 = \quad \underline{£32} \text{ (credit stores)}$$

23,400 kg of cost of sales

$$\therefore \quad \frac{23,400}{25,000} \times £500 = \underline{£468} \text{ (credit P and L)}$$

$$\text{(debit variance account) } \underline{£500}$$

Stocks are now revalued from standard to actual cost
$(1,600 \text{ kg} \times £1 \cdot 50 = £2,400) = £2,400 - £32$
$$= £2,368 \text{ (actual cost)}$$

At the beginning of the next accounting period stocks are revalued back to standard price, by debiting stores account and crediting variance account.

Students should note that if material stocks are valued at actual cost, the price variance is based on materials used.

Also materials issued to production are valued at standard cost.

(iii) Standard costing ratios can be used for departmental comparisons:

$$\text{Efficiency ratio} = \frac{\text{Standard hours of actual production}}{\text{Actual hours worked}} \times 100$$

$$= \frac{2,300}{2,320} \times 100 = 99 \cdot 14\%$$

$$\text{Capacity ratio} = \frac{\text{Actual hours worked}}{\text{Budgeted hours}} \times 100$$

$$= \frac{2,320}{2,400} \times 100 = 96 \cdot 67\%$$

$$\text{Activity ratio} = \frac{\text{Standard hours of actual production}}{\text{Budgeted hours}} \times 100$$

$$= \frac{2,300}{2,400} \times 100 = 95 \cdot 83\%$$

Activity ratio   = Efficiency ratio × capacity ratio

95·83%   = 99·14% × 96·67%

All ratios are less than 100%, meaning they are adverse.

9.0 CONCLUSION

In this chapter a formula approach to the computation of variances has been used because of its speed when applied to examination questions.

Students must use their own discretion about which variances should be calculated when asked to provide management with meaningful control information.

CHAPTER FOURTEEN

Further Variance Analysis

1.0 MATERIAL MIX AND YIELD VARIANCES

When a product is made of two or more raw materials, whose proportions are changeable, then it is useful to analyse the material usage variance into a materials mix and yield variance.

Example 1

A, B, and C are three ingredients of a chemical compound D. The standard cost card for the production of 1,000 litres of D is as follows:

Material	Quantity (kg)	Price	Standard cost
A	2,000	£2	£4,000
B	4,000	4	16,000
C	6,000	6	36,000
	12,000		£56,000
Normal loss	2,000		
Output	10,000 kg		

Actual data

Material	Quantity (kg)	Price
A	2,100	£2
B	4,000	4
C	5,900	6
	12,000	
Actual loss	2,100	
Output	9,900	

Compute the relevant variances.

SOLUTION

(a) *Price variance.* Actual and standard price are the same, and therefore there cannot be a price variance.

(b) *Mix variance.* This is found by comparing the actual mix with the actual quantity of materials used in a standard mix. The difference is multiplied by the standard price.

Material	Actual mix (kg)		Standard mix (kg)	Standard price (£)
A	2,100	$\frac{1}{6}$	2,000	2 = 200 *adverse*
B	4,000	$\frac{1}{3}$	4,000	4 = nil
C	5,900	$\frac{1}{2}$	6,000	6 = 600 *favourable*
	12,000	(This is now put into standard proportions)	12,000 Mix variance	= 400 *favourable*

This favourable mix variance has arisen because less of the most expensive material *C* was used than planned. A greater proportion of the cheaper material *A* was used than planned.

(c) *Yield variance.* This can be calculated in one of two ways. Students must understand both approaches.

(i) (Expected yield − actual yield) weighted average standard cost per unit of material

$$(10,000 - 9,900)\ £5 \cdot 60 \quad = \quad \underline{£560}\ adverse\ yield\ variance$$

$$\left(\frac{£56,000}{10,000}\right)\text{kg}$$

(ii) By comparing the standard input for actual output, with the actual input in budgeted proportions. The difference is multiplied by the standard price.

Material		Standard input for actual output (kg)	Actual input in budgeted proportions) (kg)		Standard price (£)	
A	$\frac{1}{6}$	1,980	2,000		2 = 40	adverse
B	$\frac{1}{3}$	3,960	4,000		4 = 160	adverse
C	$\frac{1}{2}$	5,940	6,000		6 = 360	adverse
		*11,880	12,000	yield variance	= 560	adverse

*12,000 kg of input is required for an output of 10,000 kg

$\therefore \dfrac{9,900}{10,000} \times 12,000$ kg of input is required for an actual output of 9,900 kg

= *11,800 kg — standard input for actual output. This is put into budgeted proportions.

The yield variance measures the difference between what is put into the process and what should have been put into the process based on actual good output produced. It represents an abnormal loss.

(d) *Usage variance.* This is computed by comparing the actual mix with the standard input for actual output. The difference is multiplied by the standard price.

Material	Standard input for actual output (kg)	Actual mix (kg)	Standard price (£)	Usage variance (£)
A	1,980	2,100	2	240 adverse
B	3,960	4,000	4	160 adverse
C	5,940	5,900	6	240 favourable
	11,880	12,000		160 adverse

Usage = mix + yield
£160 *adverse* = £400 *favourable* + £560 *adverse*

Many products consist of more than one material, for example, a table with a wooden top and four metal legs. The division of the usage variance into a mix and yield effect would be ridiculous, as it is absurd to consider producing tables with two tops and three legs. It is only meaningful to make the division when the nature of the product or process allows for some deviation from the standard mix.

2.0   SALES MIX AND QUANTITY VARIANCES

Where management sells more than one product, and it is possible to control the proportions of the products sold, the sales volume variance can be analysed into a sales mix and quantity variance.

Example 2

Nit-Faster are importers of domestic knitting machines. Currently they import and distribute two models, the Super NF-PC and the Family NF. Twelve months ago, using the sales forecast produced by the general sales manager, the managing director compiled the following table of information of contribution margins for each model and the total contribution for the firm:

Budgeted sales and contribution for the 12 months commencing 1st July 19X5

	Super NF-PC			Family NF			Total		
	Units	*Price*	*Total*	*Units*	*Price*	*Total*	*Units*	*Price*	*Total*
Sales	10,000	£210	£2,100,000	6,000	£100	£600,000	16,000	£168·75	£2,700,000
Variable									
costs	10,000	140	1,400,000	6,000	70	420,000	16,000	113·75	1,820,000
Contribution		70	700,000		30	180,000		55	880,000

The managing director has just received details of the actual performance for the 12 months concerned. These show that the unit prices and costs were as forecast, making the unit contribution for each of the models as was budgeted. However, a closer examination of the figures which are provided below shows that although total unit sales have fallen short of the estimates the total contribution is greater than that forecast.

Actual sales and contribution for the 12 months ended 30th June 19X5

	Super NF-PC			Family NF			Total		
	Units	*Price*	*Total*	*Units*	*Price*	*Total*	*Units*	*Price*	*Total*
Sales	12,000	£210	£2,520,000	2,000	£100	£200,000	14,000	£194·29	£2,720,000
Variable									
costs	12,000	140	1,680,000	2,000	70	140,000	14,000	130·00	1,820,000
Contribution		70	840,000		30	60,000		64·29	900,000

Required:
Analyse the favourable contribution variance in two forms:

    (a) a way which differentiates between the quantity and mix variances, and

    (b) an approach which shows the physical volume variance for the individual models.

SOLUTION
Standard and actual selling prices are the same, therefore there is no price variance.

    (a) *Sales volume variance.* This is calculated in the normal way as described in the previous chapter.

Product	Actual quantity units	Budgeted quantity units	Standard profit or Standard contribution		
Super	(12,000	− 10,000)	× £70 = £140,000	*favourable*
Family	(2,000	− 6,000)	× £30 = £120,000	*adverse*
		Sales volume variance	= £20,000	*favourable*

    (b) *Sales mix variance.* This variance is calculated in a similar way to the material mix variance.

Product	Actual mix units	Standard mix units	Standard profit or Standard contribution	
Super	$\left(12,000 - \dfrac{10}{16} \times 14,000 = 8,750\right)$		£70 = £227,500	*favourable*
Family	$\left(2,000 - \dfrac{6}{16} \times 14,000 = 5,250\right)$		£30 = £97,500	*adverse*
	14,000	14,000		
		Sales mix variance	= £130,000	*favourable*

The favourable mix variance is a result of selling more of Super, the more profitable product, than planned.

    (c) *Sales quantity variance.* This variance compares the total actual sales with the total budgeted sales and values the difference at the weighted average standards profit or contribution per unit.

(Total actual quantity − total budgeted quantity) weighted average standard contribution/unit

= (14,000 units − 16,000 units) £55 = £110,000 *adverse*

The adverse quantity variance shows the effect on profits of selling less overall than planned (for all products).

Sales volume	=	mix	+	quantity
£20,000 *favourable*	=	£130,000 *favourable*	+	£110,000 *adverse*

Students should know how to compute the above variances using sales revenue instead of sales units.

(d) *Sales revenue method (using example 2)*. In this method it is important to note that revenue is measured at standard sales price, not actual sales price. Actual revenue = actual units × standard price. In this example we are fortunate that actual and standard prices are the same.

(e) *Sales volume variance*

Product	Actual revenue	Budgeted revenue	Profit or contribution	Sales ratio
Super	$\left(2,520 - £2,100\right)$	×	$£\dfrac{700}{2,100}$	= £140,000 *favourable*
Family	$\left(200 - 600\right)$	×	$\dfrac{180}{600}$	= £120,000 *adverse*
			Sales volume variance =	£20,000 *favourable*

(f) *Sales mix variance*

Product	Actual mix £ (actual units × standard prices)	Standard mix £	Standard contribution/ sales
Super	$\left(2,520 - \dfrac{2,100}{2,700} × 2,720 = 2,115.55\right)$	$£\dfrac{700}{2,100}$	= £134,816 *favourable*
Family	$\left(200 - \dfrac{600}{2,720} × 2,720 = 604{\cdot}45\right)$	$\dfrac{180}{600}$	= £121,335 *adverse*
	2,720	2,720·00	
		Sales mix variance =	£13,481 *favourable*

(g) *Sales quantity variance*

$$\left(\begin{array}{c} \text{Total actual revenue} \\ \text{at standard selling} \quad - \quad \text{Total budgeted revenue} \\ \text{price} \end{array}\right) \begin{array}{c} \text{Standard weighted} \\ \text{average contribution/} \\ \text{sales ratio} \end{array}$$

$$(\pounds2,720 - \pounds2,700)\frac{880,000}{2,700,000} = \pounds6,519 \ favourable$$

Sales volume	=	Mix	+	Quantity
$\therefore \pounds20,000$ *favourable*	=	$\pounds13,481$ *favourable*	+	$\pounds6,519$ *favourable*

Students will observe that the sales volume variance is the same under both methods. However, the quantity and mix variances will differ under each method. In the physical (units) method the proportions of units sold of each product are controlled. In the revenue method proportions of revenue from each product are controlled.

3.0   PLANNING AND OPERATIONAL VARIANCES

In the traditional calculation of variances an actual cost is compared to a standard cost. This standard would normally have been established well before the start of the current period and in some cases could be over a year old. It is clear that internal and external circumstances affecting the production and selling aspects of the organisation could have changed in this period, with some of these changes being outside the control of the organisation.

Consider the purchase of raw materials. A standard cost may have been set originally at £2·00/kg. It is now ten months later and the management accountant is analysing the variances for, say, period 9. If the actual price paid in the period was £3·00/kg, traditional variance analysis would compute an adverse material price variance based on the difference of £1/kg, and presumably attribute responsibility to the purchasing officer. Although he obviously has some control over material costs, does he have control over the variance? The variance depends not just on the actual figure, but on the original standard. How was this established? In setting the original standard, management may have made use of historical costs and estimated future inflation rates. Due to factors entirely outside the control of the company, a world shortage may have arisen in the meantime, which caused the average market price to rise to, say, £2·80. With efficient buying and by making maximum use of quantity discounts the purchasing officer could, perhaps, have acquired the material for, say, £2·75. The introduction of this figure now enables the traditional variance to be analysed into a *controllable* and *non-controllable* element. Clearly the difference between the £3·00 actual cost and the £2·75 could be regarded as controllable, and the difference between the £2·75 and the original standard of £2·00 as probably non-controllable. This division must help facilitate responsibility accounting as it is examining the root cause of the variance.

Example 3

Lent Ltd budgets to sell 20,000 units at £20 per unit and variable costs of £8 per unit.

Actual sales were 20,000 units and variable costs were £160,000. Sales revenue was only £10 per unit. In retrospect it is realised that the standard sales price of £20 was too high, and a price of £9 per unit should have been set.

Analyse the variances.

SOLUTION

Budgeted contribution	−	actual contribution	= Total variances
£240,000	−	£40,000	= £200,000 *adverse*

Operational sales price variance

20,000 units were sold at £10/unit	= £200,000
should have sold at £9/unit	= £180,000
	£20,000 *favourable*

Planning sales price variance
(Planned sales price − revised sales price) actual sales = (20 − £9) 20,000 units
= £220,000 *adverse*

Operational	+	planning	= Total
£20,000 *favourable*	+	£220,000 *adverse*	= £200,000 *adverse*

Example 4

The management team of Thorpe Ltd feel that standard costing and variance analysis have little to offer in the reporting of some of the activities of their firm. The accountant of Thorpe Ltd states:

Although we produce a range of fairly standardised products, prices of many of our raw materials are apt to change suddenly and comparison of actual prices with a predetermined, and often unrealistic, standard price is of little use. For some of our products we can utilise one of several equally suitable raw materials and we always plan to utilise the raw material which will, in our opinion, lead to the cheapest total production costs. However we are frequently caught out by price changes and the material actually used often proves, after the event, to have been more expensive than the alternative which was originally rejected.

For example, consider the experience over the last accounting period of two of our products, alpha and beta. To produce a unit of alpha we can use either 5 kg of gamma or 5 kg of delta. We planned to use gamma as it appeared it would be the cheaper of the two and our plans were based on a cost of gamma of £3 per kg. Due to market movements the actual prices changed and if we had purchased efficiently the costs would have been:

gamma	£4·50 per kg
delta	£4·00 per kg

Production of alpha was 2,000 units and usage of gamma amounted to 10,800 kg at a total cost of £51,840.

Product beta uses only one raw material, epsilon, but again the price of this can change rapidly. It was thought that epsilon would cost £30 per tonne but in fact we only paid £25 per tonne and if we had purchased correctly the cost would have been less as it was freely available at only £23 per tonne. It usually takes 1·5 tonnes of epsilon to produce 1 tonne of beta but our production of 500 tonnes of beta used only 700 tonnes of epsilon.

So you can see that with our particular circumstances the traditional approach to variance analysis is of little use and we do not use it for materials although we do use it for reporting on labour and variable overhead costs.

Required:

(a) Analyse the material variances for both alpha and beta utilising

    (i)   traditional variance analysis; and

    (ii) an approach which distinguishes between planning and operational variances.

(b) Write brief notes which

    (i)   explain the approach to variance analysis which distinguishes between planning and operational variances;

    (ii) indicate the extent to which this approach is useful for firms in general and for Thorpe Ltd in particular; and

    (iii) highlight the main difficulty in the application of this approach.

SOLUTION

(a) (i) *Traditional variances (actual versus original budget)*

Alpha

Usage variance = (actual quantity − standard quantity) standard price
(10,800 kg − 10,000 kg) £3 = £2,400 *adverse*

Price variance = (actual price − standard price) actual quantity
= (£4·80 − £3·00) 10,800 kg = £19,440 *adverse*

£21,840 *adverse*

Beta

Usage variance = (actual quantity − standard quantity) standard price
= (700 tonnes − 750 tonnes) £30 = £1,500 *favourable*

Price variance = (actual price − standard price) actual quantity
= (£25 − £30) 700 tonnes = £3,500 *favourable*

£5,000 *favourable*

(ii) *Operational variances (actual versus revised (based on hindsight) budget)*

Alpha

Usage = (10,800 kg − 10,000 kg) £4·50 = £3,600 *adverse*
Price = (4·80 − £4·50) 10,800 kg = £3,240 *adverse*

£6,840 *adverse*

Beta
Usage = (700 tonnes − 750 tonnes) £23   = £1,150 *favourable*
Price   = (£25 − £23) 700 tonnes   = £1,400 *adverse*

£250 *adverse*

Planning variances (revised versus original budgets)

Alpha
Controllable variance
   = (£4·50 − £4·0) 10,000 kg   =   £5,000 *adverse*
(could have planned a cheaper material − delta)

Uncontrollable variance = £3 − £4·0) 10,000 kg   = £10,000 *adverse*

£15,000 *adverse*

Beta
Uncontrollable variance = (£23 − £30) 750 tonnes =   £5,250 *favourable*

Alpha	− traditional	= operational	+ planning
	£21,840 *adverse*	= £6,840 *adverse*	+ £15,000 *adverse*
Beta	—£5,000 *favourable*	+ £250 *adverse*	+ £5,250 *favourable*

(b) (i) Planning variances test management's forecasting ability by comparing the original standard (ex-ante) and the revised standard based on known factors (ex-post).

Operational variances indicate management's current level of operating efficiency by comparing actual with an up-to-date standard (revised standard).

(ii) They are useful in the following ways:

(1) in times of inflation when there are rapid price level changes those variances due to inflation can be distinguished from others;

(2) they distinguish between controllable and non-controllable variances; and

(3) they show the effects of setting unrealistic targets.

(iii) Difficulties in this approach are:

(1) a resistance to change from the traditional approach to the modern one as the latter more easily exposes controllable errors;

(2) the difficulty in obtaining accurate information about what the revised standard should be; and

(3) the assumption that the alternatives are perfect substitutes for the materials actually used, e.g., can delta be used instead of gamma?

4.0 THE PRO-RATING OF VARIANCES

As explained in the previous chapter a raw material price variance of, say, £3,000 adverse must be pro-rated between closing stocks of raw materials and production of finished units. Say 25% of £3,000 adverse, i.e., £750 adverse is transferred to the raw materials stock account.

Production variances		(10,000 units) — Production
Raw material usage	£5,000 *favourable*	(5,000 units) — Closing stock
Raw material price 75% of 3,000	2,250 *adverse*	
Labour cost	2,250 *adverse*	
Fixed overheads	4,000 *adverse*	
	3,500 *adverse*	

	Pro-rated variances
5,000 units closing stock 33⅓%	£1,167 *adverse*
10,000 units cost of sales 66⅔%	£2,333 *adverse*
	£3,500 *adverse*

Stock of raw material and finished units are valued at actual cost:

Raw material, for example	£8,000	standard
	750	pro-rated
	£8,750	actual

Finished units, for example	£7,000	standard
	£1,167	pro-rated variances
	£8,167	actual

Also	Standard profit	
	(2,333) — Pro-rated variances	
	Actual profit	

5.0 CONCLUSION

Students will come across other methods of calculating the mix, quantity and yield variances. Most of these methods are acceptable as long as the logic underlying the technique is understood.

CHAPTER FIFTEEN

The Interpretation and Investigation of Variances

1.0 INTRODUCTION

Variance analysis highlights areas of strength and weakness, but does not indicate what action, if any, should be taken. A manager must be able to interpret correctly the significance of variances before he can initiate control action.

2.0 PROBLEMS ENCOUNTERED IN THE INTERPRETATION OF VARIANCES

(a) Because of the various pressures on a budgetary control system inaccuracies can arise in the recording of actual results (material, labour and machine time used). This undermines the credibility of the variances reported.

(b) Efficiency variances will depend on the tightness or looseness of the standards set, and therefore any decisions regarding these variances must be taken in the light of the standards used.

(c) There may be interdependence between variances; for example, buying cheaper material will result in a favourable price variance, but may adversely affect the material usage and labour efficiency variances.

(d) Inflation poses a problem. If standard average price levels have been set then in the first half of the year actual prices will be below standard prices, resulting in favourable price variances. However, in the second half of the year actual will exceed standard, causing adverse price variances. If the standards are based on current price levels, they will have to be continually revised otherwise adverse price variances will just as continually arise.

(e) Some variances are controllable, so that action can be taken, and the system is brought back on course. Other variances may be uncontrollable, resulting in the revision of budgets.

(f) The size of a variance is important. Tolerance limits are set so that only variances which exceed these limits are reported.

   Tolerance limits can be either subjectively or statistically established.

Statistical control charts

Historical data is used to calculate the standard deviation which determines the confidence limits in the chart.

Example 1

It has been estimated that the mean time (taken as the standard time) to complete an operation is 120 minutes, with a standard deviation of 24 minutes. Management have decided to set warning limits at mean ± 1·96 standard deviations, and action limits at mean ± 2·57 standard deviations. These limits have been set subjectively with regard to the estimated likelihood of the process being out of control.

   The warning and action limits would therefore be:

Warning limits   upper: 120 + (1·96 × 24) = 167·04 minutes
                  lower: 120 − (1·96 × 24) =   72·96 minutes

Action limits   upper: 120 + (2·57 × 24) = 181·68 minutes
                  lower: 120 − (2·57 × 24) =   58·32 minutes

These are illustrated in Fig. 21. The crosses indicate the actual results as they become available. *A* represents an adverse variance, *B* a favourable variance; *C* indicates a warning that the situation is perhaps starting to get out of control, bringing management's attention to what may turn out to be a case for investigation; *D* shows that action is now required to correct the process. Management could now resort to comparing the expected costs and benefits of investigation.

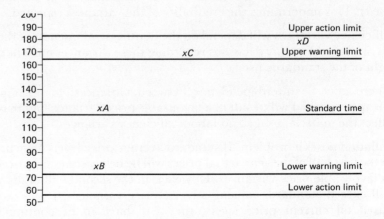

Fig. 21. *Example of a statistical control chart.*

The problem with this technique is that the wider the tolerance limits the greater the risk of controllable variances being undetected. However, if narrow control limits are set too many uncontrollable variances may be investigated.

A cumulative (multiple period) approach can be employed which detects trends earlier than existing-period variances.

(g) Costs of investigation: a cost/benefit approach can be used as follows:

Investigate the variance if $C < (1 - P)L$

Where C = cost of investigation;
L = benefits derived from control action;
P = probability of variance being uncontrollable, $\therefore 1 - P$ indicates the probability of it being controllable.

Example 2

A £2,000 adverse labour efficiency variance is reported. Costs of investigation are £500 and estimated savings are £2,000. Costs of corrective action if variance is controllable will be £600. Probability of the variance being uncontrollable is 0·4. Should it be investigated?

SOLUTION
$$from \ C < (1 - P)L$$
$$£500 < (1 - 0.4)\ (£2,000 - £600)$$
$$\therefore \text{investigate}$$

Also the expected value can be calculated:

Uncontrollable $0.4 \times (500)$ $= £(200)$
Controllable 0.6×900 $= £540$ $(£2,000 - £600 - £500 = £900)$

$$EV = +£340 \ \therefore \text{investigate}$$

The limitations of this approach are as follows:

(i) estimation of the probabilities;

(ii) estimations of the savings;

(iii) the assumption that investigation of a controllable variance leads to its immediate elimination.

(h) Composite variances: this is concerned with who is responsible for a particular variance.

Example 3

Standard/unit 5 kg of material at £4/kg
Actual 100 units, 550 kg of material, at £5/kg

Who is responsible for the variances?

SOLUTION

Price variance $\quad = (£5 - £4)\ 550\ \text{kg} \qquad = \underline{£550}\ adverse$
(the purchasing manager's responsibility).

Usage variance $\quad = (550\ \text{kg} - 500\ \text{kg})\ £4\ = \underline{£200}\ adverse$
(the production manager's responsibility).

However, there is a composite variance (not reported in traditional methods) which shows that in addition to the above the production manager should be responsible for some of the price variance — the extra usage at the excess price.

$$50\ \text{kg} \times £1 = \underline{£50}\ adverse$$

3.0   CONCLUSION

The above list of problems regarding the interpretation of variances is not exhaustive. Management will have to consider these problems deeply before initiating control action.

CHAPTER SIXTEEN

Process Costing

1.0 INTRODUCTION

This chapter has been introduced into the book in order to enable students to revise process costing, a costing topic, in the light of some recent examination questions involving the valuation of stocks of semi-finished products using "equivalent units".

2.0 EQUIVALENT UNITS

Example 1

Process A has no opening work-in-progress, but 8,000 units of material are put into the process in May. Suppose 7,000 units are completed during the month, leaving 1,000 semi-finished units at the month end. These units are complete for material but only 50% complete for labour and overheads.

Raw material

Say the cost is £16,000. This can be apportioned:

$$\frac{1,000}{8,000} \text{ to work-in-progress} \qquad \frac{7,000}{8,000} \text{ to completed production}$$

£16,000 spread over 8,000 units gives a material cost of £2/unit (1,000 × £2 to stock and 7,000 × £2 to completed production).

Labour and overheads

Here 8,000 units entered the process, but only 7,000 are complete; 1,000 units are 50% finished, and this is the equivalent of 500 completed units. Thus the labour cost incurred by the process is divided among 7,500 completed units (7,000 finished and 500 equivalent units).

If the labour and overhead cost was £22,500, then £22,500 ÷ 7,500 units = £3, is the unit cost per equivalent unit. Completed production is charged with 7,000 × £3 and closing stock 500 × £3.

	Units	£		Units	£
		Process A — May			
Material	8,000	16,000	Completed production	7,000	35,000
Labour and overheads		22,500	Stock c/f	1,000	3,500
	8,000	£38,500		8,000	£38,500

Stock

1,000 units at £2	£2,000
500 units at £3	1,500
	£3,500

Completed production

Material	—	7,000 units at £2	£14,000
Labour and overheads	—	7,000 units at £3	21,000
			£35,000

Let us extend our example into the month of June. Cost data for process A is as follows: 12,000 new units are introduced at a cost of £4/unit of material. Labour and overheads costs are £33,000 for the month. 11,000 units are completed during the month. Closing stock is 2,000 units which are 25% complete.

Equivalent units

Opening stock	1,000 complete for material, but 50% complete for labour and overheads — they require 500 equivalent units of labour/overhead expenses to complete them.
Introduced and completed	10,000 — equivalent units — material 10,000 labour/overheads — 10,000
Closing stock	2,000 — equivalent units — material — 2,000 labour/overheads — 500

The total equivalent units for June are material 12,000 and labour/overheads 500 + 10,000 + 500 = 11,000. The costs per unit = £33,000 ÷ 11,000 units = £3 per unit.

	Units	£	*Process A — June*	Units	£
Stock	1,000	3,500	Completed production	11,000	75,000
Material	12,000	48,000			
labour/ overheads		33,000	Stock c/f	2,000	9,500
	13,000	£84,500		13,000	£84,500

Closing stock

2,000 units complete for material (2,000 at £4)	£8,000
500 equivalent units (25%) of labour/overhead at £3/unit	1,500
	£9,500

Completed production

Opening stock finished off	£3,500 brought down plus 500 equivalent units at £3 = £5,000
Units put into process and completed during June	10,000 units of material at £4 = £40,000 10,000 units of labour/overheads at £3 = £30,000
£5,000 + £40,000 + £30,000	= £75,000

If waste occurs in a process, then the cost of waste is absorbed by the good production, so that the number of equivalent units over which the process cost is averaged will be reduced.

Example (2) combines process costing and standard costing.

3.0   PROCESS COSTING AND STANDARD COSTING

Example 2

Equinox is the main product of the Solstice Chemical Corporation. The product is manufactured in two processes with all the output from process 1 (chemical C) being transferred to process 2. Additional raw material (chemical D) is added at the start of processing in process 2 and the finished product is packed, in standardised containers, and dispatched to the finished goods store. A standard costing system is used and this is integrated with the company's financial accounting system.

The following standards apply:

Process 1 *Standard specification for* *1,000 kg of C*			*Process 2* *Standard specification for* *1,000 kg of Equinox*		
Direct material			Direct material		
400 kg of A at £0·36		£144	1,050 kg of C at £0·70		£735
700 kg of B at £0·08		56	50 kg of D at £0·50		25
Direct labour			Direct labour		
25 hours at £4·00 per hour		100	5 hours at £4·00 per hour		20
Variable overhead			Variable overhead		
25 direct labour hours at £8·00		200	5 direct labour hours at £9·20		46
Fixed overhead			Fixed overhead		
25 direct labour hours at £8·00		200	5 direct labour hours at £14·00		70
			Packing material		4
		£700			£900

The standards allow for a normal loss in volume of 10% of the good output in each process; this loss occurs at the *beginning* of the processing.

The following details apply for the operations of a particular week:

Purchases of raw materials:
8,000 kg of A at £0.39 per kg	£3,120
16,000 kg of B at £0·05 per kg	800
1,500 kg of D at £0·54 per kg	810

	Process 1		*Process 2*	
Direct material issued to production				
	A	8,000 kg	C	22,000 kg (transferred from process 1)
	B	17,000 kg	D	930 kg
Direct labour	530 hours at £4·10 = £2,173		110 hours at £3·80 = £418	
Variable overhead	£4,134		£912	
Fixed overhead	£4,900	(actual)	£1,510	(actual)
	£5,000	(budgeted)	£1,660	(budgeted)
Packing material			£95	

Production and work-in-process	kg	Degree of completion	kg	Degree of completion
Opening work-in-process	2,100	50%	1,050	50%
Output (completed production)	22,000	100%	17,000	100%
Closing work-in-process	2,675	30%	3,225	25%

Direct material price variances are calculated when the material is purchased. Raw material stocks are, therefore, recorded at standard cost and issued to production at standard cost. All other production expenses are charged at "actual" from the expense accounts to the process accounts and any variances are transferred from the process accounts to appropriate variance accounts. Such transfers are made weekly. Output transferred from process 1 to process 2 is transferred at standard cost and work-in-process is valued on this basis.

You are required:

(a) to write up the process accounts for process 1 and process 2;

(b) to comment on the mix of raw materials used in process 1 during the week;

(c) to comment on the profitability of process 2 if chemical C can be sold at £0·90 per kg and the market price of Equinox is £1·05 per kg.

SOLUTION

(a)   *Workings for process account 1*

Calculation of equivalent units		Equivalent units	
	Units	Materials	Labour and overheads
Opening work-in-process	2,100	2,100	1,050 (50%)
Opening work-in-process completed	2,100	0	1,050 (50%)
Other completed work (22,000 − 2,100)	19,900	19,900	19,900
Output of C to process 2	22,000	19,900	20,950
Closing work-in-process	2,675	2,675	802·5 (30%)
Equivalent units of work done		22,575	21,752·5

As the degree of completion of materials is not given in the question, then it is assumed that opening and closing work-in-process are 100% complete as to materials.

Stock valuation	*(at standard cost)*	
Opening stock	2,100 equivalent units of material at £(144 + 56)⟶£200 per 1,000 units	£420
	1,050 equivalent units of labour and overhead at £500 per 1,000 units	525
	£(100 + 200 + 200)	£945
Closing stock	2,675 equivalent units of material at £200 per 1,000 units	£535
	802·5 equivalent units of labour and overhead at £500 per 1,000 units	401.25
		£936·25
Finished output	22,000 kg of C at £700 per 1,000 units	£15,400

Workings for process account 2

Calculation of equivalent units		*Equivalent units*		
	Units	Materials	Labour and overheads	
Opening stock— work-in-process	1,050	1,050	525	(50%)
Opening work-in-process	1,050	0	525	(50%)
Other completed work (17,000 – 1,050)	15,950	15,950	15,950	
Output of Equinox	17,000	15,950	16,475	
Closing work-in-process	3,225	3,225	806·25	(25%)
Equivalent units of work done		19,175	17,281·25	

It is assumed that the opening and closing work-in-process are 100% complete as to materials.

Stock valuation (at standard cost)

Stocks are not packed and therefore their standard cost will exclude packing material. Standard material cost is (£25 + £735) = £760 per 1,000 equivalent units, and the standard labour and overhead costs are (£20 + £46 + £70) = £136 per 1,000 equivalent units.

Opening stock	1,050 equivalent units of material at £760 per 1,000 units	£798·0	
	525 equivalent units of labour and overhead at £136 per 1,000 units	71·4	
			£869·4
Output of Equinox	17,000 kg at £900 per 1,000 kg		£15,300
Closing stock	3,225 equivalent units of material at £760 per 1,000 units	£2,451	
	806·25 equivalent units of labour and overhead at £136 per 1,000 units	109·65	
		£2,560·65	

Calculation of variances

Material   Price variance does not appear in the process account.

Usage variance   = (actual quantity − standard quantity) standard price

(For C)   = (22,000 − 20,133·75) 0.7

$$\left(19,175 \times \frac{1,050}{1,000}\right)$$

= £1,306·38 *adverse*

(For D)   = (930 − 958·75) 0·5

$$\left(19,175 \times \frac{50}{1,000}\right)$$

= £14·38 *favourable*

Labour

Rate variance   = (actual rate − standard rate) actual hours paid
= (£3·80 − £4·0) 110
= £22·00 *favourable*

Efficiency variance = (actual hours worked − standard hours) standard rate

= (110 − 86·40625) £4

$$\left(17,281·25 \times \frac{5}{1,000}\right)$$

£94·38 *adverse*

Variable overhead

Efficiency   = (actual hours worked − standard hours) standard overhead rate

$= (110 - 86 \cdot 40625)\ £9 \cdot 20$

$= £217 \cdot 06$ *adverse*

Expenditure

110 hours actually cost	£912
110 hours should have cost ($110 \times £9 \cdot 2$)	1,012
	£100 *favourable*

Material

Price variance does not appear in the process account, but rather in the raw material account.

Usage variance   = (actual quantity − standard quantity) standard price

(For A) $= (8,000 - 9,030)\ £0.36$

$$\left(22,575 \times \frac{400}{1,000}\right)$$

$= £370 \cdot 8$ *favourable*

(For B)   = (actual quantity − standard quantity)   standard price

$= (17,000 - 15,802 \cdot 5)\ £0 \cdot 08$

$$\left(22,575 \times \frac{700}{1,000}\right)$$

$= £95 \cdot 8$ *adverse*

Labour

Rate variance   = (actual rate − standard rate) actual hours paid

$= (£4 \cdot 10 - £4)\ 530$

$= £53$ *adverse*

Efficiency   = (actual hours worked − standard hours)   standard rate

$= (530 - 543.8125)\ £4$

$$\left(21,752 \cdot 5 \times \frac{25}{1,000}\right)$$

$= £55 \cdot 25$ *favourable*

Variable overhead

      Efficiency   = (actual hours worked − standard hours)
      standard overhead rate

$$= (530 - 543.8125) \pounds8$$
$$= \pounds110.50 \text{ favourable}$$

      Expenditure   = 530 hours actually cost   £4,134
                          530 hours should have cost
                            (530 × £8)   4,240

                                              £106 *favourable*

Fixed overhead

Expenditure variance   = (actual fixed overheads − budgeted fixed overheads
                             = (£4,900 − £5,000)
                             = £100 *favourable*

Efficiency variance   = (actual hours worked − standard hours) standard fixed
                                overhead rate
                             = (530 − 543.8125) £8
                             = £110.50 *favourable*

Capacity variance   = (actual hours worked − budgeted hours) standard fixed
                                overhead rate
                             = (530 − 625) £8

$$\left(\frac{\pounds5,000}{8 \text{ hours}}\right)$$

                             = £760 *adverse*

Process account 1

Opening work-in-process	£945.00	Output of C to process 2	£15,400.00
Direct labour	2,173.00	*Adverse variances*	
Variable overhead	4,134.00	Material B usage	95.80
Fixed overhead	4,900.00	Labour rate	53.00
Material A		Fixed overhead capacity	760.00
(8,000 kg at £0.36)	2,880.00		
Material B			
(17,000 kg at £0.08)	1,360.00		
Favourable variances			
Material A usage	370.80		
Labour efficiency	55.20		

Variable overhead efficiency	110·50		
Fixed overhead efficiency	110·50		
Variable overhead expenditure	106·00		
Fixed overhead expenditure	100·00	Closing work-in-process	936·20
	£17,245·00		£17,245·00

Fixed overhead

Expenditure variance	= (actual fixed overheads − budgeted fixed overheads = (£1,510 − £1,660) = £150 *favourable*
Efficiency variance	= (actual hours worked − standard hours) standard fixed overhead rate = (110 − 86·40625) £14 = £330·31 *adverse*
Capacity variance	= (actual hours worked − budgeted hours) standard fixed overhead rate = (110 − 118·57142) £14 ↑ $\left(\dfrac{£1,660}{£14}\right)$ = £120 *adverse*

Packing materials variance Only finished units are packed therefore the actual costs relate to the 17,000 kg of Equinox.

17,000 kg cost £95, but should cost $17,000 \times \dfrac{4}{1,000} = £68$.

$$\text{Variance} = £95 - £68 = \underline{£27}\ adverse$$

Process account 2

Opening work-in-process	£869·40	Output of Equinox	£15,300·00
Direct labour	418·00	*Adverse variances*	
Variable overhead	912·00	Usage — material C	1,306·38
Fixed overhead	1,510·00	Labour efficiency	94.38
Packing material	95·00	Variable overhead	
Material C (17,000 kg		efficiency	217·06

from process 1)	15,400·00	Fixed overhead efficiency	330·31
Material D (930 kg		Fixed overhead capacity	120·00
at £0·50)	465·00	Packing material cost	27·00
Favourable variances			
Material C — usage	14·38		
Labour rate	22·00		
Variable overhead			
expenditure	100·00		
Fixed overhead		Closing work-in-process	2,560·65
expenditure	150·00		
	£19,955·78		£19,955·78

(b) (i)   *The mix variance*

(Actual mix — Actual mix in standard proportions) Std. price

Material A	$\left(8,000 - \left(\dfrac{4}{11}\right) 9,090\cdot9\right)$	£0·36	$= £392\cdot72$ *favourable*
Material B	$\left(17,000 - \left(\dfrac{7}{11}\right)15,909\cdot1\right)$	£0·08	$=$ 87·27 *adverse*
	25,000 25,000		£305·45 *favourable*

(ii)   *The yield variance*

$$22,575 \text{ equivalent units did use} \qquad 25,000 \text{ kg}$$
$$\text{but should use}\left(22,575 \times \frac{1,100}{1,000}\right) = \quad 24,832\cdot5 \text{ kg}$$
$$\underline{\qquad\qquad} $$
$$167\cdot5 \text{ kg}$$

Standard weighted average price per kg

of A and B is $\dfrac{£200}{1,100 \text{ kg}}$

∴ Yield variance $= 167\cdot5 \text{ kg} = \dfrac{£200}{1,100} =$ $\qquad$ £30·45 *adverse*

Total usage variance $= £275\cdot00$ *favourable*

The favourable mix variance is a result of buying less of the more expensive material A than planned (the actual cost of A was £0·03/kg above the standard price).

However, if the output from process 1 (chemical C) is of low quality because of its content being mainly that of material B, the cheaper material, then the labour efficiency and material usage variances in process 2 may be adversely affected.

(c) Decisions about further processing should be based on a comparison between the incremental revenue and incremental costs of further processing, for example

Sale of Equinox	$= (1,000\,\text{kg} \times £1\cdot05)$	$=$	£1,050
Sale of C	$= (1,050\,\text{kg} \times £0\cdot90)$	$=$	945
	Incremental revenue	$=$	105

Incremental costs

Material D	£25		
Direct labour	20		
Packing material	4		
Variable overhead	46		(95)
(Further processing)	$\longrightarrow$ incremental gain	$=$	£10

It is therefore more profitable to produce Equinox than chemical C, assuming that fixed overheads are not incremental.

CHAPTER SEVENTEEN

The Learning Curve

1.0 INTRODUCTION

The learning curve principle was first applied in the aircraft industry in the 1920s, where it was discovered that the more an activity was practised, the more proficient operators became at performing the activity. Initially the amount of learning was substantial, but as the individual's expertise increased the amount of outstanding learning decreased and the learning curve "flattened out".

The learning curve theory is most applicable when a high degree of manual skilled labour is required and there is opportunity for repetition of process. It allows costs to be predicted and is therefore extremely useful in standard costing and decision-making.

2.0 THE CALCULATION

The following principle applies: as the cumulative quantity of output doubles, the average time per unit will fall to a fixed percentage of the previous time.

Example 1

An 80% learning curve is in effect, and the first unit requires 100 hours to produce. Find the time required to produce 5 units.

SOLUTION

Number of units	Average time/ unit	Cumulative time	Incremental time	Average time/ extra unit	
1	100	100	100 for 1	100	
2	80% ↗ 80	160	60 for 1	60	
4	80% ↗ 64	256	96 for 2	48	Falling
8	80% ↗ 51.2	409·6	153·6 for 4	38.4	
16	80% ↘ 41	656	246·4 for 8	30·8	

The average time/unit (Y) can be plotted against the number of units (x) (*see* Fig. 22).

Graphically it can be seen that the average time per unit for 5 units is 60 hours, and therefore the time required to produce 5 units is [$5 \times 60 \times 300$ hours].

An alternative, more accurate, approach is to use a formula, based on an exponential expression.

$$Y = ax^{-b}$$

Where Y = average time/unit

$\quad\quad\quad a$ = number of hours that the first unit requires

$\quad\quad\quad x$ = number of units

$\quad\quad\quad b$ = the index of learning, which represents a rate of increase of productivity.

$\therefore Y = 100(5)^{-0·3219*}$

$\therefore Y = 59·57$ hours

$\therefore$ time required to produce 5 units = $5 \times 59·57 = 297·85$ hours.

$*b = \dfrac{\log 0·8 \text{ (80\% curve)}}{\log 2 \text{ (doubling effect)}} = 0·3219*$

Example 2

Smith Ltd operates an 80% learning rate. It has been asked to quote for 60 units of a product to be assembled to the specific requirements of a customer. Estimates for the assembly of the first unit are:

Direct materials	£20,000
Direct labour	8,000
Variable overhead	4,000

Fixed overhead is absorbed at £1/labour hour.

Wages are £4/hour. Estimate the marginal costs of making the 60 units.

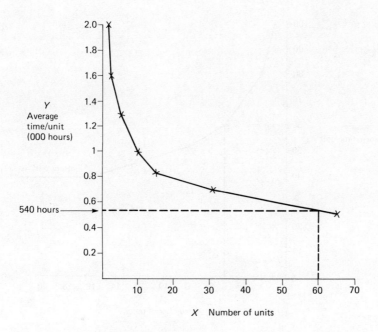

Fig. 22. *Example of a learning curve.*

SOLUTION

Units	Average time/unit hours	Cumulative time hours
1	2,000	2,000
2	1,600	3,200
4	1,280	5,120
8	1,024	8,192
16	819·2	13,107
32	655·4	20,973
64	524·3	33,556

This may be plotted graphically as in Fig. 23.

Estimated Marginal Costs (60 units)

Direct materials	£1,200,000	
Direct labour	129,600	(540 hours × 60 units × £4)
Variable overhead	240,000	
	£1,569,600	

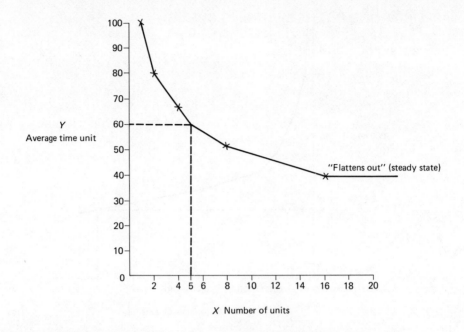

Fig. 23. *Using the learning curve to estimate marginal costs.*

Students should note that a cumulative learning curve can also be used to determine the cumulative hours for 60 units (*see* Fig. 24).

From Fig. 24 it can be seen that for 60 units the cumulative hours are approximately 32,400, which equals (540 hours × 60 units) from the earlier graph.

You may use either graph to find an approximate time.

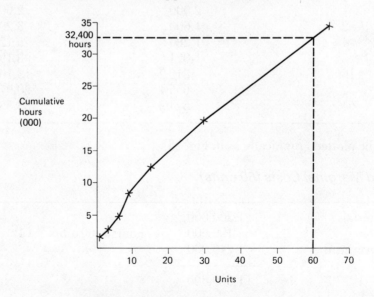

Fig. 24. *Cumulative learning curve.*

3.0   APPLICATIONS OF THE LEARNING CURVE

3.1   The setting of standard costs

The learning curve phenomenon must be recognised, otherwise a standard may be set when the cumulative output is low, resulting in a high cost being set — one that is too near the cost of the first unit. Favourable variances will emerge. If standards are set during the steady state (that state where there is little outstanding learning), adverse variances arise, due to the costs set being too low.

3.2   The setting of wage incentive schemes

If these schemes ignore the learning curve effects, then employees will need to be compensated during the early stages of learning, for the lower than normal (steady state) level of performance, which is owing to lack of familiarity and experience in the early stages of production rather than any lack of motivation or ability.

3.3   Work scheduling and overtime decisions

As the learning effect is realised output per employee increases. Production schedules, machine capability and materials' availability must be carefully maintained to avoid potential bottlenecks and stockouts. Also overtime may be required in the early stages of learning to compensate for poor efficiency.

3.4   Budgeting cash flows

When the learning curve applies, increases in output will not attract a proportionate increase in variable costs. Direct labour, material, and variable overheads per unit will reduce due to greater efficiency and less scrap material. A new level of finance for this output must be planned.

3.5   Pricing

It is important when pricing follow-up orders to recognise that labour, material and variable overhead (if activity based) costs will reduce as the company goes down its learning curve.

Students should note that, if variable overheads are not activity based but recovered on a labour/cost basis, then although the overhead charge to a customer is less the cost to the firm will not have decreased.

4.0   LIMITATIONS OF THE LEARNING CURVE

(a) It is only applicable in labour intensive operations, which are repetitive and reasonably skilled.

(b) Employees must be motivated in order to learn.

(c) It assumes that there is a stable labour mix with a negligible labour turnover.

(d) Breaks between production runs must be short, or learning is forgotten.

(e)   Technological change, for example, robots performing skilled jobs, reduces the significance of the learning curve application.

(f)   The learning rate is difficult to determine accurately. It ranges from 60% to 90%; 70% to 80% experience curves for the whole company are most frequently found.

Students will realise that a 50% learning curve is impossible, otherwise extra units would take no extra time to make.

5.0   CONCLUSION

If an industry is subject to continual technological change, it is beneficial to risk heavy research and development investment in order to become a leader as opposed to a follower, so that output is increased and lower production costs are achieved because of the learning curve effect. Selling prices can therefore be lowered and the firm becomes more competitive and captures a larger share of the market.

CHAPTER EIGHTEEN

Decentralisation and Performance Evaluation

1.0 INTRODUCTION

Because of the increase in the number of business mergers and acquisitions during the last two decades, business organisations have increased in complexity. As the organisation grows in size successful management of it by a central group of people becomes more difficult. In order to overcome this problem the modern trend is towards decentralisation, that is, the breaking down of the organisation into subunits where individual managers have the freedom to make their own decisions.

The main objectives of decentralisation are as follows:

(a) *goal congruency:* that the objectives of each divisional manager remain in accordance with overall company policy;

(b) *autonomy:* that the subunits retain the freedom to make their own decisions;

(c) *performance evaluation:* that objective evaluation of divisional managerial performance is achieved.

2.0 PRECONDITIONS FOR EFFECTIVE DECENTRALISATION

Wherever possible the following conditions should exist:

(a) Operational independence, that is, separate production facilities;

(b) Divisional control over pricing and expenditure;

(c) Central policies to integrate and coordinate divisions;

(d) Clearly defined areas of responsibility;

(e) The output of one division is not the input of another division.

The greater the degree of independence between subunits, the more easily effective decentralisation is attained.

3.0 ADVANTAGES OF DECENTRALISATION

(a) Frees top management from everyday decision-making thereby enabling it to concentrate on strategic planning, policy formulation, and providing overall direction.

(b) More decision-making provides better training for managers.

(c) Optimises decision-making by ensuring that only those personnel thoroughly acquainted with an aspect of the firm make decisions concerning it.

(d) There is a more rapid response to environmental changes and opportunities by eliminating administrative bottlenecks, which are inherent in a centralised firm.

(e) Motivational advantages include:

   (i)   increased status for a divisional manager with wider responsibilities;

   (ii)   more control over the factors which determine his performance;

   (iii) the smaller subunit is more personalised and therefore fosters good labour relations.

4.0 DISADVANTAGES OF DECENTRALISATION

(a) A more elaborate and therefore expensive communication system is required.

(b) Possible loss of economies of scale if each division is an autonomous unit manufacturing similar products. (For example, duplication of assets and services, and loss of discounts as a result of not buying centrally in bulk).

(c) Problems in objectively measuring divisional performance.

(d) Problems in establishing an optimal transfer pricing system where the division supplies another within the group.

(e) Dysfunctional decision-making: this arises if a manager makes a decision that is beneficial to his own division, but which is suboptimal to the organisation as a whole. Such decisions are likely when there is lack of motivation, and interdependence exists between subunits.

5.0 COST, PROFIT, AND INVESTMENT CENTRES

5.1 Cost centre

A cost centre is a centre where the responsibility for costs lies. Its main objective is to facilitate responsibility accounting. However, it is important that managers are only made responsible for costs over which they have some control.

5.2 Profit centre

A profit centre is a centre where responsibility lies for costs and revenue. Its main objective is to maximise the profitability of divisions and thereby that of the organisation as a whole. Problems arise in the setting of a fair transfer pricing system for divisional transfers within the organisation.

5.3 Investment centre

An investment centre is a centre where responsibility lies for costs, revenue, and investments. The main problem is whether major investments should be made at divisional level or centrally.

Students should note that although profit centres are associated with decentralisation, their existence does not prove that a firm is decentralised. A manager may be held responsible for the profits of his division and yet have no decision-making power to improve profitability.

6.0 INTRODUCTION TO PERFORMANCE EVALUATION

The following techniques can be employed for measuring divisional performance:

    (a) standard costing and variance analysis;

    (b) net profit;

    (c) value added;

    (d) ratio analysis:

        (i)   return on investment;

        (ii)   contribution/sales;

        (iii) "other" ratios;

    (e) residual income.

7.0 TECHNIQUES OF PERFORMANCE EVALUATION

7.1 Standard costing and variance analysis

This method is dealt with in detail in Chapter 13. It involves the setting of predetermined cost estimates in order to provide a basis for comparison with actual performance. Any differences arising are called *variances*, and where necessary control action should be taken.

7.2 Net profit

This measure of performance has the following disadvantages:

    (a) As it is unrelated to a divisional investment, any intergroup or interfirm comparison is meaningless.

(b) Net profit is divisional revenue less total costs. Total cost would include direct divisional cost plus allocated central costs of the organisation. This goes against the grain of decentralisation. It is better to use divisional revenue less divisional costs as a measure of divisional performance, or divisional revenue less divisional controllable costs as a measure of divisional managerial performance.

7.3 Value added

This is the sales value of goods or services minus the cost of materials, goods and services introduced into the firm. It can also be described as the increase between the value of the goods and services which finally emerge as the result of its activities.

Statement of value added: year to 31/12/X1

	£m
Turnover	100
Bought in materials and services	60
Value added	40
Applied the following way:	
To pay employees:	
Wages, pensions, benefits	25
To pay providers of capital:	
Interest and dividends	3
To pay government:	
Taxation	5
To provide for maintenance and expansion of assets:	
Depreciation	2
Retained profits	5
	40

Value added has the following advantages:

(a) It shows the distributions which have been attributed to the various participants from the fund of added value created.

(b) Profit has problems of definition. Value added may therefore provide a communication benefit.

(c) Added value ratios may provide control measures, for example value added/number of employees, value added/capital employed.

(d) The ratio of added value per £ of labour cost might act as a basis for productivity payments.

(e) It emphasises that the success of a business depends upon its ability to add value, and that the cost of bought-in materials and services is merely passed on to the customer. Profit only comes out of added value.

7.4 Ratio analysis

(a) *Return on investment (ROI)*

$$ROI = \frac{return}{investment} \times 100$$

Although problems exist in defining the return and the investment, the return is usually net profit before deducting taxation, and excluding interest payable and income from trade investments. The investment is usually capital employed excluding intangibles and trade investments. The capital employed can be at either gross or net book values. Students should be aware that ROI is the same as *ROCE (return on capital employed)* — the accounting rate of return. The ROI can be analysed into further ratios as follows:

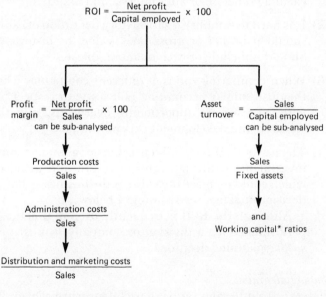

Working capital ratios include:

$$\text{average collection period} = \frac{debtors}{credit\ sales} \times 365$$

$$\text{stock turnover} = \frac{average\ stock}{cost\ of\ goods\ sold} \times 365$$

current ratio = current assets : current liabilities

quick asset ratio = current assets (less stock) : current liabilities

(i) *Advantages of ROI*

    (1) It uses financial accounting measurements which should be readily understood by management.

    (2) It is a relative measure indicating the average level of return on assets.

    (3) It can be used as a basis for further ratios which are used for analytical purposes.

    (4) It may be used in interfirm comparisons, provided that the firms whose results are being compared are of comparable size and of the same industry.

(ii) *Limitations of ROI*

    (1) It is hard to establish a satisfactory definition of profit — should it be calculated before or after interest and taxation?

    (2) It is hard to establish a satisfactory definition of capital employed — should it be net or gross book value, or historic or current cost? Should it include or exclude intangible assets?

    (3) When comparing ratios of different companies it is necessary that they use similar accounting policies with respect to valuing stocks and fixed assets, apportioning overheads, and the treatment of research and development expenditure, etc.

    (4) The use of ROI may influence divisional management to select only investments with high rates of return and to reject opportunities which could increase the value of the business (that is, dysfunctional decision-making, see Example 4 below).

    Although the ROI is frequently used in practice as a measure of performance for a division or company it must never be used for *making* planning decisions.

(b) *Contribution/sales ratio*

Although the profit to sales ratio is a useful measure of overall profitability, it cannot be used to measure the effects on profit of changes in sales volume, and is therefore inappropriate for decision-making purposes.

    However, the contribution to sales ratio is an important aid for making such decisions.

Example 1

Z Ltd makes two products A and B, with results as follows:

	£	A £	£	B £
Sales		600,000		400,000
Variable costs	510,000		320,000	
Fixed costs	30,000		48,000	
	———	(540,000)	———	(368,000)
Profit		£60,000		£32,000

Z Ltd expects to have extra production capacity to make either £100,000 of sales of A, or £80,000 of sales of B (assume that the current sales price remains constant for both products). Which product should be made and sold?

SOLUTION

A		B
10%	Profit to sales	8%
15%	Contribution to sales	20%

Using the profit to sales ratio: A, 10% of £100,000 = £10,000; compared with B, 8% of £80,000 = £6,400. However as the fixed costs are unaffected by the decision it is more appropriate to use the contribution to sales ratio: A, 15% of £100,000 = £15,000; B, 20% of £80,000 = £16,000. B generates more contribution from the additional sales and is therefore preferable to A.

   (c) *"Other ratios"*
      The following ratios, although not traditional financial ratios, can be useful to all grades of management because of their specific application to certain types of analysis:

     (i)   standard costing ratios (efficiency, capacity, and production volume ratios);

     (ii) sales per salesman;

     (iii) sales per metre of shelf/floor space;

     (iv) sales per £ of advertising;

     (v) sages per employee;

     (vi) other expenses per employee;

     (vii) costs per tonne of delivering goods.

Example 2

During 1960 Alfred Williams retired from the army and with his gratuity purchased a small retail wool shop which he called by his wife's name. Since then he has run the shop with no assistance other than that from his wife Olive. During 1975 he was asked by the Retail Association of Wool Shops whether he would be prepared to submit his annual accounts, for these to be combined in an anonymous manner with those of other firms, to enable comparisons of trading results to be made.

Mr Williams agreed and sent along his accounts for the year ended 31st March 1975, which were as follows:

Olive's Wool Shop:
Profit and Loss Account for the year ended 31st March 1975

Sales		£10,145
Less: Cost of goods sold		6,087
Gross profit		4,058
Expenses:		
Wages	£325	
Rates	125	
Heating and light	370	
Insurances	80	
Advertising, printing, stationery	510	
Miscellaneous expense	275	
Depreciation	400	
		2,085
Net profit (before taxation)		£1,973

The following additional information had to be supplied:

(a) Whether the premises were owned or rented and, if the latter, the amount of the rent.

(b) Details of the time that the owner and other members of his family spent working in the shop. In their case, Mr Williams worked for 40 hours each week and his wife for 30.

(c) Details of equipment used in the shop (cost, date of purchase, estimated life).

(d) The amount shown on the capital account. This was £4,750 at the commencement of the year in question.

Subsequently Mr Williams received the following statement of the "average" accounts for the wool shops contributing to the scheme, with his own results as "adjusted" by the Association.

	Olive's Wool Shop	Average wool shop
Sales	£10,145	£12,440
Less: Cost of goods sold	6,087	6,470
Gross profit	4,058	5,970

Expenses:

Management expenses	£2,000	1,850
Wages	865	610
Rates	125	120
Heating and light	370	345
Insurances	80	90
Advertising, printing etc.	510	280
Miscellaneous expenses	275	250
Depreciation	400	400
Interest on capital	475	480
Rent	500	500
	5,600	4,925
Net profit (loss) (before taxation)	(£1,542)	£1,045

Mr Williams and his wife were perplexed at these figures, as from their own accounts they had felt that they were doing very well.

You are required to provide:

(a) an explanation of the purpose of the exercise and of the reasons for each of the adjustments to the original profit statement.

(b) a comparison of the results of Olive's Wool Shop with those for similar shops which indicates those areas which Mr Williams should investigate. How should Mr Williams view these individual problem areas in order to improve the overall performance of his business?

SOLUTION

(a) The Retail Association of Wool Shops have altered the original accounts to include notional (or imputed) items of costs which were not previously reflected in the accounts in order that Olive's Wool Shop can be fairly compared with the average wool shop.

Profit as shown on original statement		£1,973
Less: Expenses not shown:		
Wages (£865 − £325)	£540	
Management expenses	2,000	
Rent	500	
Interest on capital	475	
		3,515
Net loss as shown on adjusted statement		£(1,542)

Reasons for the inclusion of those notional expenses

(i)   *Management expenses:* the amount Mr Williams would have to pay a manager for the work he does himself. This represents the amount he could obtain if he worked elsewhere in the same capacity.

(ii) *Wages:* the amount is an estimate of the wages for the hours worked by his wife if an outsider were employed.

(iii) *Interest on capital:* it is assumed that if the capital had been invested elsewhere it would have generated a return of at least 10%.

(iv) *Rent:* as the premises are owned an amount is included which represents the return which could be obtained if the shop were rented out to another organisation.

(b) *Comparison of results*
The following ratios can now be used to compare trading results:

Olive's Wool Shop		Average wool shop	
$\text{ROI} \left[\frac{(1,542)}{4,750} \times 100\right]$	= (32%)	$\left[\frac{1,045}{4,800} \times 100\right]$	= 22%
$\text{Asset turnover} \left[\frac{10,145}{4,750}\right]$	= 2·1	$\left[\frac{12,440}{4,800}\right]$	= 2·6
$\text{Net profit margin} \left[\frac{(1,542)}{10,145} \times 100\right]$	= (15·2%)	$\left[\frac{1,045}{12,440} \times 100\right]$	= 8·4%
Gross profit margin	40%		48%
Sales volume	82%		100%
Expenses/sales	55%		40%
(Advertising, printing and stationery)/sales	5%		2·25%

From the above the following areas require investigation:

(i)   The sales volume is only 82% of the average and the asset turnover ratio is lower than average. More sales must be generated.

(ii) The gross profit margin is lower than average. This could indicate that the mark-up is too low. However, the low mark-up should have increased sales. Perhaps the wrong type of goods are being purchased. A review of Olive's stock control policy must also be undertaken.

(iii) The ratio of expenses/sales is higher than average. On further analysis it is the cost of advertising, printing, etc. that causes the most concern.

(iv) Mr Williams must try to study the effect of different pricing policies on asset turnover ratios and profit margins. Also it must improve on its present buying policy, and be more sensitive to customer requirements.

(c) *Residual income (RI)*

Residual income is the operating income of a division, less the "imputed" interest on the assets used by the division.

Example 3

Division A has capital employed of £50,000, net income of £15,000 and a cost of capital of 14%.

Net income	=	£15,000
Imputed interest	=	(7,000) (14% of £50,000)
		———
Residual income		£8,000
		———

The residual income approach is similar to that of the net present value (NPV) approach, a discounted cash flow technique, which maximises shareholders' wealth and is therefore in the best interests of the company as a whole. The ROI approach can lead to dysfunctional decision-making.

Example 4

Division X and division Y are both currently considering an outlay on new investment projects.

	Division X	*Division Y*
Investment outlay	£100,000	£100,000
Net outlay return	£16,000	£11,000
Current ROI divisional		
assets	18%	11%

The group's cost of capital is 13%.
  Should the projects be accepted or rejected?

SOLUTION
  (i) *Using ROI*
      The ROI for the projects is 16% for X, and 11% for Y. Project X would therefore be rejected as it is less than the current ROI of 18%, and project Y accepted as it is not less than the current 11% return.

(ii) *Using RI*

	X £	Y £
Assets	100,000	100,000
Imputed interest	13,000	13,000
Net income	16,000	11,000
RI	£3,000	£(2,000)

Project X would be accepted and Y rejected.

This conclusion is consistent with the NPV approach. (Students unfamiliar with DCF techniques can ignore the following computation.)

Project X: NPV $=$ (100,000) $=$ $+\dfrac{16,000}{0.13}$ (in perpetuity)

          Gain $=$ $+ £23,077$

Project Y: NPV $=$ (100,000) $+$ $\dfrac{11,000}{0\cdot13}$ (in perpetuity)

          Loss $=$ $- £15,385$

A typical residual income statement for a division is as follows:

Divisional performance statement

		£
Revenue		x
Less: Variable costs		x
Contribution		x
Less: Controllable fixed costs		x
Controllable profit		x
Less: Interest on controllable investment		x
Controllable residual income		x
Less: Uncontrollable costs (allocated HO charges)	x	
Less: Interest on non-controllable investment	x	
		x
		x
Net residual income		x

Advantages of RI

(a) Charging a cost of capital (company's required rate of return) ensures that divisional management are constantly aware of the opportunity cost of funds.

(b) Charging each division with the firm's cost of capital ensures that decisions taken at divisional level will be compatible with the interests of the organisation as a whole.

(c) By maximising RI, growth is achieved where opportunities are available which earn a rate of return in excess of the cost of capital.

(d) It avoids dysfunctional decision-making, as a project would not be rejected because it would lower the divisional average rate of return, if it earned a higher rate of return than the company's cost of funds.

Disadvantages of RI

There may be difficulties in:

(a) defining the value of the assets on which the interest charge is based, as with ROI;

(b) identifying controllable and uncontrollable factors at divisional level;

(c) defining the cost of capital;

(d) deciding on whether to use a single group cost of capital or specific divisional costs of capital. The former is normally used as it enhances divisional goal congruency.

8.0 CONCLUSION

Students should now see that although the trend is towards decentralisation a healthy balance must be struck between centralisation and decentralisation, as the former results in top management being overburdened with everyday decision-making, and the latter in a lack of goal congruency between subunits and the organisation as a whole.

Furthermore, students must be familiar with all the different types of measures of performance. The functions of these measures are to:

(a) encompass the widest possible definition of performance;

(b) be fair;

(c) motivate divisional management towards goal congruency;

(d) reflect the results of decisions taken in the interests of both the short-term and long-term objectives of the organisation;

(e) reflect the degree of managerial control at divisional level — it is therefore important that the design of measures is linked to the level of autonomy of the division, and

(f) reflect the quality of performance by the divisional manager.

CHAPTER NINETEEN

Transfer Pricing

1.0 INTRODUCTION

A transfer price is that notional value placed on goods and services transferred from one division to another within a large business organisation.

The reasons for implementing a transfer pricing system can be summarised as follows:

(a) To record intracompany transfers, thereby maintaining a check on the flow of resources within the organisation.

(b) To enable the performance (profitability) of a division to be evaluated, by compensating it for benefits provided for other divisions and charging it for benefits received.

(c) To motivate managers into maximising the profitability of their divisions, while acting in the best interests of the organisation as a whole.

(d) International groups may try to manipulate transfer prices between countries in order to minimise the overall tax burden.

The above reasons illustrate that transfer pricing aims to improve decision-making in a decentralised organisation. Thus the three objectives of decentralisation (goal congruency, performance evaluation and autonomy) should be satisfied by the system of transfer pricing.

Comprehensive example 1

D Ltd includes two divisions. Division A manufactures a component which is used by Division B to produce a finished product. For the next period, output and costs have been budgeted as follows:

	Division A	*Division B*
Component units	50,000	
Finished units		50,000
Total variable costs	£250,000	£600,000
Fixed costs	150,000	200,000

The fixed costs are separable for each division.

You are required to advise on the transfer price to be fixed for Division A's component under the following circumstances.

Circumstance 1
Division A can sell the component in a competitive market for £10 per unit. Division B can also purchase the component on the open market at that price.

SOLUTION
A transfer price can be arrived at which is equal to the sum of the incremental (marginal) costs of producing the components plus the opportunity cost to the *whole organisation* of not being able to use the components in the next most profitable way.

Transfer price = £5 (marginal costs) + £5 (contribution forgone by transferring internally as opposed to selling on the open market)

= £10

This approach appears to be the same as that of using the market price. However circumstance 2 will illustrate otherwise.

Circumstance 2
As per the situation described in circumstance 1, but assuming that Division B currently buys the component from an external supplier at the market price of £10 and there is a reciprocal agreement between the external supplier and another Division, C, within the group. Under this agreement the external supplier agrees to buy one product unit from Division C, at a profit of £4 per unit to that division, for every component which Division B buys from the supplier.

SOLUTION
Transfer price = £5 (marginal costs) + £5 (contribution forgone as in 1)
+ £4 (profit forgone by Division C as Division B will acquire its units from Division A instead of the external supplier)

= £5 + £9   (opportunity cost to the whole organisation)

= £14

This price should result in the manager of Division B continuing to buy from the external supplier at the market price of £10. However, the price of £14 is right from the viewpoint of the organisation as a whole, since if the component is transferred internally not only will Division A forgo an external profit of £5, but Division C will also forgo an external profit of £4. It is assumed that Division C could not achieve the same profit by selling elsewhere.

Example 2

Where a division has spare capacity it may be in the group's best interest that all or part of the transfer be internal as opposed to external (*see* Fig. 25).

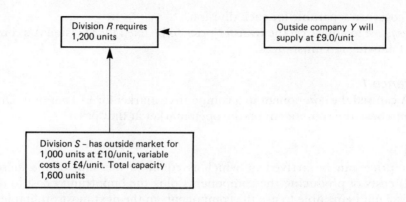

Fig. 25. *Transfer pricing with spare capacity.*

(a) *Cost statement of the group where R acquires all 1,200 units from Y*

External sales (of Division S)	(1,000 units at £10)		£10,000
Costs:			
(of Division S)	(1,000 units at £4)	£4,000	
(of Division R)	(1,200 units at £9)	10,800	
			(14,800)
		net cost	£(4,800)

(b) *Cost statement of the group where R acquires all 1,200 units from S*

External sales (of S)	(400 units at £10)		£4,000
Costs:			
(of S)	(1,600 units at £4)		(6,400)
		net cost	£(2,400)

(c) *Cost statement of the group where R acquires 600 units from Company Y and 600 units from S*

External sales (of S)	(1,000 units at £10)		£10,000
Costs:			
(of S)	(1,600 units at £4)	£6,400	
(of R)	(600 units at £9)	5,400	
			(11,800)
		net cost	£(1,800)

Students will note that the costs and sales between R and S will cancel out and therefore do not appear in the above group statements.

Because Division S has spare capacity it is in the best interest of the group that Division R acquires some of its requirements internally from S, and some from Company Y. However, it will be necessary to use a dual pricing system so that another transfer price can be used in order to motivate Division S to supply the spare capacity units to Division R. Perhaps a market price or negotiated market price could be used for performance evaluation purposes, and the above cost statement (c) for decision-making aspects as £1,800 provides the least cost to the group.

Students should compare the example above with circumstance 2.

Circumstance 3 (Example 1)

Circumstances 1 and 2 do not apply as there is no external market for the component produced by Division A, and Division B's product is selling in a very competitive market at £28 per unit. Both decision-making and performance evaluation aspects should be considered.

SOLUTION

Transfer price = £5 (marginal costs)   + £0   (as there is no external market there can be no opportunity cost to the firm as a whole)

= £5

Using a transfer price of £5/unit the following results will appear:

	Division A		Division B		Whole Organisation
Transfer to B	£250,000	Sales	£1,400,000	Sales	£1,400,000
		Costs:		Costs:	
Own costs	(400,000)	Own 800,000		A 400,000	
		From A 250,000		B 800,000	
			(1,050,000)		(1,200,000)
Loss	£(150,000)	Profit	£350,000	Profit	£200,000

Students will note that the £250,000 transfer price in A, and transfer cost in B, cancel out and do not appear in the profit statement for the whole organisation. Profits can only be made by the whole organisation on sales to the outside market (not on internal sales).

A transfer price of £5, although it will ensure that decisions taken by the manager of Division B are in the best interests of the organisation as a whole, will do nothing to motivate the manager of Division A (which shows a loss) or to enable the performance of Division A to be evaluated. Another transfer pricing system can therefore be agreed for the purpose of subsequent evaluation and reward of performance.

For the purpose of evaluating results, a transfer price could be agreed which divides the overall profit of £200,000 in an equitable manner between the two divisions. On the basis of total costs (other bases could be used if fair and agreed to), the profit could be shared in the ratio of 1:2, so that Division A receives £66,667 and Division B receives £133,333 of the profit.

The transfer price needed to achieve these profits can be calculated in the following way:

Division A — loss (150,000) ∴ contribution needed
  to generate a profit of   £66,667
                = 150,000 + 66,667   =   £216,667
                                             50,000 units

             Contribution (£216,667 ÷ 50,000 units)   =   £4·33/unit
             Variable costs (marginal)   =   £5·00/unit

             Transfer price (selling price)   =   £9·33/unit

Using a transfer price of £9·33/unit (approximately)

	Division A		Division B		Whole organisation
Transfer to B	£466,667	Sales		£1,400,000	Sales	£1,400,000
		Costs:			Costs:	
Own costs	(400,000)	Own	800,000		A 400,000	
		From A	466,667		B 800,000	
				(1,266,667)		(1,200,000)
Profit	(£66,667)	Profit		£133,333	Profit	£200,000

It can be seen that a change in the transfer price has no effect on the profits of the organisation as a whole, but only on the distribution of the profits between the divisions.

This system of using a transfer price of £5/unit for decision-making purposes, and a transfer price of £9·33/unit for performance evaluation aspects, is called *dual pricing*.

Circumstance 4 (Example 1)

If the transfer from Division A to Division B is made at full cost, what is the minimum price that Division B could sell the finished product for, and would this price be in the best interest of the organisation as a whole?

SOLUTION

Students will remember (from our discussion of pricing, Chapter 9) that when the goods are to be made, the minimum price is equal to the incremental costs of making the goods.

	Transfer costs from A		Variable costs of B
∴. Minimum price =	£400,000	+	£600,000
	(full cost)		
=	£1,000,000 ÷ 50,000 units	=	£20/unit

However, it is beneficial to the whole firm to set a minimum price at £250,000 (variable costs of A) + £600,000 (variable costs of B)

$$= \quad £850,000 \div 50,000 \text{ units} \quad = \quad \underline{£17/\text{unit}}$$

It can be seen that transferring at full costs results in Division B's treating the fixed costs of Division A as variable costs, which in turn leads to dysfunctional decision-making. Division B might reject an offer of £19/unit as it is below its minimum price, and thereby cause the firm as a whole to lose (£19 + £17 = £2 contribution/unit.

2.0   METHODS OF TRANSFER PRICING

2.1   Market price

This method is used whenever possible, as it puts the transferor (selling) and transferee (buying) divisions on the same footing as independent contractors, and satisfies the three criteria of decentralisation — goal congruence, performance evaluation and autonomy.

   (a) *Advantages*

   (i)   Competition of the market place should enhance the economic efficiency of the transferor division and thereby reduce inefficiency in the form of excessive costs from being passed on to the transferee division.

   (ii) The buying division, like the selling division, is autonomous and can therefore subject the latter to the same appraisal as it would an outside supplier.

   (iii) Subject to the price being acceptable intercompany trading should result in a better quality of service, dependability of supply, and more flexibility.

   (b) *Disadvantages*

   (i)   If the goods or services are highly specialised a market price may not exist.

(ii)   Perfect competition may not be possible because of branding or lack of full information.

(iii) Market prices can fluctuate considerably and the problem arises as to whether long-run average or existing (current) prices should be used. Current prices are normally chosen as it is considered better to evaluate managerial performance in the light of prevailing conditions be they good or bad.

(iv)   It can be expensive to continually acquire up-to-date market prices in a complex market place.

(v)   A transfer price at market value may not induce a division to use up spare capacity.

(vi)   A negotiated market price may have to be used to allow for the fact that internal transfers are less costly than external sales because of less advertising, lower transport costs, no bad debts, etc.

2.2 Full cost

This is a popular method because of its convenience and consistency with absorption costing. However, students should be aware of the following:

(a)   Standard costs should be used in preference to actual costs as the latter can result in inefficiencies in the form of costs being passed on to the transferee.

(b)   A mark-up (profit) will be added to the full cost in order to provide incentives for internal transfers. There may be difficulty in arriving at a fair mark-up.

(c)   The fixed costs of the transferor division are converted into a variable cost for the transferee, which may lead to dysfunctional decision-making.

2.3 Marginal costs

For decision-making purposes a possible transfer price is one based on marginal (incremental) costs of the goods plus any opportunity cost to the firm as a whole (of not being able to use them in the next most profitable way). However, the following points should be noted:

(a)   Opportunity cost is sometimes difficult to identify except where it is zero.

(b)   If the opportunity cost is zero then a profit element, arrived at on an equitable basis, will have to be added to the marginal cost for motivational purposes.

(c)   Marginal costs are difficult to ascertain accurately as they do not form part of the conventional cost accounting data, and continually change as output levels change.

(d)   Variable costs plus a profit margin can be used, but do not allow for any recovery of a division's fixed costs.

2.4 Linear programming

This is particularly useful where the transferor division cannot satisfy all the demand from transferee divisions because of limitations on its capacity and on resource availability.

A linear programming model is, therefore, necessary in order to arrive at an optimal plan. Since the shadow price of a scarce resource is the contribution per unit of the transferred product, the transfer price is calculated by adding the shadow price and the marginal cost per unit of the transferred product.

The linear programming approach has the following limitations:

(a) It is difficult to obtain accurate cost data.

(b) Linear programming is an expensive method as a new optimal plan must be produced every time there is a change in the demand for the product or a change in the resource mix.

(c) There are assumptions to be made in the method of linear programming.

(d) Divisional autonomy is reduced as the linear programming solution is normally imposed by head office on all the divisions concerned.

There are two other methods of transfer pricing — an imposed transfer price, and a negotiated transfer price, but these are seldom used for obvious reasons.

An imposed transfer price by head office may be necessary, as a last resort, in order to settle divisional conflict. However, it destroys divisional autonomy and is regarded as a retrograde step towards centralisation.

A negotiated transfer price, one arrived at by consultation between divisional managers, can be very time-consuming, lead to divisional preoccupation and thereby dysfunctional decision-making.

Also students should be aware that a system of dual pricing may be used, where one transfer price is employed for decision-making purposes, and another transfer price is used for, say, performance evaluation reasons.

3.0 CONCLUSION

Students will realise that transfer pricing is a complex topic. It is very difficult to arrive at a transfer price which satisfies all the relevant criteria of decentralisation. Flexibility is required.

CHAPTER TWENTY

Quantitative Analysis in Management Accounting

1.0 INTRODUCTION

Quantitative techniques are often used in planning and decision-making areas of management accounting, but to a lesser extent in performance evaluation and control aspects where behavioural factors are more important than sophisticated techniques.

They are useful therefore as additional tools to be used by the accountant when they are appropriate and cost-effective.

The management accountant must be aware of the techniques and their assumptions and limitations. It is important that they do not alter underlying principles or aims, but facilitate the practice of accounting in particular circumstances.

The quantitative techniques which are of importance to the management accountant include the following:

(a) linear programming for decision-making, particularly on resource allocation;

(b) the economic batch order quantity in inventory control;

(c) discounted cash flow techniques in investment appraisal;

(d) network analysis for planning purposes;

(e) calculus in pricing decisions;

(f) the use of probabilities and expected values for decision-making;

(g) the learning curve in setting standards;

(h) simulation for model building.

Students should study the ensuing examples, which are a collection of past examination questions, involving the use of quantitative techniques in management accounting situations.

2.0 EXAMPLES OF QUANTITATIVE TECHNIQUES

Example 1

The sales forecast is frequently a critical factor in the budgeting process. Sometimes the periodic sales of an organisation are found to be serially correlated. When this happens the method of extrapolating past sales information may be helpful in the provision of a sales forecast. Refinements to extrapolation include: use moving averages; the weighting of these averages by a constant which acts as a surrogate to combine the effects of most of the other variables which influence the organisation's sales. In the process of weighting moving averages, the sales for the future period, $S_{(t + 1)}$, are assumed to be related to the average sales for a past number of stated years, $(n + 1)$, multiplied by some constant, K, i.e.

(1)
$$S_{(t + 1)} = \frac{K(S_{(t)} + S_{(t-1)} \dots + S_{(t - n)})}{(n + 1)}$$

One of the disadvantages of this method is that it gives equal weighting to each item in the average. To overcome this disadvantage the technique of moving weighted averages with decreasing weightings may be used. This technique provides greater weightings to the more recent items in the series.

Better Results Ltd has been using formula (1) to make its sales forecast, with $K = 1 \cdot 5$, and $n = 2$. However, the firm is considering a refinement of this approach. Two suggestions have been made as to how this could be done. *Both would still use $K = 1 \cdot 5$ and $n = 2$.*

The first proposal is that the sales of the year preceding the forecast should be weighted by 2, to provide the following formula:

(2)
$$S_{(t + 1)} = \frac{K(2S_{(t)} + S_{(t-1)} + S_{(t - 2)})}{4}$$

The second suggestion is that the sales of the year preceding the forecast should be weighted by 3, and the year before this by 2, to provide the formula:

(3)
$$S_{(t + 1)} = \frac{K(3S_{(t)} + 2S_{(t - 1)} + S_{(t - 2)})}{6}$$

Sales for the company over the past 8 years have been as follows:
65; 78; 101; 129; 164; 208; 269 and 343 in the most recent year.

You are required to provide:

  (a) Calculations showing the forecasts for Better Results Ltd's sales for *years 4 to 8, using each of the three formulae shown above.* Present your results in tabular form.

  (b) A report to Better Results Ltd to indicate which of the above formulae you would recommend it to use. *Give clearly the reasons for your recommendation,* stating any assumptions that you have made. In your report provide details of any *other sources of information about demand* that you think the firm should consider before their final forecast of sales for use in the next period's budget is made.

SOLUTION

(a)

Years	Actual sales	Appendix Model 1	Model 2	Model 3
1	65	—	—	—
2	78	—	—	—
3	101	—	—	—
4	129	122	129	131
5	164	154	164	167
6	208	197	209	213
7	269	251	266	270
8	343	321	341	347

$$\text{Model 1} = \frac{1 \cdot 5(S_t + S_{t-1} + S_{t-2})}{3}$$

$$\text{Model 2} = \frac{1 \cdot 5(2S_t + S_{t-1} + S_{t-2})}{4}$$

$$\text{Model 3} = \frac{1 \cdot 5(3S_t + 2S_{t-1} + S_{t-2})}{6}$$

(b)
To:
The Managing Director,   XY Accountants
Better Results Ltd,   Address
Address   Date

Re: sales forecasting procedures

Dear Sir

The results as illustrated in the enclosed appendix show that both of the proposed models which use moving weighted averages with decreasing weightings provide better forecasts than the model currently used which is based upon simple moving averages. Because of the past, and expected future growth of sales, the current model's forecasts fall and will continue to fall behind actual sales achieved. The constant K would have to be increased and continually revised as long as sales continued on an upward trend.

Both the proposed models would require less frequent revision, as they automatically deal, to a certain extent, with sales growth. Model 2 gives a heavier weighting to sales nearest the forecast period and is therefore slightly better than model 3. This is because the smoothing gives a greater weighting to the nearest grown sales element. However we recommend that you test both models 2 and 3 so that should the pattern of growth change one of these models would become noticeably superior to the other.

Although these models may appear to provide precise results other factors must be considered. Since other budgets are geared to the sales budget, any inaccuracy in sales forecasting could result in drastic consequences to your firm.

Such factors include: competition, pricing policies, sales promotion, population (size, age distribution, geographical movements), incomes, economic and political situations. This market information could be obtained from your own sales force, business colleagues, and market researchers.

We would conclude by recommending the use of one of the moving weighted average models, and consideration of the above factors before taking the forecasts from the model as the basis for sales in your budgets.

Yours faithfully

XY Accountants

Example 2

(a) Corpach Ltd manufactures three products for which the sales maxima, for the forthcoming year, are estimated to be:

	Product 1	Product 2	Product 3
	£57,500	£96,000	£125,000

Summarised unit cost data are as follows:

	Product 1	Product 2	Product 3
Direct material cost	£10·00	£9·00	£7·00
Variable processing costs	8·00	16·00	10·00
Fixed processing costs	2·50	5·00	4·00
	£20·50	£30·00	£21·00

The allocation of fixed processing costs has been derived from last year's production levels and the figures may need revision if current output plans are different.

The established selling prices are:

	Product 1	Product 2	Product 3
	£23·00	£32·00	£25·00

The products are processed on machinery housed in three buildings:

Building A contains type A machines on which 9,800 machine hours are estimated to be available in the forthcoming year. The fixed overheads for this building are £9,800 per annum.

Building B1 contains type B machines on which 10,500 machine hours are estimated to be available in the forthcoming year.

Building B2 also contains type B machines and again 10,500 machine hours are estimated to be available in the forthcoming year.

The fixed overheads for the B1 and B2 buildings are, in total, £11,200 per annum.

The times required for one unit of output for each product on each type of machine, are as follows:

	Product 1	Product 2	Product 3
Type A machines	1 hour	2 hours	3 hours
Type B machines	1·5 hours	3 hours	1 hour

Assuming that Corpach Ltd wishes to maximise its profits for the ensuing year, you are required to determine the optimal production plan and the profit that this should produce.

(b) Assume that, before the plan that you have prepared in part (a) is implemented, Corpach Ltd suffers a major fire which completely destroys building B2. The fire thus reduces the availability of type B machine time to 10,500 hours per annum and the estimated fixed overhead for such machines, to £8,200. In all other respects the conditions set out, in part (a) to this question, continue to apply.

In his efforts to obtain a revised production plan the company's accountant makes use of a linear programming computer package. This package produces the following optimal tableau:

Z	$X1$	$X2$	$X3$	$S1$	$S2$	$S3$	$S4$	$S5$	
0	0	0	0	0·5	1	0	0·143	− 0·429	1,150
0	0	1	0	− 0·5	0	0	− 0·143	0·429	1,850
0	0	0	0	0	0	1	− 0·429	0·286	3,800
0	0	0	1	0	1	0	0·429	− 0·286	1,200
0	1	0	0	1	0	0	0	0	2,500
1	0	0	0	1·5	0	0	2·429	0·714	35,050

In the above: Z is the total contribution,
$X1$ is the budgeted output of product 1,
$X2$ is the budgeted output of product 2,
$X3$ is the budgeted output of product 3,
$S1$ is the unsatisfied demand for product 1,
$S2$ is the unsatisfied demand for product 2,
$S3$ is the unsatisfied demand for product 3,
$S4$ is the unutilised type A machine time
and $S5$ is the unutilised type B machine time.

The tableau is interpreted as follows:

Optimal plan — Make 2,500 units of product 1,
1,850 units of product 2
and 1,200 units of product 3.

Shadow prices — Product 1 £1·50 per unit,
Type A machine time £2·429 per hour
Type B machine time £0·714 per hour.

Explain the meaning of the shadow prices and consider how the accountant might make use of them. Calculate the profit anticipated from the revised plan and comment on its variation from the profit that you calculated in your answer to part (a).

(c) Explain why linear programming was not necessary for the facts as set out in part (a) whereas it was required for part (b).

SOLUTION

(a) Products	1	2	3
Sales in £	57,500	96,000	125,000
Selling price £	23	32	25
∴ Sales in units	2,500	3,000	5,000

Machine time required for these units					
Type A — hours	2,500	6,000	15,000	=	23,500
Type B — hours	3,750	9,000	5,000	=	17,750

Available hours for A = 9,800, for B = 21,000.

Type A machine time is the limiting key factor, and the optimal mix will be determined by ranking the products according to the unit contribution per hour of type A machine time.

Products	1	2	3		
Unit contribution £	5	7	8		
Contribution per hour of type A machine time £	5	3·5	2·67		
∴ Ranking order	1	2	3		
Optimal mix in units	2,500	3,000	433·33		
Type A hours required	2,500	6,000	1,300	=	9,800 available hours
Contribution £	12,500	21,000	3,466·67	=	£36,966·67
		Less: Fixed overheads (11,200 + 9,800)		=	£21,000·00
			Profit		£15,966·67

(b) *New profit calculation*

Products			
1	2,500 units at £5		£12,500
2	1,850 units at £7		12,950
3	1,200 units at £8		9,600
			35,050
	Less: Fixed overheads		
	(8,200 + 9,800)		(18,000)
		Profit	£17,050

Although the contribution has fallen by £1,917, the profit has increased by £1,083. This is because the fixed overheads saved by the fire (£3,000) exceed the lost contribution of £1,917 by £1,083.

Interpretation of the tableau

The shadow price of £1·50 for product 1 shows that if the demand for product 1 could be increased by 1 unit, total profit could be increased by £1·50. The extra unit of product 1 would produce a contribution of £5, but to make the unit would require forgoing half a unit of product 2 and this would cost $\frac{1}{2} \times$ £7 = £3·50. The net gain is £1·50.

The shadow price of £2·429 for type A machine time shows that an additional hour of this time would increase profits by £2·429. This is acquired by making 0·429 of a unit more of product 3 and 0·143 of a unit less of product 2. These figures are in the column of the tableau that contains the shadow price.

The shadow price of £0·714 for type B machine time shows that an additional hour of this time would increase profits by £0·714. This is achieved by making 0·429 of a unit more of product 2 and 0·286 of a unit less of product 3. These figures feature in the column of the tableau that contains the shadow price.

(c) In part (a) there existed only one constraint so that it was possible to rank products by means of contribution per unit of limiting factor. However, in part (b), due to the fire, more than one constraint arose and linear programming was required to obtain a solution.

Example 3

CR Ltd specialise in supplying cash registers to a number of grocery supermarket chains. The company's product has a reputation for reliability and the low number of requests for service calls from its customers has enabled it to operate with a small service division.

At present the grocery chains arrange for worn cash register ribbons to be replaced by their own employees on an ad hoc basis. However, a number of CR Ltd's customers have indicated that they would appreciate the provision of a specialist service to undertake the replacement of ribbons.

The management accountant of CR Ltd has made investigations and is of the opinion that 17 store groups would be prepared to subscribe to a ribbon maintenance contract. Between them these store groups account for a total of 1,000 cash registers, with each of their high street stores operating on average ten registers. The management accountant bases his estimates upon the provisions of a planned maintenance replacement system at a contract price of £30 per cash register per annum. The contract price would be inclusive of all the costs of replacing ribbons. The ribbons on all cash registers in a store at the date of the scheduled replacement visit would be changed.

In the event of ribbon failure in between such visits an emergency replacement service would be provided as part of the contract. If CR Ltd decides to offer this service its existing service division would have to be enlarged. The fixed costs of this division would be increased by £5,000 per quarter. The average variable costs for the service time and travelling expenses for each planned visit to a store are estimated at £4 however many cash registers have to be dealt with. The average variable cost of an emergency visit would be £2. Only cash registers with failed ribbons would be dealt with during emergency visits and it is unlikely that simultaneous failures will occur to facilitate grouping. Ribbons normally cost CR Ltd £1 each but it is expected that a 25% discount could be negotiated from the ribbon manufacturer for the larger quantities that would be procured if a planned maintenance system was offered.

A recent survey has shown that a ribbon's life pattern has been as follows:

Life (interval between replacement in months)	Proportion of ribbons with this life
1	0·1
2	0·5
3	0·4

You are required to state:

(a) what should be the optimal planned replacement interval if CR Ltd decides to offer the contract replacement service;

(b) the annual profit/loss that the new venture would contribute to the company and the approximate number of registers that would have to be included in the scheme if CR Ltd was to be no worse off financially;

(c) what benefits are likely to arise to the supplier of, and the customers using, such a service.

Note: In your answer ignore taxation, the cost of capital and inflation.

SOLUTION

(a) In order to arrive at the optimal replacement interval it is necessary to compare costs for replacement periods over a common life cycle, for example, three months.

   (i) *Cost statement for replacement each month over a three-month cycle*

Variable costs:	
Ribbons (1,000 × £0·75 × 3 (month cycle))	£2,250
Visits (100 stores* × £4 × 3 months)	1,200
	£3,450

$$\frac{*1,000\ \text{cash registers}}{10\ \text{registers/store}} = 100\ \text{stores}$$

   (ii) *Cost statement for replacement every other month over a three-month cycle*

Variable costs:	
Bulk replacements:	
Ribbons $\left(1,000 \times £0\cdot75 \times 1\frac{1}{2}\ \left[\begin{array}{l}3\ \text{month cycle}\\ \overline{2}\ \text{every other month}\end{array}\right]\right)$	£1,125·00
Visits (100 stores × £4 × 1½ times)	600.00
Replacement of failures:	
Ribbons (100 × £0·75 × 1½)	112·50
Visits (100 stores × £2 × 1½)	300·00
	£2,137·50

   (iii) *Cost statement for replacement every three months over a three-month cycle*

Variable costs:	
Bulk replacements:	
Ribbons (1,000 × £0·75 × 1)	£750·00
Visits (100 stores × £4 × 1)	400·00
Replacement of failures:	
Ribbons (610* × £0·75 × 1)	457·50
Visits (610 visits × £2 × 1)	1,220·00
	£2,827·50

*The 610 ad hoc replacements are a result of 100 ribbons failing at the end of the first month, plus 500 of the original 1,000 failing in the second month, plus the failure of 10% of the 100 replaced during the first month of the quarter (100 + 500 + 10 = 610). Failures during the third month can be disregarded as bulk replacement will take place at the end of this month.

From the above it can be seen that the optimal replacement period is every other month.
 The fixed costs which are common to all three alternatives are irrelevant to the replacement decision.

(b) *Annual profit/loss statement for the optimal replacement period*

Revenue (1,000 registers at £30 each)	£30,000
Variable costs	
(£2,137·5 × 4 quarters)	8,550
Contribution =	21,450
Less: Fixed costs (£5,000 × 4) =	20,000
Net profit =	£1,450

$$\text{Breakeven point (in units)} = \frac{\text{Fixed costs}}{\text{Contribution per unit}} = \frac{£20,000}{(£21,450 \div 1,000)} = 933 \text{ registers}$$

(c) *Benefits of using such a service*

For supplier

(i)   Increased customer goodwill.

(ii) Beneficial to marketing its main activity, supplying cash registers.

(iii) Improvement in the provision of market information.

(iv) Better utilisation of existing service staff.

(v)   Improved cash flows if premiums are paid in advance for the replacement contracts.

For customer

(i)   No responsibility for maintaining stocks of ribbons.

(ii) Able to budget their costs for ribbon replacement.

(iii) Have fewer ribbon failures at critical times.

Example 4

Optimum Ltd makes a single product, the Opt. Opts sell for £30 each and demand is running at 1,000 units per annum, evenly distributed over the year. Technical features in production necessitate batch production methods to supply the expected demand. Currently the company produces in batches of 200 units, although this quantity is not determined by the technology. The cost card for the production of one Opt provides the following information:

Material cost		£6·00
Labour costs:		
Machining 2 hours @ £1·75	£3·50	
Assembly 1 hour @ £1·25	1·25	
Packing ½ hour @ £0·50	0·25	
	———	5·00
Other direct costs		
Two machine hours @ £4·00		8·00
Overheads		3·00
		———
		£22·00

On investigation you find that the overheads are comprised of elements for:

(a) the labour costs associated with the preparation time required for each batch of Opts of 4 hours, which is carried out by the packing staff;

(b) machine set-up costs of £40 per batch — this service is provided by an outside firm;

(c) the absorption of other fixed overheads.

Opts are stacked three high on pallets which require storage space 1 metre square (m^2) and are stored in a warehouse. The rent of the warehouse was negotiated many years ago at the favourable price of £10 per square metre. However, as demand for Opts has been dropping the firm has been increasingly able to sublet its surplus warehouse space for £24 per square metre. Recently Optimum Ltd's labour force has been reduced, although there is still plenty of spare capacity in the organisation as far as all classes of its labour are concerned. Nevertheless, the management has no intention of causing further redundancies. You may assume that the opportunity cost of interest on stock holdings is negligible.

You are required to:

(a) Compute the optimum batch size of Opts to the produced, explaining the formula you have used, commenting briefly on any assumptions you have made and relevant costs you have introduced.

(b) Comment briefly on the size of the average stock of Opts held, in the light of your answer to (a) above.

SOLUTION

(a) When an organisation produces larger and fewer batches although the set-up costs are reduced, holding costs are increased. The converse applies when fewer and smaller batches are produced; this reduces holding costs and causes an increase in set-up costs associated with the production of more batches.

The optimum number in a production batch is found where the aggregate of set-up and holding costs for a period is minimised. The optimum batch size can be obtained from the following model:

$$Q = \sqrt{\frac{2CD}{iP \text{ or } (H)}}$$

Where:

Q = the optimum batch size to produce (in the case of ordering the optimum order quantity).

D = annual demand for the product.

C = the initial fixed costs associated with each batch (in the case of manufactured products the set-up costs, and in the case of purchased goods the cost of placing an order).

H = the annual cost of holding one unit of stock. This is obtained from the annual cost of holding stock expressed as a percentage of the value of the stock concerned (i), multiplied by the cost of a unit of production or stock (P).

The assumptions made in arriving at the above formula are as follows:

(i)   the demand rate is constant and known with certainty,

(ii)   zero lead time (immediate replenishment);

(iii) no stock-outs;

(iv)   a constant purchase price.

In this question $Q = \sqrt{\dfrac{2 \times 1,000 \times 40}{8}} = 100$ optimum batch size.

The above relevant costs have been used for the following reasons:

(i)   The preparation time of the packing staff is not relevant because of the spare capacity as far as labour is concerned and because no redundancies are envisaged.

(ii)   It is impossible to work out holding costs as a percentage of product cost, and therefore H is the opportunity cost of one square metre of warehouse space which is £24 divided by the three Opts stacked on it = £8/Opt. The original £10/m² is a sunk cost and therefore irrelevant.

(b)   *Current policy (assuming a 50-week year)*   *New policy*

$\dfrac{200}{1,000} \times 50 \text{ weeks} = \dfrac{\text{order every}}{10 \text{ weeks}}$ $\dfrac{100}{1,000} \times 50 \text{ weeks} = \dfrac{\text{order every}}{5 \text{ weeks}}$

Average stock

$= \dfrac{200}{2} = \underline{100 \text{ units}}$ $= \dfrac{Q}{2}$ $\dfrac{100}{2} = \underline{50 \text{ units}}$

The above figures suggest that it is preferable to carry a lower average stock but to order more frequently. This would suggest that the costs of ordering are cheap in relation to the costs of holding stock.

CHAPTER TWENTY-ONE

Management Information Systems and Communication

1.0 INTRODUCTION

A management information system (MIS) is a system which enables management to provide the appropriate information at optimal cost so managers can manage.

Although a specialist top-level group will design, monitor and control the information needs of an organisation, an MIS is not a self-contained department, but rather a system which permeates throughout the whole enterprise.

In order to facilitate understanding of this topic it is best to consider systems and information separately.

2.0 SYSTEMS

A system comprises three interrelated parts: inputs, processes or operations, and outputs which achieve objectives. In an information system *the inputs* are labour, capital and technology, the *process* is the conversion of these inputs to provide information, and *the output* is the publication of this information — for example, management reports.

Systems can either be *"open loop"*, where output produced does not control the system and control is taken externally, or *"closed loop"*, where output starts control action by influencing the input.

Most businesses are closed loop and use the output as feedback in order to adjust input, where necessary, and thereby exercise control action to improve the situation.

There are three types of systems:

(a) *Deterministic (mechanistic) systems:* where the outputs that will arise from certain specified inputs can be perfectly predicted; very few businesses behave in this predictable way.

(b) *Probabilistic (stochastic) systems:* where outputs can only be predicted in terms of the probability of an occurrence.

(c) *Self-organising or adaptive systems:* where systems are capable of continually adapting to the environment. A business organisation must adjust to those environmental changes — technological, legal, economic and political — which threaten its survival.

2.1 A closed loop (feedback) system

Figure 26 shows an example of a closed loop (feedback) system (for example, standard costing variance reports). In Fig. 26 management organises its resources (inputs) to achieve the plan. Actual results (output), conveyed in management reports (sensors), are compared against the plan, by managers. This means of comparison is called *a comparator* and can take the form of equipment (computer) or clerical workers. Where variances arise, and after investigation control action is deemed necessary, corrective action to amend the inputs will be taken. This control action can be a manager's set of control instructions and is called *an effector*.

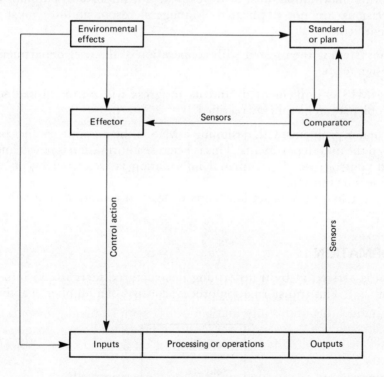

Fig. 26. *A closed loop (feedback) system.*

The environmental effects — such as legislation, competition, consumer behaviour, material and wage costs — influence both inputs, and the plan.

Students should note that the above system, like a petty cash or inventory control system, is a subsystem of an accounting system, which in turn is a subsystem of a management control system of a business.

In any of these systems feedback must be quick in order that any control action taken can be effective.

3.0   THE DESIGN OF A MANAGEMENT INFORMATION SYSTEM

The design of a management information system (MIS) would involve the following stages:

Stage (1) It is necessary to analyse the managers' functions, the type of decisions made, the time contraints on these decisions, the need for accuracy, and the different managerial levels in the organisation which will demand different decision needs;

Stage (2) this step will consider the exact information requirements;

Stage (3) a balance must be struck between the cost and time constraints;

Stage (4) the data processing techniques of recording, processing, communicating and storing information must be developed. It is important that information and decisions are not duplicated. Managers' responsibilities must be clearly identified;

Stage (5) the system is then tested with cooperation of the user departments and the design team.

Stage (6) the MIS is implemented, and its progress will be monitored so that any problems can be quickly rectified.

One of the major problems with designing a MIS is the possible conflict between the designers and the user departments. This is because information is power and therefore secrecy and control over departmental information is treasured by managers who resent outside intervention.

However, freedom of information tends to lead to a more democratic leadership style.

4.0   INFORMATION

Information is arrived at by transforming unstructured facts (data) into structured facts (*see* Fig. 27). This transformation process consists of a number of activities:

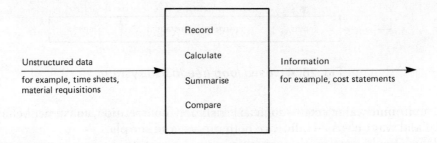

Fig. 27. *Transformation of data into information.*

(a) *Recording:* identifying and transcribing facts about events and transactions;

(b) *Classifying:* encoding collections of data into "like items", for example, sales by types of goods;

(c) *Sorting:* screening, and encoding data into categories;

(d) *Calculating:* adding, subtracting, multiplying, dividing, comparing, arranging the basic data;

(e) *Summarising:* arranging transaction data in a condensed form, such as averages, ratios, "totals";

(f) *Reproducing:* printing and issuing the results of these processes.

4.1 Management information systems

The management information system carries out the above transformation, and the following paragraphs describe the effective requirements of a good MIS.

(a) Managers should be supplied with information which is relevant to their needs.

(b) Wherever possible the reporting of information should work on the "exception" principle, otherwise an information overload can arise which confuses managerial decision-making.

(c) The MIS should reflect the structure of the organisation, so that the right people receive the appropriate information. Top management will require strategic information, which includes departmental profitability, total cash requirements and capital budgeting needs.

Middle management use tactical information, such as variance reports, and labour turnover details. Such information is expressed in monetary and non-monetary terms and prepared more frequently than strategic information.

Lower management need operational information, such as labour hours worked by each employee, and amounts of material absorbed into production. This type of information is frequently required (daily) and will be very detailed.

(d) The MIS must be quick in order that effective control action can be taken.

(e) The system's objectives should be clearly defined, embracing all activities within the firm; it must not be a self-contained function.

(f) In a dynamic business environment a MIS has to be flexible to changing volume and information requirements.

(g) Information supplied should incorporate the effects of uncertainty. Initially information reduces the level of uncertainty. Thereafter the incremental value falls until data simply reinforces what is already known. The information is not cost-effective when this happens (*see* Fig. 28).

(h) The MIS should promote non-dysfunctional decisions, that is, prevent suboptimisation. This can be achieved by supplying managers with information which illustrates the consequences of possible decision outcomes on the organisation as a whole, not just on their particular departments.

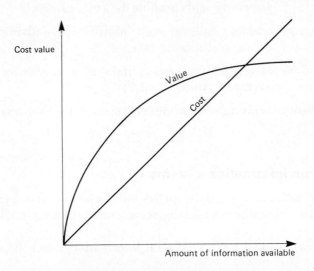

Fig. 28. *Cost-effectiveness of information*

(i) Communication problems ("*noise*") can arise owing to mistakes in source data, incorrect coding and decoding, transmission losses, misclassification, misinterpretation and deliberate tampering. One way of overcoming this problem is to employ more than one channel of communication, for example, support a telephone conversation with a letter.

   If the MIS is computerised (and it should be, providing computerisation is cost-effective) the above errors are reduced by verification at the data capture stage, validation checks at the input stage, software and hardware controls and internal control procedures.

(j) Information should flow vertically (down and up) between superior and subordinate, and horizontally between departments.

(k) It is important that information is expressed in the correct format. Reports should be properly headed and paragraphed and written in clear, logical, unambiguous language which is commensurate with the recipient's level of understanding. Summaries and recommendations must be impartially submitted, and professional opinions distinguished from facts. Working schedules and graphs (bar charts, pie charts, Z-charts, and flow charts) should be relegated to appendices.

(l) Wherever possible qualitative information will be quantified, and if this is impossible then such information will be supplied in addition to quantitative information.

(m) There are various channels of communication in an organisation — such as telephone, "face-to-face" meetings, letters, telex, magnetic tapes and discs. Where confidentiality is necessary the system must ensure that the appropriate channel is used.

(n) Information must be comprehensive; in other words, its sources will include those from within the firm and from the outside environment, such as competitors, consumers, and government. Where uncertainty exists, probabilities and other decision-making criteria, are used.

(o) Information should be accurate (within the realms of materiality).

4.2   Problems associated with management in formation systems

The major problems associated with designing an effective MIS are as follows:

(a) accuracy may have to be sacrificed, to a degree, in order to obtain feedback as quickly as possible for control and decision-making purposes;

(b) factual information is required, yet when necessary this must be supported by qualitative, subjective information;

(c) information must be comprehensive, yet detailed (volume versus detail);

(d) all the above effective requirements are expensive, and the system must be cost effective. Its cost effectiveness is difficult to determine.

5.0   CONCLUSION

A management information system is the sensory device, which, if properly designed and controlled, will improve decision-making for a firm, and thereby result in better profitability, reduced costs, and wiser utilisation of resources.

CHAPTER TWENTY-TWO

Cost Reduction Schemes

1.0 INTRODUCTION

Cost reduction results in costs being reduced from some predetermined norm, while maintaining the functional value of the product or service. It is usually carried out on an ad hoc basis, but should be an ongoing process, otherwise short-term cuts may cause costs to increase in the long term.

Cost reduction should be distinguished from cost control, as the latter contains costs within some predetermined target, for example, standard costing and budgetary control.

Unnecessary costs arise because of lack of ideas, lack of information, inefficiency, and a general resistance to change. The particular areas which are in need of cost reduction include: material costs, labour costs and finance costs. Although a cost reduction programme could cover the whole organisation, it should only be applied where potential benefits outweigh the costs of the scheme.

2.0 COST REDUCTION TECHNIQUES

2.1 Work study

This technique investigates work, existing or proposed, in order to find more efficient methods of performing tasks. Its objectives are to establish standards, and develop and install optimal work methods. It is of particular importance in problem areas, where bottlenecks, high volumes of rejected work, low morale and low productivity exist.

Work study can be divided into two areas: method study and work measurement.

(a) *Method study:* involves the following stages:

(i) Area of study is defined, using cost/benefit considerations.

(ii) Information is collected by observation, interviews, flow-charts and management reports.

(iii) Alternative methods of performing work are considered.

This process will involve analysing the current methods used, and the following questions may be asked:

Is the job necessary? Are all parts of it essential? Is the best equipment being used? Could the job be replaced by machinery? Are there adequate controls? Are there bottlenecks? Is the job being performed to an acceptable standard?

(iv) The best alternative is developed and installed.

(v) Feedback is obtained and progress is monitored.

(b) *Work measurement:* finds the time it should take an average worker to perform a specific job at a standard level of performance (allowing for relaxation periods and contingencies). Statistical sampling techniques can be applied to mass labour.

Work measurement follows method study, and should be carried out openly, with no criticisms or threats of redundancies.

2.2 Value analysis

This technique examines all aspects of an existing product or component in order to reduce costs whilst maintaining or improving its quality. Value engineering applies this to the design stage of a new product.

Value analysis is of particular importance in areas of design, planning, buying and manufacturing. Its stages are the same as those described above in method study, except that in stage 3 the following questions may be asked:

Is the product needed? Are all its features necessary? Is there a superior alternative product? Can it be bought elsewhere more cheaply? Can it be standardised? Can a cheaper material be used in its manufacture? Is material bought in the right batch order quantity? Are components and products stored in the best possible way?

When considering standardisation, which will result in longer production runs, and therefore lower unit costs, management must recognise the effects on customer goodwill of a reduction in variety of product.

3.0 PROBLEMS WITH A COST REDUCTION SCHEME

(a) It is usually carried out on an ad hoc basis, but should be a continual process.

(b) It may be limited to a small area, but should embrace all activities, where cost-effective.

(c) There is a resistance by some employees, who feel threatened and pressurised by such schemes.

(d) These schemes must be carried out objectively by experts, whose services are expensive.

(e) It may be applied hurriedly to gain short-run benefits, resulting in bad long-term consequences.

4.0 CONCLUSION

Cost reduction schemes are designed to reduce expenditure. They should be long-term cost-effective exercises, which cover all important aspects of an organisation, including areas such as energy costs and capital expenditure.

CHAPTER TWENTY-THREE

Cost/Benefit Analysis

1.0 INTRODUCTION

Cost/benefit analysis (CBA) has been defined as an analytical tool in decision-making which enables a comparison to be made between the estimated cost of a project and the estimated value and benefits which may arise from the project.

It is widely used in the public sector, and sometimes in the private sector. Examples of its application include the allocation of scarce resources between health, education, and environmental departments.

Cost/benefit analysis differs from financial analysis by being much broader in its application; for example, in the CBA of a London Transport department the benefits taken into consideration included reduced congestion on nearby roads and the travelling time and vehicle operating costs (from reduced traffic flow) of those who continued to use their cars instead of the transport line. Another example arises when a company considers building a plant. Cost/benefit analysis would recognise the social costs of possible pollution on the health of the population.

2.0 COST/BENEFIT ANALYSIS METHOD

(a) Objectives must be clearly agreed and stated, and all problems identified.

(b) Alternative solutions are ascertained.

(c) Any constraints are noted and assumptions must be specified, for example, the life of a project and the discount rate (cost of capital) to be used.

(d) Incremental costs, including opportunity costs, must be estimated.

(e) Both quantitative and qualitative benefits must be estimated.

(f) An optimal solution is found by comparing and ranking alternatives in order of cost/benefit ratios. If the benefits are qualitative then judgements must be made.

3.0 CONCLUSION

Unlike marginal costing, a conventional management accounting technique, cost benefit analysis is much wider in its application and attempts to recognise the reality of all the decision-making variables. Because of this, it is often criticised as being too subjective. However, it plays an important role in creating an awareness of social and business costs and benefits.

APPENDIX ONE

Index to Examination Questions and Suggested Answers

Examination Questions

The following questions are provided to give each student the chance to answer examination standard questions under timed conditions. Students should read the relevant chapter and then attempt the questions associated with it — allowing themselves some 35 minutes in which to read and to answer the problem. Students should not check with our answer until they have made their attempt. Only by making mistakes can they hope to understand their weaknesses and thus discover what areas need special care and attention during their studies.

COST CLASSIFICATION

1.

Slick Sales Ltd have a sales force structure based upon a national sales manager situated in Birmingham, and 15 representatives who cover the kingdom. The sales force, including the sales manager, are all provided with the same sort of car. This costs £3,200 when new and there is a replacement programme when it is traded in after two years for a guaranteed £1,200. The salesman covering the lowest mileage, which is 18,000 miles annually, operates in the London area. The one with the highest mileage travels 40,000 miles throughout the Scottish Highlands. The sales manager has averaged an annual 25,100 miles over the last three years. The annual average mileage of the complete sales team works out at 30,000 miles per vehicle.

Members of the sales force are allowed to use their cars for local private journeys at no cost to them. However, if they wish to use their company car for a long holiday journey, they are expected to make a contribution towards the annual running costs of the vehicle, based upon the mileage that they cover while on holiday.

The average annual cost of operating a salesman's vehicle is:

Petrol and oil	£1,200
Road tax	40
Insurance	160
Repairs (see note (a))	240
Miscellaneous (see note (b))	100
	£1,740

Notes:

(a) *Annual repairs include £80 for regular maintenance. Tyre life is around 30,000 miles and replacement sets cost £120. No additional repair costs are incurred during the first year of a vehicle's life because a special warranty agreement exists with the supplying garage to cover these. However, on average £200 is paid for repairs in the second year. Repair costs are averaged over the two years with regular maintenance and repairs being variable to mileage rather than time.*

(b) *This includes such things as subscriptions to motoring organisations, cleaning vehicles, parking fees, allowances for garaging, etc.*

You are required to provide the following:

(a) Computations showing the cost of operating the organisation's highest and lowest mileage vehicles each year.

(b) The salesman based at London wishes to take his car on a holiday tour of Wales and the Lake District. He expects to cover 1,800 miles. Suggest ways in which the contribution that he should pay to Slick Sales Ltd for the use of the car during this tour could be calculated.

It is important that you clearly state any assumptions that you make when answering the various parts of this question.

(c) The sales manager has to make a special journey to Ireland to carry out negotiations with a potential large new customer. If he takes his car he will have to cover an additional mileage to that normally incurred in a year. This will be 151 miles to the ferry, where he will have to pay £35 for the return ferry fare for himself and his car, and then travel for another 100 miles on the other side to his ultimate destination. He could fly directly to the potential customer's offices for £60 return. Which method of transportation would you advise him to use?

Note: the cost of capital, taxation considerations and inflation can all be ignored in answers to this question.

2.

Figure 29 represents nine cost–volume relationships. They have been drawn on the following bases and assumptions:

(a) the independent variable is productive activity;

(b) the dependent variable is total cost;

(c) the graphs are not necessarily drawn to scale;

(d) the zero point is at the intersection of the axes;

(e) the period being considered is a year;

(f) each relationship which is represented should be interpreted as being independent of those shown on other diagrams.

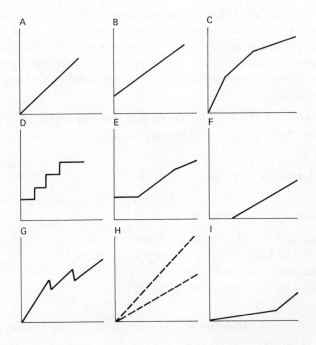

Fig. 29. *Nine different cost–volume relationships.*

You are required to provide:

(a) A brief statement of which relationship each diagram could represent, together with an example, taken either from your reading or own experiences, of a cost that could follow the pattern illustrated. In your answer, clearly indicate which diagram you are discussing.

(b) A brief discussion of how a knowledge of the major cost–volume relationships can be helpful to the management accountant.

COST ESTIMATION

3.

The following data relates to Warp Ltd which processes a single type of chemical. Overhead processing costs for the last thirteen accounting periods (of four weeks each) have been as follows:

Period	1	2	3	4	5	6	7	8	9	10	11	12	13
Overhead costs (£)	770	820	810	830	960	900	940	950	940	870	800	820	790
Output (in tonnes)	120	150	160	170	200	170	200	200	180	160	140	150	140

You are required to devise a formula to assist in the preparation of the overhead budget for the following year.

OVERHEAD AND ABSORPTION COSTING PRINCIPLES

4.

The following information relating to the month of June is extracted from the cost records of the Holborn Manufacturing Co. Ltd., which makes mechanical toys, the parts of which are made in Department A and assembled in Department B.

	Total	Department A	Department B
Direct materials consumed	£6,500	£5,000	£1,500
Direct labour	£70,000	£30,000	£40,000
Direct labour hours worked	80,000	30,000	50,000
Machine hours worked	30,000	25,000	5,000
Factory rent, heat, light	£1,500		
Supervision wages	£600	£250	£350
Depreciation of machinery	£500		
Power	£400		
Repairs to machinery	£175	£122	£53
Indirect labour	£500	£350	£150
Departmental horsepower	400	300	100
Book-value of plant	£5,000	£4,000	£1,000
Floor area (square feet)	20,000	10,000	10,000
Number of machines — ratio between departments		2	1

The costs of batch X 252 have been booked as follows:

Materials	£320	£270	£50
Labour	£6,500	£2,500	£4,000

Direct labour hours worked on batch X 252 were 2,500 in Department A, 5,000 in Department B. Machine hours worked on this batch were 1,250 in Department A and 600 in Department B.

You are required to:

    (a) Advise how overhead expenses might be apportioned to batch X 252.

    (b) Consider objections which might be raised against the bases and methods of apportionment used.

    (c) Calculate the cost of each unit in batch X 252, assuming there are 1,000 units in the batch.

    (d) Discuss briefly the purposes which might be served by such cost accounting statements.

5.

The Isis Engineering Company operates a job order costing system which includes the use of predetermined overhead absorption rates. The company has two service cost centres and two production cost centres. The production cost centre overheads are charged to jobs via direct labour hour rates which are currently £3·10 per hour in production cost centre A and £11·00 per hour in production cost centre B. The calculations involved in determining these rates have excluded any consideration of the services that are provided by each service cost centre to the other.

    The bases used to charge general factory overhead and service cost centre expenses to the production cost centres are as follows:

    (a) general factory overhead is apportioned on the basis of the floor area used by each of the production and service cost centres;

    (b) the expenses of service cost centre 1 are charged out on the basis of the number of personnel in each production cost centre;

    (c) the expenses of service cost centre 2 are charged out on the basis of the usage of its services by each production cost centre.

The company's overhead absorption rates are revised annually prior to the beginning of each year, using an analysis of the outcome of the current year and the draft plans and forecasts for the forthcoming year. The revised rates for the next year are to be based on the following data:

	General factory overhead	Service cost centres		Production cost centres	
		1	2	A	B
Budgeted overhead for next year (before any reallocation)	£210,000	£93,800	£38,600	£182,800	£124,800
Percentage of factory floor area	—	5	10	15	70
Percentage of factory personnel	—	10	18	63	9
Estimated usage of services of service cost centre 2 in forthcoming year	—	1,000 hours	—	4,000 hours	25,000 hours

Budgeted direct labour hours for next year (to be used to calculate next year's absorption rates)	—	—	—	120,000 hours	20,000 hours
Budgeted direct labour hours for current year (these figures were used in the calculation of this year's absorption rates)	—	—	—	100,000 hours	30,000 hours

(a) Ignoring the question of reciprocal charges between the service cost centres, you are required to calculate the revised overhead absorption rates for the two production cost centres. Use the company's established procedures.

(b) Comment on the extent of the differences between the current overhead absorption rates and those you have calculated in your answer to (a). Set out the likely reasons for these differences.

(c) Each service cost centre provides services to the others. Recalculate next year's overhead absorption rates recognising the existence of such reciprocal services and assuming that they can be measured on the same bases as those used to allocate costs to the production cost centres.

(d) Assume that:

   (i) General factory overhead is a fixed cost.

   (ii) Service cost centre 1 is concerned with inspection and quality control with its budgeted expenses (before any reallocations) being 10% fixed and 90% variable.

   (iii) Service cost centre 2 is the company's plant maintenance section with its budgeted expenses (before any reallocations) being 90% fixed and 10% variable.

   (iv) Production cost centre A is labour intensive with its budgeted overhead (before any reallocations) being 90% fixed and 10% variable.

   (v) Production cost centre B is highly mechanised with its budgeted overhead (before any reallocations) being 20% fixed and 80% variable.

In the light of these assumptions, comment on the cost apportionment and absorption calculations made in parts (a) and (c) and suggest any improvements that you would consider appropriate.

MARGINAL AND ABSORPTION COSTING

6.

The Waverley Co. Ltd has been set up in order to manufacture and sell three products,
A, B and C. Details of planned production and sales quantitites for each of these for the
next two years are shown below:

Planned activity — units (000s)

	Year 1			Year 2		
	A	B	C	A	B	C
Production	30	20	10	30	20	10
Sales	24	16	4	24	10	12

The proposed pattern of production is considered to be the normal long-term pattern
but the sales expected in the first two years are not representative of the anticipated
long-term position.

It is expected that the sales price and the variable cost per unit will be stable for at
least two years. The details of these are:

	Sales price (per unit) £	Variable cost (per unit) £
A	8	2
B	12	4
C	12	3

The manufacturing process requires that all production be subjected to both manual
operations and mechanical processing. Details of labour and machine production
hours required for each unit produced are:

	Labour hours (per unit)	Machine hours (per unit)
A	2	1
B	3	1
C	2	2

Total fixed production overhead costs will be £280,000 in each year.

The managing director wishes to ascertain both the total profit (before administration costs, etc.) expected for each of the first two years and the profitability of each product. Accordingly he has asked each of the three applicants for the job of management accountant to produce the information he requires but is surprised that the figures they produce display little similarity. It appears that one candidate has utilised direct costing whereas the other two have utilised absorption costing but with each using a different basis for overhead recovery. Before making a decision as to whom to employ the managing director wishes to ascertain which one of the sets of figures provided is "correct" and which two sets are, therefore, "wrong" and so seeks your advice.

You are required to:

    (a) Prepare the three statements the managing director is likely to have received and which show:

        (i)   the total profit (before considering administration costs, etc.) for each of the first two years; and

        (ii) the profitability of each product.

    (b) Comment on the reasons for any similarities and/or differences in the three sets of figures provided in (a) above. In your comments suggest any improvements which could be made to the application of the absorption costing methods. Advise the managing director which candidate's set of figures provides the "correct" answer and which are "wrong".

    (c) It is decided to increase the production of the first year only, by 20% in order to provide additional buffer stocks. Calculate the cost to Waverley Ltd of holding such additional stocks for a full year if the appropriate cost of financing the additional stocks is 12% per annum (ignore any obsolescence and costs of storage).

7.

The Miozip Company operates an absorption costing system which incorporates a factory-wide overhead absorption rate per direct labour hour. For 19X0 and 19X1 this rate was £2·10 per hour. The fixed factory overhead for 19X1 was £600,000 and this would have been fully absorbed if the company had operated at full capacity, which is estimated at 400,000 direct labour hours. Unfortunately, only 200,000 hours were worked in that year so that the overhead was seriously underabsorbed. Fixed factory overheads are expected to be unchanged in 19X2 and 19X3.

The outcome for 19X1 was a loss of £70,000 and the management believed that a major cause of this loss was the low overhead absorption rate which had led the company to quote selling prices which were uneconomic.

For 19X2 the overhead absorption rate was increased to £3·60 per direct labour hour and selling prices were raised in line with the established pricing procedures which involve adding a profit mark-up of 50% onto the full factory cost of the company's products. The new selling prices were also charged on the stock of finished goods held at the beginning of 19X2.

In December 19X2 the company's accountant prepares an estimated profit and loss account for 19X2 and a budgeted profit and loss account for 19X3. Although sales were considered to be depressed in 19X1, they were even lower in 19X2 but, nevertheless, it seems that the company will make a profit for that year. A worrying feature of the estimated accounts is the high level of finished goods stock held and the 19X3 budget provides for a reduction in the stock level at 31 December 19X3 to the (physical) level which obtained at 1 January 19X1. Budgeted sales for 19X3 are set at the 19X2 sales level.

The summarised profit statements for the three years to 31 December 19X3 are as follows:

Summarised profit and loss accounts

	Actual 19X1		Estimated 19X2		Budgeted 19X3	
Sales revenue		£1,350,000		£1,316,250		£1,316,250
Opening stock of finished goods	£100,000		£200,000		£357,500	
Factory cost of production	1,000,000		975,000		650,000	
	1,100,000		1,175,000		1,007,500	
Less: Closing stock of finished goods	200,000		357,500		130,000	
Factory cost of goods sold		900,000		817,500		877,500
		450,000		498,750		438,750
Less: Factory overhead underabsorbed		300,000		150,000		300,000
		150,000		348,750		138,750
Administrative and financial costs		220,000		220,000		220,000
	Loss	(£70,000)		£128,750	Loss	(£81,250)

You are required to:

(a) Write a short report to the board of Miozip explaining why the budgeted outcome for 19X3 is so different from that of 19X2 when the Sales Revenue is the same for both years.

(b) Restate the profit and loss account for 19X1, the estimated profit and loss account for 19X2 and the budgeted profit and loss account for 19X3 using marginal factory cost for stock valuation purposes.

(c) Comment on the problems which *may* follow from a decision to increase the overhead absorption rate in conditions when cost-plus pricing is used and overhead is currently under-absorbed.

(d) Explain why the majority of businesses use full costing systems while most management accounting theorists favour marginal costing.

Note: Assume in your answers to this question that the value of the £ and the efficiency of the company have been constant over the period under review.

COST–VOLUME–PROFIT ANALYSIS

8.

The Holee College teaches wholly through the correspondence method. This is done by the production of self-study packs which enable students to prepare for professional qualifications.

Each course of study was sold at the price of £15 last year and a total of 10,000 units were produced and sold. The production costs of the various courses offered by the College are the same.

The variable cost of producing a study course last year was:

Direct materials	£5·00
Direct labour	6·00
Other direct costs	0.60
Variable overheads	0·40
Total variable cost	£12·00

The fixed overhead for the Holee College during the year was £20,000.

During the coming year the costs of the organisation are expected to increase by the following:

	%
Direct materials	20·00
Direct labour	16·67
Other direct costs	67·00
Variable overhead	25·00
Fixed overhead	5·00

Market research has shown that when the company increases the price of its courses to its students, as long as the increase is kept below 17·5% this is unlikely to have an effect on the number of units sold. However, for every 1% that prices are raised above a 17·5% increase the number of units sold can be expected to fall by 2%.

Your are required to provide for the coming year:

(a) The selling price of the study courses if the number of study courses sold and the annual profits are to remain as before.

(b) The number of units that the organisation would have to sell if it did not change the price charged for these, but maintained the profit level attained in the previous year.

(c) A brief analysis of a situation where, when prices are changed, the number of units sold is affected. The data provided in the above example can be used to illustrate your analysis.

9.

A. Merchant's trading operations for the last two years ending 31st December are summarised below:

	Year 1 £	Year 2 £
Sales	200,000	231,000
Cost of goods sold	160,000	189,000
Gross profit	40,000	42,000
Operating expenses	10,000	9,500
Net profit	£30,000	£32,500

Mr Merchant is very disappointed with the recent year's results particularly as his selling prices were 10% higher than in the previous year and his operating expenses £500 lower. He has asked you to explain why "a 15% increase in turnover has produced only an 8% increase in net profit", and to offer such advice as you consider appropriate.

You are required to prepare an appropriate analysis of these figures, and to write a brief report for your client, explaining the figures and advising on future action.

10.

The accounts of the Globe Manufacturing Co. Ltd for the year ending 31st December are expected to be as follows:

Sales		£800,000
Deduct:		
Direct material	£200,000	
Direct labour	160,000	
Variable overhead:		
Material	£40,000	
Labour	36,000	
Other	24,000	
	100,000	
Fixed overhead	100,000	
		560,000
Profit		£240,000

During the current year, production has been running at 80% of capacity, and the marketing director has estimated that in the following year:

(a) if prices were reduced by 5%, the volume of sales would increase by 25%, thereby enabling full productive capacity of the factory to be used; or

(b) even without a price reduction, sales volume could be increased by 10%, this being the measure of the unsatisfied demand at the current price level.

A recent wage award in the major supply industry is expected to reflect itself in increased costs of direct material and it is estimated that three-quarters of the direct material used in the following year will cost 5% more than current prices. Other price increases will affect the remaining direct materials, all the indirect materials and the other variable expenses, by an estimated 3%. A review of administrative and establishment costs is expected to result in an overall reduction of £5,000 in the fixed overhead for the following year.

The current hourly wage rates are £0·8 for the direct workers and £0.6 for the indirect workers. Negotiations with the trade unions representing the whole labour force have resulted in an increase of £0·05 per hour for all workers from 1st January the following year, in return for a productivity deal which provides that:

(a) for increased output up to 100% capacity, no more hours will be worked than have been worked in the current year;

(b) if it is decided to increase production only up to the level needed to satisfy the demand at existing prices, then workers representing 10% of the direct and indirect labour hours for the current year will be transferred to similar employment in an associated company which is short of labour.

You are required to prepare statements showing:

(a) the profit for the following year of each of the marketing director's two proposals;

(b) (i)   Profit/volume ratios;

   (ii) Net profit/turnover ratios;

   (iii) Labour productivity indices (taking the current year at 100), in respect
         of the current year and for each of the alternative proposals for the
         following year; and

(c) Your comments, briefly, upon your findings.

11.

The Arithmetical Engineering Co. Ltd manufactures a range of products. While
compiling the budget for the next financial year the management realises that a
decision has to be made concerning the method of manufacture of one product, a
precision-made hand razor. This product is designed to sell for £1. A choice must be
made between three alternative production processes, and the management seeks to
find the most profitable method.

   The following information relates to the three processes, A, B and C.

	A	B	C
Variable cost per product	80p	85p	90p
Fixed costs of process	£95,000	£60,000	£37,500

Maximum production in any process is one million razors.

You are required to:

(a) present the information in the form of a profit graph to highlight factors
    significant to this decision, commenting on the information in the light of the
    problem under consideration,

(b) discuss other matters which you would take into account before deciding
    which process to use, and

(c) present a breakeven graph for process B.

12.

(a) Comment briefly on the information provided by a breakeven chart.

(b) State the assumptions underlying the construction of a breakeven chart.

(c) Discuss the usefuiness of the breakeven chart as an aid to profit-planning.

(d) How useful is a breakeven chart in a multiproduct company?

13.

The accountant's approach to cost–volume–profit analysis has been criticised in that,
among other matters, it does not deal with the following:

(a) situations where sales volume differs radically from production volume;

(b) situations where the sales revenue and the total cost functions are markedly non-linear;

(c) changes in product mix;

(d) risk and uncertainty.

Explain these objections to the accountant's conventional cost–volume–profit model and suggest how they can be overcome or ameliorated.

DECISION-MAKING UNDER CONDITIONS OF CERTAINTY

14.

The budget of Whisker Ltd provides for the manufacture and sale of 10,000 whisks per month, the unit standard cost being £6, made up as follows:

Direct material	£2·50
Direct labour	1·00
Variable overhead	0·50
Fixed overhead	2·00
	£6·00

the selling price of the whisk being £8·00.

Production and sales for periods 1, 2 and 3 were as follows:

	Period 1	Period 2	Period 3
Production	10,000	8,000	11,000
Sales	8,000	9,000	12,000

Production can be increased to 11,000 units without a corresponding increase in fixed overheads.

You are required to:

(a) Prepare operating statements for the three periods,

   (i)   assuming the company uses absorption costing

   (ii) assuming the company uses marginal costing.

(b) Comment on the differences between the two systems as regards:

   (i)   stock valuations

(ii)   period profit, and

(c)   State briefly the recommendations of SSAP 9 concerning the valuation of stock and the inclusion of overhead costs.

15.

The Easytune Radio Co. Ltd, which manufactures the "Easytune" radio receiver, commenced trading on 1 April. The company's budget for each four-week period is as follows:

Sales — 20,000 receivers		£400,000
Manufacturing cost of goods sold:		
Variable costs	£240,000	
Fixed overhead	60,000	
		300,000
Gross profit		100,000
Selling and distribution costs (fixed)		20,000
Net profit		£80,000

The following data relates to the first two trading periods:

	Period 1 units	Period 2 units
Production	24,000	18,000
Sales	18,000	21,000

You are required to:

(a)   Prepare operating statements for each of the two periods:

(i)   where fixed manufacturing overhead is absorbed into product cost at the budgeted rate and selling and distribution costs are treated as period costs;

(ii)   where all fixed costs are treated as period costs.

(You are to assume that the selling price, fixed costs and the unit variable costs for the two periods are in line with budget.)

(b)   Comment briefly upon the results revealed by your statements.

16.

Golden Ltd is considering whether to manufacture a new product, Zippo, for one year. Components for the product will be manufactured in a new factory to be specially leased for the purpose at £10,000 a year. Zippos will be assembled in the existing factory, utilising the same production lines as the firm's other products. The estimated costs per Zippo are shown below:

	Component manufacture	Assembly
Material	£0·20	—
Labour	0·20	£0·10
Factory supplies	—	0·10
Variable overhead	0·30	0·30
Total direct cost	0·70	0·50
Fixed overhead (250% of direct labour)	0.50	0.25
Administrative overhead (50% of total direct cost)	0·35	0·25
Total cost	1·55	£1·00
Add: Total assembly cost	1·00	
Total cost per Zippo	£2·55	

When operating at maximum capacity, the components factory can supply sufficient parts for 24,000 Zippos per year. Surplus capacity after meeting the assembly division's requirements will be used to produce sets of Zippo components for a supermarket which will market them under a different name. The cost of such components will be identical to those produced for the assembly division's use. The supermarket is willing to pay £1 per set of components.

A market research study has suggested that only two prices for Zippo should be considered, £3·60 and £3·10 per unit. Sales at these prices are estimated to be 15,000 and 22,000 units respectively.

Of the fixed overhead charged to Zippos 20% relates to the historical cost depreciation of machinery. The machines in the assembly plant do not depreciate in use.

Capacity in the assembly division is already used fully and it is estimated that one unit of an existing product, yielding £1 over and above its variable cost, will have to be sacrificed for each unit of the new product assembled.

The estimated total overhead costs (excluding depreciation) of the component factory are: lease £10,000, other fixed overhead £1,000, and administrative costs £5,000.

The machines needed to manufacture the components are available within the firm.

They have a value of £10,000 in the firm's books and could be sold for £4,000. If retained on their existing work, they will need to be replaced (at a cost of £15,000) in one year's time. If transferred to Zippo production, they will have to be scrapped (proceeds nil) at the end of the year.

You are required to:

(a) Briefly advise management whether they should manufacture Zippos and, if so, at what volume and price, add a brief note on your treatment of fixed overhead.

(b) Pay particular attention to the layout of numerical data used in your recommendation.

17.

Wizard Ltd, which is a good customer of Witch Ltd, has asked Witch to produce 400 units of a special variation of one of the standard products that it buys from Witch. It costs £10 to produce each unit of the standard product which is sold at £12.

Although Witch is not geared up to make the modification and variations required, it decides for "customer relationship" reasons to agree to go ahead and supply the order. It will be able to produce 100 of the special units each 40-hour week, but will require special machinery for the purpose. There are three alternative ways of obtaining this machinery, and these, and the costs associated with them, are as follows:

(a) *Adapting existing machinery*
The existing machinery which could be adapted is not being used at present although it is envisaged that in approximately three months it will be required in its present form for a contract currently being negotiated.

Costs of adapting this machinery would be £500, and after the order has been completed it would cost £600 to remove the adaptations and replace worn parts, etc., in order to return the machine to its current value. The machinery, which could be adapted, originally cost £10,000 five years ago and is being depreciated at £1,000 per annum. A special insurance policy would have to be held while it was operated in its adapted form, the premium being 2% of the value of the machine when adapted. The current value of the machine is £3,000.

Variable operating costs associated with using the adapted machinery would be: labour £1 per hour and maintenance 50p per hour.

(b) *Hiring specialist machinery*
The charge for hiring suitable machinery which includes maintenance and insurance, but no labour costs, is £5 per production hour with a minimum hire charge of £300 per week.

(c) *Purchasing specialist machinery*
To buy a new machine would cost £5,000. Operating, maintenance and insurance costs would be on the same basis as for the adapted one.

The manufacturers of the machinery estimate that it loses value at the rate of £2·00 for every unit produced and on this basis they are prepared to repurchase any machinery sold by them, after deducting a further 10% of the residual value to cover transaction expenses.

You are required to:

(a) Prepare a report to the management of Witch Ltd advising them which of the alternative courses of action would be most beneficial, based upon the previous information. Indicate ways in which your recommended course of action might be further improved.

In your report suggest a price to be charged to Wizard Ltd for the modified product, mentioning the factors which should be considered before a final decision is taken.

(b) Suppose that Wizard Ltd was willing to place a continuing order for the modified product. In this new situation broadly explain the alterations needed to produce a long-run cost analysis of the alternatives.

Note: You should ignore the cost of capital, taxation and inflation in your deliberations.

18.

(a) The Noddy Company Limited has received a special order for product 123. The company does not normally produce this product; however, it has decided to accept this order, provided it is profitable, for two reasons:

(i) to use up spare capacity and surplus materials, and

(ii) to use it as a test case to determine whether or not the company should add 123 to its product range and produce in anticipation of orders.

You have been asked for your opinion on the material prices which should be used for inclusion in the cost estimates for the special order and for continuous production and you are required to give this, in non-technical language, in respect of each of the following four materials which are required for the production of 123.

(i) *Material A:*
The order requires 500 kg of material A. Material A is an unstable byproduct of another of the company's manufacturing processes and can be sold on the open market. Production of A is very irregular and the selling price received fluctuates widely. It has been as high as £1 per kg but on occasions it has cost the company 5p per kg to have it taken away and destroyed. During the last few months the selling price has dropped steadily and last month it was only 6p per kg.

(ii) *Material B:*
This material, which requires special storage, was used by the company, but no longer is, although there are still 2,000 kg in stock and only 1,000 kg are needed for the special order. At the end of the last financial year this was valued at 25p per kg and, although the current market price is 30p per kg, the best price that the company was recently offered was 27p per kg.

(iii) *Material C:*
The company uses this material regularly at a rate of approximately 500 kg per week. At present there are 5,000 kg in stock at an average purchase price of 50p per kg. The standard price used for this in the

company's standard cost calculations is 52p per kg and the current market price is 51p per kg.

(iv) *Material D:*
This material is also used by the company and has a marked seasonal price variation. The average purchase price of the stock on hand at present is 75p per kg. If some of this is used for the special order the company will have to go to the market sooner than expected when the price is estimated to be nearer to 72p per kg than the 67p per kg which was the anticipated next buying price.

(b) Farmer Giles approached Fatten-him-Up Stock Feeds to supply him in bulk by contract over the next year with a special cattle-feed mix. He is prepared to pay £2,500 during the period for the amount of feed he requires. The following estimates have been made by the company's cost accountant for the cost of supplying the cattle-feed mix:

(i) *Materials*
The company will have to mix two materials, "lush" and "bulk", to make the mix.

(1) It has sufficient "lush" in stock for the mix. This cost £1,000 a few months ago. However, "lush" is only used on special orders. Although it would now cost £2,000 to buy, as there is little use for the material, the company was considering selling it for only £500.

(2) "Bulk" would have to be purchased for the contract at £1,000.

(ii) *Labour and supervision*

(1) The firm uses casual labour for mixing. This is paid £1 per hour. The casual labour would have to work 500 hours on this contract during the coming year. However, the supply of casual labour is not completely elastic and it seems that 200 of these hours would be worked as overtime. Overtime is paid at time-and-a-half.

(2) Quality control supervisors will be expected to spend 100 hours checking the mix. They are paid salaries of £80 for a 40-hour week. Existing supervisors will be able to cope with the supervision of this special mix so no new supervisors will be employed.

(iii) *Plant and machinery*
The special cattle-feed will be made over the next year using a mixer which cost £5,000 five years ago. When purchased it had an estimated life of ten years and is being depreciated over this period using the straight-line method.
    The machine has no other use and no scrap value.

(iv) *Overheads*
General overheads for the firm will be unchanged whatever products are produced. These are apportioned to all products at 100% of direct labour costs (excluding quality control supervisors' salaries but including overtime payments).

You are required to

    (a) Provide statements:

        (i)   using conventional cost-accounting to match revenue with costs;

        (ii)   clearly stating whether the company should accept Farmer Giles's order.

    (b) Explain the reasons for the differences between the two statements.

19.

Rappup Ltd is engaged solely in costing other manufacturers' metal fabrications with a preservative. The fabrications are at no time the property of Rappup Ltd and their value does not appear in that company's accounts. Rappup Ltd have prepared the following budget for the six months ending 31 December:

Budget	Quantity	Value
Preservative	50,000 cans	£600,000
Direct labour	150,000 hours	150,000
Variable overhead		450,000
Factory cost		1,200,000
Fixed overhead		750,000
Total cost		1,950,000
Profit		390,000
Sales		£2,340,000

Variable overhead can be assumed to vary in direct proportion to direct labour hours.

    Early in May the company was asked to quote for coating for a new customer, the contract to be completed by 31 August. The technical director estimates that each fabrication unit will require one can of preservative and seven direct labour hours to complete, and asks the accountant to calculate a selling price. The Board, however, are concerned because difficulty has always been experienced in obtaining regular supplies of preservative and labour is in short supply in the summer months because of the incidence of holidays.

You are required to:

    (a) Calculate on each of the following assumptions a price for the new contract, below which it would not pay to sell:

        (i)   assuming normal absorption costing principles with fixed overhead cost based on factory cost and a profit loading based on total cost;

    (ii)   assuming direct material is the major factor limiting production;

    (iii) assuming direct labour is the major factor limiting production.

(b) State which price you would recommend and why. Would you differ in your recommendation if delivery was requested in December? Give reasons.

20.

The board of directors of KF Limited, manufacturers of three products, A, B and C, have asked for advice on the production mixture of the company.

You are required to:

(a) Prepare a statement to advise the directors of the most profitable mixture of the products to be made and sold; the statement should show:

    (i)   the profit expected on the current budgeted production; and

    (ii) the profit which could be expected if the most profitable mixture were produced.

(b) Direct the directors' attention to any problems which are likely to arise if the mixture in (a)(ii) above were to be produced.

The following information is given:

		Product A £	Product B £	Product C £
Data for standard costs, per unit element of cost:				
Direct materials		10	30	20
Variable overhead		3	2	5

Direct labour: Department	Rate per hour £	hours	hours	hours
1	1·00	14	8	15
2	2·00	$2\frac{1}{2}$	3	5
3	1·00	8	4	15

	Product A	Product B	Product C
Data from current budget:			
Production in units per year	10,000	5,000	6,000
Selling price per unit	£50	£68	£90
Fixed overhead per year: £200,000			
Forecast by sales director of maximum possible sales for the year in units	12,000	7,000	9,000

However, the type of labour required by department 2 is in short supply and it is not possible to increase the manpower of this department beyond its present level.

21.

The Reno Auto Ltd recently suffered a strike by production labour that lasted for two weeks. During that time no cars were produced. The company issued a press statement to the effect that the cost of the strike was £500,000. This figure was estimated on the basis of lost production of 1,000 vehicles, each of which could have been sold for £500, a total loss of turnover of £500,000. The company's accountant feels that this figure overstates the cost of the strike and produces the following statement to support his view:

Expenses avoided:	
Materials (£100 per car)	£100,000
Production labour (£50 per car)	50,000
Depreciation of machinery	175,000
Overheads: 200% on production labour	100,000
	425,000
Loss of sales revenue	500,000
Cost of strike	£75,000

The following additional information is available:

(a) Depreciation of machinery is based on the straight-line method of calculation. However, the plant manager estimates that the machinery will fall in value by £20,000 each week, regardless of the level of production. He feels that, in addition, its value will fall by £15,000 for every 100 cars that are produced.

(b) Overhead expenses are recovered at the rate of 200% on production labour. Most of the overhead expenses are unaffected by the level of production, for example, rent, rates, maintenance and staff wages, but some, such as power and lighting, vary directly with production. The general manager estimates that the latter type of overhead expense amounts to £1,000 for every 100 cars produced.

(c) During the period of the strike the maintenance staff, whose wages are included in the fixed overhead expenses, carried out a major overhaul on one of the company's machines using materials costing £1,000. This overhaul would normally have been performed by an outside contractor at a price, including materials, of £10,000.

(d) The sales manager feels that about one half of the production lost could be made up and sold in the next month by the production labour working overtime. Labour is paid at the rate of time-and-a-half for overtime working.

You are required to advise a major shareholder, who doubts the validity of both the press statement and the accountant's statement, as to the true cost of the strike.

22.

The budgeted product profitability report of Midland Ltd for each of its products for the forthcoming year is as follows:

Product	V £000	W £000	X £000	Y £000	Z £000	Total £000
Sales	4,400	4,900	6,500	5,100	9,100	30,000
Manufacturing costs:						
Materials	220	660	1,320	1,100	1,650	4,950
Labour	500	800	1,500	1,400	1,800	6,000
Production overhead						
—variable	250	350	400	500	720	2,220
Production overhead						
—fixed	350	600	1,100	1,000	950	4,000
	1,320	2,410	4,320	4,000	5,120	17,170
Transport and delivery costs:						
Transport	120	360	720	600	650	2,450
Packaging	200	100	200	100	300	900
	320	460	920	700	950	3,350
Selling and advertising expenses:	720	545	525	555	755	3,100
Administration	660	735	975	765	1,365	4,500
Total cost	3,020	4,150	6,740	6,020	8,190	28,120
Profit/(loss)	1,380	750	(240)	(920)	910	1,880

The management accountant provides the following additional information concerning the basis on which the above report was prepared:

(a) Material costs are a combination of variable material cost and a 10% surcharge which is added to the basic variable material cost in order to recover the fixed costs of storage and stores administration.

(b) Labour is to be considered a variable cost.

(c) Fixed production overhead comprises some directly attributable fixed costs which are allocated to their appropriate product together with an apportionment of general fixed production overhead. The general fixed production overhead amounts to £3,000,000 and is apportioned in proportion to labour costs, i.e. 50% of labour costs. The attributable fixed cost is avoidable if the product to which it relates is not produced.

(d) Transport charge comprises a fixed cost of £450,000 and a variable charge. The fixed cost is apportioned to products in proportion to their material costs.

(e) Selling and advertising expenses comprise advertising expenses directly related, and therefore directly attributed, to each product and a sales commission which equals 5% of sales revenues. Advertising costs are avoidable fixed costs.

(f) Administration is a fixed cost and is apportioned in proportion to sales revenue.

(g) Packaging is a variable cost.

The managing director feels that products X and Y should not be produced as they each result in a loss.

The marketing manager makes two points:

(a) Sales of any product can be increased by up to 40% of the sales figures contained in the above report merely by pursuing an additional extensive advertising campaign. If any product were selected to have its sales increased the additional advertising campaign would cost three times the currently planned cost of advertising that product.

  The relationship between advertising costs and increased sales applies to each product and is a proportional relationship; for example, sales could increase by 20% if advertising were increased by 150%.

(b) By reducing sales (and production) of product X the demand for either V or W will rise depending upon which product is offered as a substitute for X. If V is offered as the substitute then each £1 reduction in sales of X will cause an increase in sales of V of £0·45. If W is the substitute then each £1 reduction in sales of X will cause an increase in sales of W of £0·50.

You are required to:

(a) Advise the managing director of the desirability of ceasing production of products X and Y and prepare a statement which shows the effect that not producing X and Y will have on the profits of Midland Ltd.

(b) (i) Show the effect of pursuing the advertising campaign mentioned by the marketing manager in order to increase sales of each product by 40%. Indicate which products it would be worthwhile advertising.

   (ii) If only £1,200,000 is available for advertising indicate which products should then be advertised.

(c) Decide whether sales (and production) of X should be reduced in favour of either V or W. If so, which product should be offered as a substitute for X? Show the effect of reducing sales of X to zero.

(d) Give two examples of an attributable fixed production overhead cost.

23.

Itervero Ltd, a small engineering company, operates a job order costing system. It has been invited to tender for a comparatively large job which is outside the range of its normal activities and, since there is surplus capacity, the management are keen to quote as low a price as possible. It is decided that the opportunity should be treated in isolation without any regard to the possibility of its leading to further work of a similar nature (although such a possibility does exist). A low price will not have any repercussions on Itervero's regular work.

The Estimating Department have spent 100 hours on work in connection with the quotation and they have incurred travelling expenses of £550 in connection with a visit to the prospective customer's factory overseas. The following cost estimate has been prepared on the basis of their study:

Inquiry 205H/81: Cost Estimate

Direct material and components:	
2,000 units of A @ £25 unit	£50,000
200 units of B @ £10 per unit	2,000
Other material and components to be bought in (specified)	12,500
	64,500
Direct labour:	
700 hours of skilled labour @ £3·50 per hour	2,450
1,500 hours of unskilled labour @ £2 per hour	3,000
Overhead:	
Department P — 200 hours @ £25 per hour	5,000
Department Q — 400 hours @ £20 per hour	8,000
Estimating department:	
100 hours @ £5 per hour	500
Travelling expenses	550
Planning department:	
300 hours @ £5 per hour	1,500
	£85,500

The following information has been brought together:

Material A: This is a regular stock item. The stock holding is more than sufficient for this job. The material currently held has an average cost of £25 per unit but the current replacement cost is £20 per unit.

Material B: A stock of 4,000 units of B is currently held in the stores. This material is slow moving and the stock is the residue of a batch bought seven years ago at a cost of £10 per unit. B currently costs £24 per unit but the resale value is only £18 per unit. A foreman has pointed out that B could be used as a substitute for another type of regularly used raw material which costs £20 per unit.

Direct labour: The workforce is paid on a time basis. The company has adopted a "no redundancy" policy and this means that skilled workers are frequently moved to jobs which do not make proper use of their skills. The wages included in the cost estimate are for the mix of labour which the job ideally requires. It seems likely, if the job is obtained, that most of the 2,200 hours of direct labour will be performed by skilled staff receiving £3·50 per hour.

Overhead — department P: Department P is the one department of Itervero Ltd that is working at full capacity. The department is treated as a profit centre and it uses a transfer price of £25 per hour for charging out its processing time to other departments. This charge is calculated as follows:

Estimated variable cost per machine hour	£10
Fixed departmental overhead	8
Departmental profit	7
	£25

Department P's facilities are frequently hired out to other firms and a charge of £30 per hour is made. There is a steady demand from outside customers for the use of these facilities.

Overhead — department Q: Department Q uses a transfer price of £20 for charging out machine processing time to other departments. This charge is calculated as follows:

Estimated variable cost per machine hour	£8
Fixed departmental overhead	9
Departmental profit	3
	£20

Estimating department: The Estimating Department charges out its time to specific jobs using a rate of £5 per hour. The average wage rate within the department is £2·50 per hour but the higher rate is justified as being necessary to cover departmental overheads and the work done on unsuccessful quotations.

Planning department: This department also uses a charging-out rate which is intended to cover all departmental costs.

You are required to:

(a) Restate the cost estimate by using an opportunity cost approach; make any assumptions that you deem to be necessary and briefly justify each of the figures that you give.

(b) Discuss the relevance of the opportunity cost approach to the situation described in the question and consider the problems which are likely to be encountered if it is used in practice.

(c) Discuss briefly the general applicability of opportunity cost in business decision-making where a choice exists among alternative courses of action.

24.

Styric plc is a divisionalised company. Two of its manufacturing divisions are Y Division and Z Division. These divisions are housed in a single leased building on which the lease is due to expire in two years' time. Y Division manufactures the microprocessor which is used as a component in the Styric Controlmaster which is manufactured by Z Division. The microprocessor is transferred from Y Division to Z Division at a transfer price of £30 per unit and 30,000 units have been transferred in each of the past two years, 19X0–X1 and 19X1–X2. Y Division is operating at 75% of its full capacity. During 19X1–X2 it has investigated the possibility of selling its product to external customers at the £30 price but there is zero demand at this price as several competitors provide comparable products at prices which are well below £30. Y Division made a loss for 19X1–X2 of £90,000.

During 19X1–X2 Z Division sold 30,000 Styric Controlmasters at the fixed price of £150 and it made a profit of £610,000 for the year. Enquiries have been made of other microprocessor suppliers and a quotation has been received from A, one of Y's competitors, offering to supply a minimum of 30,000 and a maximum of 40,000 processors per year for two years with adequate guarantees as to quality and continuity of supplies. The unit price would be £22.

The general manager of Z Division has proposed that his division be given authority to buy the mircoprocessor from outside. If Z Division is allowed to do this, it would want to take all of its requirements (that is, 30,000 per year) from A unless Y Division can cut its transfer price to £22. He suggests that if Y cannot do this it would be better for it to cease to operate and that this would have the incidental advantage of releasing additional space for Z's use. Z Division is currently seeking extra warehouse space.

The summarised profit and loss accounts of the divisions for 19X1–X2 are as follows:

Profit and loss accounts for 19X1–X2

	Y Division	Z Division
Production and sales (physical units)	30,000	30,000
Sales revenue	£900,000	£4,500,000
Direct materials	£450,000	£2,100,000
Microprocessor	—	900,000
Direct labour	90,000	240,000
Variable overhead	90,000	150,000
Fixed overhead (excluding depreciation)	285,000	300,000
Fixed overhead — depreciation	75,000	200,000
	£990,000	£3,890,000
Profit/(loss)	(90,000)	610,000
	£900,000	£4,500,000

You have been asked to investigate and advise on the foregoing proposal and during the course of your investigation you ascertain the following:

(a) The limitation of the proposed contract with A to a two-year period would be agreeable to Styric as the lease of the factory is unlikely to be renewed in two years' time and there is no wish to enter into firm commitments beyond that date. If Y is closed, most of the work force could be productively absorbed by other divisions of Styric, which operate in the vicinity, at no additional cost to those divisions.

(b) The manager of Y Division complains that his division has to bear exceptionally heavy depreciation charges and fixed overheads (including central office charges) which are beyond his control. Without these expenses he believes that Y Division could match the price quoted by A and still make a reasonable profit. He also believes that with a price of £22 it should be possible to operate at full capacity selling 25% of the output on the open market. The additional output would increase the direct material cost and variable overhead proportionately but he estimates that the total direct labour cost would only increase by 10%.

(c) The plant used by Y Division has a book value of £150,000. Its current resale value is probably £50,000; in two years' time it is estimated that it will have negligible value.

(d) The storage space required by Z Division will probably cost £10,000 per annum if rented.

(e) Y Division has in stock sufficient raw material for nine months' production if production is continued at the same level as has been achieved over the last two years. If this raw material is sold off (following a decision to close the division) it would probably fetch 25% of its cost.

You are required to:

(a) Prepare Y's profit and loss account for the ensuing two-year period on the assumption that the division continues to operate for that period but that it reduces the microprocessor transfer price to £22 and sells externally 10,000 units annually at this price (in addition to the 30,000 units to be taken annually by Z Division).

(b) Prepare a statement of the costs and benefits to Styric plc of a decision to adopt the proposal made by the general manager of Z Division instead of the plan put forward by the Y Division's manager. Ignore interest and taxation. Compare and reconcile your calculations with the results given in your answer to part (a) and comment on the differences.

DECISION-MAKING UNDER CONDITIONS OF UNCERTAINTY

25.

(a) Allegro Finishes Ltd is about to launch an improved version of its major product — a pocket-size chess computer — onto the market. Sales of the original model (at £65 per unit) have been at the rate of 50,000 per annum but it is now planned to withdraw this model and the company is now deciding on its production plans and pricing policy.

The standard variable cost of the new model will be £50 which is the same as that of the old, but the company intends to increase the selling price "to recover the research and development expenditure that has been incurred". The research and development costs of the improved model are estimated at £750,000 and the intention is that these should be written-off over 3 years. Additionally there are annual fixed overheads of approximately £800,000 allocated to this product line.

The Sales Director has estimated the maximum annual demand figures that would obtain at three alternative selling prices. These are as follows:

Selling price £	Estimated maximum annual demand (physical units)
70	75,000
80	60,000
90	40,000

You are required to prepare a cost–volume–profit chart that would assist the management to choose a selling price and the level of output at which to operate. Identify the best price and the best level of output. Outline briefly any reservations that you have with this approach.

(b) With the facts as stated for part (a), now assume that the Sales Director is considering a more sophisticated approach to the problem. He has estimated, for each selling price, an optimistic, a pessimistic and a most-likely demand figure and associated probabilities for each of these. For the £90 price the estimates are:

	Annual demand	Probability of demand
Pessimistic	20,000	0·2
Most likely	35,000	0·7
Optimistic	40,000	0·1
		1·0

On the cost side, it is clear that the standard unit variable cost of £50 is an "ideal" which has rarely been achieved in practice. An analysis of the past 20 months shows that the following pattern of variable cost variances (per unit of output) has arisen: an adverse variance of around £10 arose on four occasions; an adverse variance of around £5 arose on 14 occasions; and a variance of around 0 arose on two occasions.

There is no reason to think that the pattern for the improved model will differ significantly from this or that these variances are dependent upon the actual demand level.

From the above, calculate the expected annual profit for a selling price of £90.

(c) A tabular summary of the result of an analysis of the data for the other two selling prices (£70 and £80) is as follows:

	£70	£80
Probability of a loss of £500,000 or more	0·02	0
Probability of a loss of £300,000 or more	0·07	0·05
Probability of a loss of £100,000 or more	0·61	0·08
Probability of breakeven or worse	0·61	0·10
Probability of breakeven or better	0·39	0·91
Probability of a profit of £100,000 or more	0·33	0·52
Probability of a profit of £300,000 or more	0·03	0·04
Probability of a profit of £500,000 or more	0	0·01
Expected value of profit/(loss)	(£55,750)	£68,500

You are required to compare your calculations in part (b) with the above figures and to write a short memo to the Sales Director outlining your advice and commenting on the use of subjective discrete probability distributions in problems of this type.

(d) Assume that there is a 10% increase in the fixed overheads allocated to this product line and a decision to write off the research and development costs in one year instead of over three years. Indicate the general effect that this would have on your analysis of the problem.

26.

The Central Co. Ltd has developed a new product and is currently considering the marketing and pricing policy it should employ for it. Specifically it is considering whether the sales price should to set at £15 per unit or at the higher level of £24 per unit. Sales volumes at these two prices are shown in the following table:

Sales price £15 per unit		Sales price £24 per unit	
Forecast sales volume (000s)	Probability	Forecast sales volume (000s)	Probability
20	0·1	8	0·1
30	0·6	16	0·3
40	0·3	20	0·3
		24	0·3

The fixed production costs of the venture will be £38,000.

The level of the advertising and publicity costs will depend on the sales price and the market aimed for. With a sales price of £15 per unit the advertising and publicity costs will amount to £12,000. With a sales price of £24 per unit these costs will total £122,000.

Labour and variable overhead costs will amount to £5 per unit produced. Each unit produced requires 2 kg of raw material and the basic cost is expected to be £4 per kg. However, the suppliers of the raw material are prepared to lower the price in return for a firm agreement to purchase a guaranteed minimum quantity. If Central Co. Ltd contracts to purchase at least 40,000 kg then the price will be reduced to £3·75 per kg for all purchases. If Central contracts to purchase a minimum of 60,000 kg then the price will be reduced to £3·50 per kg for all purchases. It is only if Central guarantees either of the above minimum levels of purchases in advance that the appropriate reduced prices will be operative.

If Central Co. Ltd were to enter into one of the agreements for the supply of raw material and were to find that it did not require to utilise the entire quantity of materials purchased then the excess could be sold. The sales price will depend upon the quantity which is offered for sale. If 16,000 kg or more are sold then the sale price will be £2·90 per kg for all sales. If less than 16,000 kg are offered the sale price will be only £2·40 per kg. Irrespective of the amount sold the costs incurred in selling the excess raw materials will be, per kg, as follows:

Packaging	£0·30
Delivery	£0·45
Insurance	£0·15

Central's management team feels that losses are undesirable while high expected money values are desirable. Therefore, it is considering the utilisation of a formula which incorporates both aspects of the outcome to measure the desirability of each strategy. The formula to be used to measure the desirability is:

$$\text{``Desirability''} = L + 3E$$

where: L = lowest outcome of the strategy
E = expected monetary value of the strategy

The higher this measure the more desirable the strategy.

The marketing manager seeks the advice of you, the management accountant, to assist in deciding the appropriate strategy. He says, "We need to make two decisions now:

(a) which price per unit should be charged; is it £15 or £24 per unit? and

(b) should all purchases of raw materials be at the price of £4 per kg or should we enter into an agreement for a basic minimum quantity? If we enter into an agreement, then what minimum level of purchases should we guarantee?

As you are the management accountant, I expect you to provide me with some useful relevant figures."

You are required to:

(a) Provide statements which show the various expected outcomes of each of the choices open to Central Co. Ltd.

(b) Advise of its best choice of strategies if Central Co. Ltd's objective is:

   (i)   to maximise the expected monetary value of the outcomes;

   (ii) to minimise the harm done to the firm if the worst outcome of each choice were to eventuate;

   (iii) to maximise the score on the above mentioned measure of "desirability".

(c) Briefly comment on either:

   (i)   two other factors which may be relevant in reaching a decision; *or*

   (ii) the decision criteria utilised in (b) above.

PRICING DECISIONS

27.

French Ltd is about to commence operations utilising a simple production process to produce two products, X and Y. It is the policy of French to operate the new factory at its maximum output in the first year of operations. Cost and production details estimated for the first year's operations are:

Product	Production resources per unit		Variable cost per unit		Fixed production overheads directly attributable to product	Maximum production — units
	Labour hours	Machine hours	Direct labour	Direct materials	£(000s)	(000s)
			(£)	(£)		
X	1	4	5	6	120	40
Y	8	2	28	16	280	10

There are also general fixed production overheads concerned in the manufacture of both products but which cannot be directly attributed to either. This general fixed production overhead is estimated at £720,000 for the first year of operations. It is thought that the cost structures of the first year will also be operative in the second year.

Both products are new and French is one of the first firms to produce them. Hence in the first year of operations the sales price can be set by French. In the second and subsequent years it is felt that the market for X and Y will have become more settled and French will largely conform to the competitive market prices that will become established. The sales manager has researched the first year's market potential and has estimated sales volumes for various ranges of selling price. The details are as below:

Product X		Product Y	
Range of per unit sales prices	Sales volume	Range of per unit sales prices	Sales volume
£ £	(000s)	£ £	(000s)
Up to 24·00	36	Up to 96·00	11
24·01 to 30·00	32	96·01 to 108·00	10
30·01 to 36·00	18	108·01 to 120·00	9
36·01 to 42·00*	8	120·01 to 132·00	8
		132·01 to 144·00	7
		144·01 to 156·00*	5

*Maximum price

The managing director of French wishes to ascertain the total production cost of X and Y as, he says, "Until we know the per unit cost of production we cannot properly determine the first year's sales price. Price must always ensure that total cost is covered and there is an element of profit — therefore I feel that the price should be total cost plus 20%.

"The determination of cost is fairly simple as most costs are clearly attributable to either X or Y. The general factory overhead will probably be allocated to the products in accordance with some measure of usage of factory resources such as labour or machine hours. The choice between labour and machine hours is the only problem in determining the cost of each product — but the problem is minor and so, therefore, is the problem of pricing."

You are required to

    (a) Produce statements showing the effect the cost allocation and pricing methods mentioned by the managing director will have on:

        (i)   unit costs,

        (ii)   closing stock values, and

        (iii) disclosed profit for the first year of operations.

    (b) Briefly comment on the results in (a) above and advise the managing director on the validity of using the per unit cost figures produced, for pricing decisions.

    (c) Provide appropriate statements to the management of French Ltd which will be of direct relevance in assisting the determination of the optimum prices of X and Y for the first year of operations. The statements should be designed to provide assistance in each of the following, separate, cases:

        (i)   year II demand will be below productive capacity;

        (ii)   year II demand will be substantially in excess of productive capacity.

In both cases the competitive market sales prices per unit for year II are expected to be

    X — £30 per unit
    Y — £130 per unit

Clearly specify, and explain, your advice to French for each of the cases described (ignore taxation and the time value of money).

28.

    (a) Nantderyn Products has two main products, Exco and Wyeco, which have unit costs of £12 and £24 respectively. The company uses a mark-up of $33\frac{1}{3}\%$ in establishing its selling prices and the current prices are thus £16 and £32. With these prices, in the year which is just ending, the company expects to make a profit of £300,000 from having produced and sold 15,000 units of Exco and 30,000 units of Wyeco. This programme will have used all the available processing time in the finishing department. Each unit of Exco requires an hour of processing time in this department and every unit of Wyeco correspondingly requires half an hour.

Fixed overhead was £360,000 for the year and this has been charged to the products on the basis of the total processing hours used. All other costs may be assumed variable in relation to processing hours. In the current year it is estimated that £60,000 of the fixed overhead will be absorbed by Exco and £300,000 by Wyeco. With the existing selling prices it is considered that the potential annual demand for Exco is 20,000 units and that for Wyeco 40,000 units.

You are required to comment critically on the product mix adopted by Nantderyn Products. Calculate what would have been the optimal plan given that there was no intention of changing the selling prices.

(b) For the forthcoming year increased capacity has been installed in the finishing department so that this will no longer be a constraint for any feasible sales programme. Annual fixed overhead will be increased to £400,000 as a consequence of this expansion of facilities, but variable costs per unit are unchanged.

A study commissioned by the Sales Director estimates the effect that alterations to the selling prices would have on the sales that could be achieved. The following table has been prepared.

	Exco		Wyeco	
Price	£13·50	£18·50	£29·00	£35·00
Demand in 000s	30	10	60	20

It is thought reasonable to assume that the price/demand relationship is linear. Assuming that the company is now willing to abandon its cost-plus pricing practices if these can be shown to be deficient, you are required to calculate the optimal selling price for each product and the optimal output levels for these prices. State clearly any assumptions that you find it necessary to make.

(c) "The paradox is that, while cost-plus pricing is devoid of any theoretical justification, it is widely used in practice."

Discuss possible justifications for this use.

29.

An article in *Studies in Cost Analysis,* edited by David Solomons, is entitled "Costing and pricing: the cost accountant versus the economist", by W. T. Baxter and A. R. Oxenfeldt.

You are required to give a critical analysis of the full cost-plus pricing procedure, with your suggestions as to how any objections that you may have to it can be overcome.

JOINT PRODUCT AND BYPRODUCT COSTING

30.

The Kew Gardens Perfume Company processes a secret blend of flower petals into three products. The process works in such a way that the petals are broken down into a high-grade perfume, Musk, and a low-grade flower oil. The flower oil is then processed into a low-grade perfume, Springtime, and a cologne, Joyeux.

The company used 10,000 lb of petals last month. The costs involved in reducing the petals into Musk and flower oil were:

Direct materials	£150,000
Direct labour	90,000
Indirect costs	60,000
	£300,000

The costs of producing Springtime and Joyeux from the flower oil were:

Direct materials	£15,000
Direct labour	35,000
Indirect costs	20,000
	£70,000

Total production and sales for the month were:

Musk	10,000 ounces
Springtime	10,000 ounces
Joyeux	10,000 ounces

The selling price of Musk is £40 per ounce; of Springtime, £10 per ounce and of Joyeux £1 per ounce.

Additional costs, entirely separate for each product, of processing and selling are:

Musk	£20,000
Springtime	160,000
Joyeux	40,000
	£220,000

There were no opening or closing stocks.

You are required to:

(a) Prepare a profit statement for each product. Costs are to be assigned on the basis of the net relative sales value.

(b) Advise management, which is considering the possibility of increasing the quality of Springtime, at an increase in final processing cost of £2 per ounce. The selling price would be increased to £12 per ounce. This would result in a different product mix of Springtime and Joyeux. Every 10,000 lb of petals would then result in 10,000 ounces of Musk, 18,000 ounces of Springtime and 60,000 ounces of Joyeux. The separable costs of Joyeux and Springtime are completely variable. All prices and costs not specifically mentioned will remain unchanged. Should this alternative be selected?

BUDGETARY CONTROL

31.

The Aram Company, a subsidiary of a UK company, operates out of Selangor. It produces two products, the KL and the JB. It can be assumed that both the production and the sales of these products occur almost instantaneously and are evenly spread throughout the year. Thus no stocks are held.

In the year just about to end on 31 December 19X8 the company produced 2,000 KLs which have a retail price of M$25 each, and 10,000 JBs whose retail price has been M$10 each. These products were distributed through dealers who were allowed a 20% discount from the retail price to show them a 25% margin on cost.

Total costs of producing the two products were:

	KLs (M$)	JBs (M$)
Direct materials	15,000	25,000
Direct labour	20,000	30,000
Variable overhead	10,000	10,000
Fixed overhead*	3,000	3,000

*Apportioned on the basis of variable overhead

Next year the company aims to expand its production and sales, again keeping these in step, and has the machine capacity to enable it to achieve these new objectives. The new policies and forecasts ensuing from these, are as follows:

Revenues

(a) Retail prices will be increased by 10% from 1 January, and by another 10% on 1 July. At the same time, from the beginning of the year, an additional 5% discount from the retail price of the products will be given to distributors. This is to encourage them to push the Aram Company's products in preference to those of competitors.

(b) For the first three months, following each of the price increases, special promotional activities costing M$1,000 per month for each product will be run.

(c) The sales forecast for 19X9, based upon the combined effect of the above strategies, shows an increase in sales volume of 44% for KLs and 40% for JBs.

Costs

(a) Material prices are expected to increase by 16% from 1 April. However, because the Aram Company wil be able to order materials in larger quantities it will be able to gain an additional 10% bulk ordering discount from the invoiced price of all materials bought in the year.

(b) Wages are expected to increase by 10% from 1 January, an increase that will be in line with the UK holding company's wages policy guidelines. However, in the year just ending labour was working at full capacity. To draw forth the additional forecast production, overtime paid at time-and-a-half will have to be worked.

(c) Rent for the company's factory at Selangor will be increased by M$4,000 per annum from 1 October next. It is forecast that from the beginning of the year the input prices relating to variable overhead will increase by 5%.

You are required to provide:

(a) A profit and loss account in contribution form for the year ended 31 December 19X8.

(b) A budgeted profit statement in contribution form for the year commencing 1 January 19X9.

Draw any conclusions which you consider to be pertinent from your statements above and indicate any areas in which you feel that it is important to have additional information.

32.

C & B Ltd is a small-toy manufacturing organisation which makes and sells cuddly chicks and bunnies through a number of wholesalers. The major consumer demand for the products has two peaks — one at Christmas, the other during the spring and at Easter. Experience has shown that wholesalers, although placing forward orders, which helps the company in its formulation of manufacturing plans, tend to require delivery of the goods that they order at the last possible minute. Nevertheless, C & B Ltd has equalised the use of its production facilities throughout the year to provide its factory with a fairly even throughput. Recent actual and the budgeted figures up to June 19X9 are as follows:

Month	Sales (gross)	Overheads (including depreciation)
19X8	£	£
October (actual)	40,000	5,499
November (actual)	40,000	1,501
December (budget)	20,000	2,500
19X9 (all figures budgeted)		
January	4,000	10,000
February	4,000	2,500
March	32,000	4,500
April	20,000	3,500
May	10,000	2,500
June	20,000	3,500

Overheads include £500 per month for depreciation and also cover other items such as rent, rates and utilities. Except for depreciation, the timing of the above overhead reflects the payment period. For the purposes of profit calculation, on an accrual basis, these costs are applied monthly on the basis of a percentage of gross revenues. The percentage in the current year is 23%. The budgeted position at the bank on 1 January 19X9 is for there to be an overdraft of £10,000.

C & B Ltd offers a discount of 5% if bills are paid in the month following the sale and $2\frac{1}{2}$% if paid in the second month following the sale. Experience has shown that half its customers will take the 5% discount, one-quarter the $2\frac{1}{2}$% and one-fifth will take no discount and pay three months after the sale was made. The balance represents bad debts.

The company has equalised its purchase of raw materials which, before discounts, account for 35% of the product's sale price, buying £6,000 of this on the 1st of each month throughout the year. Materials are paid for on the 20th of the month during which they are purchased to enable the company to take advantage of a 5% settlement discount. Wages and salaries of £4,000 per month, which account for 25% of the revenue received for products, are paid during the month incurred.

Other information at hand is that the managing director's car is due to be replaced during February. The on-the-road cost of the new vehicle is £5,000. However, there will be a trade-in allowance on the old car of £2,500 if the account is settled immediately.

Making all the necessary adjustments, the management accountant draws up appropriate budgets for the first six months of 19X9. Just as these have been completed, a non-financial director calls in at the office and is shown the budgets. He observes that the budgeted profit differs from the movement in the projected cash balance and admits to some confusion on this point.

You are required to provide:

(a) The preparation for C & B Ltd of:

(i)   a profit and loss account to show the budgeted results in aggregate; and

      (ii)   a cash budget on a monthly basis,

both for the six months commencing 1 January 19X9. Clearly state any assumptions that you make.

   (b) Comments to dispel the confusion on the part of the director.

   (c) A brief discussion on the use of the information content of the documents that you have drawn up.

33.

Although Earlham Ltd currently has a fairly wide range of products, the overall mix of products closely conforms to the following breakdown of sales price:

	%	%
Sales price		100
Cost of goods sold (all variable):		
Direct materials	35	
Direct labour	20	
Variable overheads	25	
	—	80
Contribution towards profit and fixed overheads		20

There are no seasonal fluctuations and activity levels have been roughly constant for several years. The current working capital position is typical:

	£000	£000
Stocks		
Raw materials	240	
Work-in-progress	120	
Finished goods	150	
	—	510
Debtors		210
Creditors		90

The activity for the past year can be summarised thus:

	£000
Sales	1,200
Purchases of raw materials	420
Cost of goods sold	960

There is the opportunity for Earlham Ltd to increase immediately its level of activity from a sales turnover figure of £1·2 million per year to £2 million per year.

The managing director suggests that such an increase in activity level will be profitable as, he says, "the contribution of 20% on the extra sales of £800,000 is £160,000 — this will be all additional profit as our fixed costs are unaltered. As there is no capital expenditure involved then we need not worry about availability of cash — in my experience in this firm, profit generates its own level of cash."

The production and marketing directors make the following points:

(a) Expansion is into a new type of product and market, and existing activities will be largely unaffected.

(b) Credit allowed to customers of the new products will, on average, be about 30 days more than is currently allowed. This increase in the period of credit given is for sales of the expansion products only.

(c) The number of days for which raw materials are on average held in stock will be increased by 10%, again for the expansion only.

(d) The length of time stocks are in work-in-progress will be unaltered.

(e) The average length of time finished goods of the new products will remain in stock will be 20% greater than the current average.

(f) Material costs for the expansion will average out at about 40% of sales rather than the 35% for existing products. Other variable costs will be unaffected, the overall effect being that contribution will be lower.

(g) Payments to suppliers will need to be made more promptly. This will affect all suppliers and the number of days' credit taken will fall for all creditors to only 45 days.

(h) The cost of money is currently 14% per annum, therefore the proposed expansion needs to be carefully analysed to ensure that if additional cash has to be found to finance it then that expansion will be still profitable after obtaining cash.

The managing director feels that there is little evidence that the expansion will be any different in (financial) operational terms from the organisation's existing activities. He suggests, "The expansion is merely scale expansion of our existing activities and there is no reason why, for example, credit allowed should increase."

You are required to:

(a) Prepare two statements which will show whether extra cash is required in order to facilitate the budgeted expansion; the statements should be based on:

   (i) the scale expansion assumptions of the managing director — that is, assuming no change from the operating characteristics that the current activities display;

   (ii) the points raised by the production and marketing directors but excluding point (h) above.

(b) Calculate the additional profit generated per year by the expansion after considering points (a) to (h) by the two directors.

Assume that there are 360 days in a year.

Note: Marks will not be lost for reasonable rounding or approximation of figures.

34.

Electronic Products Ltd manufactures three products, extracts from the standard cost data relating to which are appended:

	Components used					
Component number	101	102	103	104	105	106
Unit cost	40p	50p	35p	60p	75p	90p
A	5	3	4	6	2	1
B	4	2	3	5	1	1
C	7	6	5	4	3	1

Component No. 106 is the metal chassis which passes through the machine shop for various drilling and bending operations before being passed to the assembly shop where the components are wired up and the product completed.

Details of standard labour and machine times are set out below and it should be noted that all machine time attracts equivalent labour time, each machine being in the charge of a machinist.

Product	Assembly shop (assemblers' hourly rate = 40p) hours	Machine shop (machinists' hourly rate = 50p) hours
A	1	0·1
B	1·25	0·15
C	1·5	0·2

The company operates a five-day week, eight hours per day, and production is evenly spread.

During four-weekly period number 1, budgeted sales are:

Product	Sales (units)	Unit selling price
A	12,000	£20
B	15,000	£24
C	10,000	£28

The stocks on hand at the beginning of period number 1 are expected to be:

Finished goods	A	2,000
	B	2,200
	C	1,800
Components	101	50,000
	102	30,000
	103	35,000
	104	45,000
	105	17,000
	106	9,000

Experience has indicated that finished goods stocks ought to be higher in order to satisfy orders more quickly and an increase in quantity of 10% is planned for the end of period number 1. On the other hand, component stocks are considered high having regard to recent improvements in delivery times and, in consequence, a reduction of 10% in the quantities held is planned for the end of the period.

At the time the budget was being prepared, the assembly shop consisted of 280 employees and the machine shop 32, and there were 40 machines available. Machine downtime for maintenance, setting, etc. is reckoned at six hours per machine per week.

You are required to prepare budgets for:

   (a) Sales (in quantity and value)

   (b) Production (in quantity)

   (c) Materials usage (in quantity)

   (d) Materials purchases (in quantity and value)

   (e) Direct labour utilisation and cost

   (f) Machine utilisation

and to comment upon any matters disclosed by (e) and (f) which need attention, suggesting possible solutions.

35.

Processors Limited, a manufacturing company in a process industry, prepares an annual budget which it updates after the first six months of each financial year. You are given the following information from which the latest annual budget will be prepared:

Manufacturing costs:
    Variable (according to quantity produced)

Materials	23,000 kg @£10·00 per kg
Labour	360,000 hours @ £0·80 per hour
Power	2,400,000 units @ £0·01 per unit

    Fixed
      Works overheads 12 months @ £20,000 per month

Distribution costs:
    Variable (according to quantity sold)
        Carriage   20,000 kg @ £2·40 per kg
    Fixed
        Transport office   12 months @ £1,000 per month
Selling costs:
        Fixed   12 months @ £7,500 per month
Administration costs:
        Fixed   12 months @ £14,000 per month
Output and sales: 20,000 kg

Selling price: calculated to show a 20% profit margin on total budgeted costs.

The financial year commences on 1 January. During the course of the year to which the above figures relate prices rise rapidly. It is decided to re-budget for the year on the assumption that as from 1 July all variable costs are increased by 5% and all fixed costs by 1%.

During the first half of the year the volume of output and sales is $2\frac{1}{2}$% above budget and it is estimated that this higher rate will be maintained for the rest of the year, if there is no change in selling price. However, if the selling price is raised, it is anticipated that every £0·20 increase in price per kg will result in a decrease of 20·5 kg in the quantity sold in the half-year. It is decided to increase price from 1 July by £2·40 per kg.

You may assume that stock levels remain constant and are not affected by changes in output or sales.

You are required to:

(a) calculate the initial selling price per kg based on the budget as first prepared (that is, ignoring events occurring after 1 January); and

(b) prepare a statement showing the revised budgeted profit for the year taking into account all the above decisions and events.

36.

Meadow Plastics Ltd, a manufacturer of moulded plastic containers, determined in October that it needed cash to continue operations. The corporation began negotiating for a one-month bank loan of £100,000 on 1 November at 15% interest. In considering the loan, the bank requested a projected profit statement and a cash budget for the month of November.

The following information is available:

Sales were budgeted at 120,000 units per month in October, December and January (in the following year) and at 90,000 units in November.

The selling price is £2 per unit. Sales are invoiced on the 15th and the last day of each month. Terms are 2% discount if payment is made within 10 days, otherwise the full amount is to be paid within 30 days (that is, 2/10 net 30). Past experience indicates sales are made evenly throughout the month. 50% of the customers pay the invoiced amount within the discount period, and the remainder pay at the end of 30 days, except for bad debts which average $\frac{1}{2}$% of gross sales.

The stock of finished goods on 1 October was 24,000 units. The finished goods stock at the end of each month is to be maintained at 20% of sales anticipated for the following month. The production process is such that there is no work-in-progress.

The stock of raw materials on 1 October was 22,800 kg. At the end of each month the raw materials stocks are to be maintained at not less than 40% of production requirements for the following month. Materials are purchased locally and only in lot sizes of 25,000 kg. Raw material purchases of each month are paid in the next month. Terms are net 30 days.

All salaries and wages are paid on the 15th and last day of each month for the period ending on the date of payment.

All manufacturing overhead and selling and administrative expenses are paid on the 10th of the month following the month in which the expenses are incurred. Selling expenses are 10% of gross sales. Administrative expenses, which include depreciation of £500 per month on office furniture and fixtures, total £33,000 per month.

The standard cost of a moulded plastic container, based on normal production of 100,000 units per month, is as follows:

Materials, $\frac{1}{2}$ kg	£0·50	
Labour	0·40	
Variable overhead	0·20	
Fixed overhead	0·10	(total budgeted = £10,000)
Total	£1·20	

Fixed overhead includes depreciation on factory equipment of £4,000 per month. Over-absorbed or under-absorbed overhead (that is, differences between £10,000 and the amount applied to production) is included in cost of sales.

The cash balance on 1 November is expected to be £10,000. Assume the bank loan is granted, and ignore tax.

You are required to prepare:

(a) schedules calculating stock budgets by months for:

    (i) finished goods production in units for October, November and December;

    (ii) raw materials purchases in kg for October and November;

(b) a projected profit statement for the month of November;

(c) a cash forecast for the month of November showing the opening balance, receipts (itemised by dates of collection), payments, and balance at end of month.

37.

Manning Wholesale Ltd ends its financial year on 30 June. You have been requested, in early July 19X7, to assist in the preparation of a cash forecast. The following information is available regarding the company's operations:

(a) Management believes the 19X6–X7 sales level and pattern are a reasonable estimate of 19X7–X8 sales. Sales in 19X6–X7 were as follows:

19X6	July	£360,000
	August	420,000
	September	600,000
	October	540,000
	November	480,000
	December	400,000
19X7	January	350,000
	February	550,000
	March	500,000
	April	400,000
	May	600,000
	June	800,000
	Total	£6,000,000

(b) The debtors at 30 June 19X7 total £380,000. Sales collections are generally made as follows:

During month of sale	60%
In the first subsequent month	30%
In the second subsequent month	9%
Uncollectable	1%

(c) The purchase cost of goods averages 60% of selling price. The cost of the stock on hand at 30 June 19X7 is £840,000, of which £30,000 is obsolete. Arrangements have been made to sell the obsolete stock in July at half the normal selling price on a "cash on delivery" basis.

The company wishes to maintain the stock, as of the first of each month, at a level of three months' sales as determined by the sales forecast for the next three months. All purchases are paid for on the 10th of the following month. Creditors for purchases at 30 June 19X7 total £370,000.

(d) Payments in respect of fixed and variable expenses are forecast for the first three months of 19X7–X8 as follows:

July	August	September
£160,620	£118,800	£158,400

(e) It is anticipated that cash dividends and ACT thereon of £40,000 will be paid each half-year, on the 15th day of September and March.

(f) During the year, unusual advertising costs will be incurred that will require cash payments of £10,000 in August and £15,000 in September. The advertising costs are in addition to the expenses in item (d) above.

(g) Equipment replacements are made at a rate which requires a cash outlay of £3,000 per month. The equipment has an average estimated life of six years.

(h) A £60,000 payment for corporation tax is to be made on 15 September 19X7.

(i) At 30 June 19X7 the company had a bank loan with an unpaid balance of £280,000. The entire balance is due on 30 September 19X7 together with accumulated interest from 1 July 19X7 at the rate of 12% per annum.

(j) The cash balance at 30 June 19X7 is £100,000.

You are required to prepare a cash forecast statement by months for the first three months of the 19X7–X8 financial year. The statement should show the amount of cash in hand (or deficiency of cash) at the end of each month. All computations and supporting schedules should be presented in clear and readable form.

38.

Wellpland Ltd operate a budget system which shows the following forecast of profitability for the half-year from 31 March.

(Figures in £000s)	*April*	*May*	*June*	*July*	*August*	*September*
Materials consumed	82	76	83	91	53	76
Wages	36	32	40	44	36	36
Depreciation	9	9	9	9	9	9
Factory expenses	7	7	7	7	7	7
Rent	5	5	5	5	5	5
Salaries and office expenses	37	39	48	35	42	47
Advertising	12	14	10	16	20	22
Sales commission	8	9	10	11	13	12
Provision for redemption of debentures	1	1	1	1	1	1
Group management charge	4	4	5	4	4	5
Total expenses	201	196	218	223	190	220
Sales	220	230	210	240	220	240
Net profit	19	34	(8)	17	30	20
Stocks of raw material at month end	75	64	56	82	47	59

The following additional information is significant:

(a) Payment for raw materials is made to suppliers two months after delivery.

(b) The lag in payment of wages is one-eighth of a month.

(c) Factory expenses are paid one month after they are incurred.

(d) Rent is payable in advance on each quarter-day.

(e) Salaries and office expenses are payable in the month in which they arise.

(f) Two months' credit is taken on advertising expenses.

(g) Sales commission is paid one month in arrear.

(h) Debtors are allowed three months' credit.

(i) A dividend and tax thereon will be paid in August amounting to £25,000.

(j) Retention money of 10% on plant installation of £300,000 at the company's factory is due for release in September, while a loan repayment to the company falls due in July in the sum of £8,000.

(k) The cash book showed an overdrawn balance of £21,500 on 1 July.

You are required to:

(a) compute a cash budget for each of the three months ended 30 September;

(b) state the areas of investigation that will concern management when seeking to improve the cash position of a business; and

(c) state how in particular the cashflow of Wellpland Ltd may be improved by the end of September.

39.

The following matters arise in the operation of a budgetary control system:

(a) A foreman is paid a bonus at the end of the year for overtime work he performed seven months previously. The bonus is charged to overhead.

(b) Consumable stores are charged to overhead as they are purchased and not as they are issued to the manufacturing process.

(c) An iron founder's pattern-making costs are consistently underestimated whenever job quotations are prepared.

(d) The salvage value of scrap from production is incorrectly forecast.

(e) Some 5% of input at a fruit-packing station is lost through normal spoilage.

(f) The salvage value of scrap from production is ignored completely.

(g) A worker is inefficient because he is new to his job.

(h) A worker is inefficient because he lacks concentration.

You are required to

    (a) Distinguish between variances reported because of defects:

        (i)   of management, and

        (ii) in the design of a budgetary control system.

        Illustrate your answer by reference to the examples quoted, and

    (b) Specify briefly what action you would take to correct each example and the difficulties you would expect to encounter. Are there any cases where you would not wish to take any action? Why?

40.

As an accountant of a company making, selling and distributing a wide range of products, you are preparing to install a system of budgetary control. In a report to your managing director:

    (a) state the factors to be taken into consideration in establishing the length of the proposed budget periods.

    (b) describe the operating of:

        (i)   a budgeting system for a given period; and also

        (ii) a continuous budgeting system on a moving-total basis.

        In your report give the advantages and disadvantages of the continuous system compared with the period system.

    (c) state your recommendations on the level of attainment that should be adopted.

41.

    (a) (i)   Define controllable cost. What two major factors help decide whether a given cost is controllable?

        (ii) Briefly describe responsibility accounting.

        (iii) What guidelines are useful in deciding what costs may be appropriately charged to a person?

    (b) Professor Argyris and others have pointed out that budgets help encourage a *departmental* orientation rather than a *plant-wide* orientation. This causes trouble because departmental executives concentrate on the correct functioning of their individual departments but pay no attention to the functioning of individual departments in relation to one another.

        For example, Argyris cites the example of the plant in which a mistake was made on a customer order. The goods were returned and a correction was made at a cost of £3,000, a large amount. Some department had to be charged with the error. But which department?

After two months of battling among the supervisors as to who was guilty, emotions became so heated that two supervisors stopped talking to each other.

The plant manager finally gave up; he decided to charge the error to no department. He explained, "I thought it might be best to put the whole thing under general factory loss. Or else someone would be hurt."

You are required to state whether you agree:

(i)   that budgets encourage too narrow an orientation.

(ii) with the action of the plant manager. Did the budget and departmental accounting system cause the trouble? Explain fully.

BEHAVIOURAL ASPECTS OF BUDGETING

42.

Describe the organisation and operation of a system of budgetary control, emphasising the importance of behavioural considerations in the development of an effective system.

INTRODUCTION TO STANDARD COSTING AND BASIC VARIANCE ANALYSIS

43.

(a) Mingus Ltd produces granoids. It revises its cost standards annually in September for the year commencing 1 December.

At a normal volume of output of 40,000 granoids its standard costs, including overheads, for the year to 30 November 19X1 were:

Cost	Standard	Per unit £	Total £000
Direct materials	5 kg @ £10 per kg	50	2,000
Direct labour	2 hours @ £5 per hour	10	400
Variable overheads	£1 per kg of direct material	5	200
Fixed overheads	£5 per hour of direct labour	10	400
		75	3,000

The actual expenditure incurred in that year to produce an actual output of 50,000 granoids was:

Cost	Total expenditure £000	Further details
Direct materials	2,880	320,000 kg @ £9 per kg
Direct labour	540	90,000 hours @ £6 per hour
Variable overheads	280	
Fixed overheads	380	
	4,080	

Due to an industrial dispute in 19X0 there was no stock-holding of materials, work-in-progress, or completed granoids at 1 December 19X0. At 30 November 19X1 there was an inventory of 10,000 completed granoids, but no work-in-progress, and no raw materials inventory.

You are required to calculate in each case the balance which would remain in the Finished Goods Inventory Account if each of the following six costing systems were used:

(i)   actual absorption costing,

(ii)   standard absorption costing with variances written-off,

(iii)   standard absorption costing with variances prorated between cost of sales and inventory,

(iv)   actual direct costing,

(v)   standard direct costing with variances written-off,

(vi)   standard direct costing with variances prorated between cost of sales and inventory.

(b) *You are required to* comment briefly in general terms on the main effects of applying to inventory valuation the various costing systems set out above, referring to your calculations in part (a) if you wish.

44.

Amalgamated Processors plc is a divisionalised organisation which operates a standard costing and budgetary planning and control system in which the preparation of detailed operating budgets is undertaken by the divisions themselves after centrally determined profit targets have been communicated to them.

The Penbrock Division of the company produces and sells a standardised component which is sold externally at £10 per unit and internally, to other divisions, at a transfer price of £9 per unit. The standard specification for this product is as follows:

Standard specification:	
2 m^2 of material A @ £0·20 per m^2	£0·40
5 units of component B @ £0·37 per unit	1·85
15 minutes of labour @ £2·00 per hour	0·50
Variable manufacturing overhead — 150% of direct labour cost	0.75
Fixed manufacturing overhead	1·50
Standard unit manufacturing cost	5·00
Central office charge	1·00
Selling and distributive overhead	1·00
Standard unit cost	£7·00

The fixed manufacturing overhead is absorbed on the basis of the "normal" monthly output of 15,000 units. The selling and distributive overhead relates solely to external sales and the monthly divisional budget for this comprises a fixed element of £9,600 and a variable element of £0·20 for each unit of budgeted external sales. The fixed selling and distributive overhead has been unitised assuming a "normal" monthly external sales level of 12,000 units. The "central office charge" element of the standard specification relates to a charge made by the "head office" for central services provided — this has also been unitised assuming the normal monthly activity level of 15,000 units. Unsold stock is carried at standard manufacturing cost.

The following details apply to the Penbrock Division for April 19X2:

Profit and loss account April 19X2

	Actual		Budget	
	Units		Units	
Sales				
External	10,000	£100,000	12,000	120,000
Internal	4,000	36,000	3,000	27,000
	14,000	£136,000	15,000	£147,000

	Actual Units		*Budget* Units	
Cost of goods				
manufactured	16,000	£85,000	15,000	£75,000
Less: Stock adjustment	2,000	10,000	—	—
	14,000	75,000	15,000	75,000
Selling and distributive				
overhead		13,000		12,000
Central office charges		15,000		15,000
Profit		33,000		45,000
		£136,000		£147,000

The "actual" cost of goods manufactured can be analysed as follows:

Material A	£6,500
Component B	31,745
4,250 labour hours @ £2·10	8,925
Variable manufacturing overhead	12,325
Fixed manufacturing overhead	25,505
	£85,000

The stores records of the Penbrock Division are kept at standard cost so that the material cost figures include both the cost of the actual direct materials used (priced at their standard cost) and the price variance on materials purchased during April. The details of usage and purchases are as follows:

Material A:	Usage	$34,000 \, \text{m}^2$
	Purchases	$30,000 \, \text{m}^2$ @ £0·19 per m^2
Component B:	Usage	78,500 units
	Purchases	90,000 units @ £0·40 per unit.

The work staff have complained that the quality of the most recently purchased batch of material A is inferior to the regular grade, that it gives rise to more waste and that it requires more time to process.

You are required to:

 (a) prepare a statement, for the general manager of the Penbrock Division, analysing the reasons for the profit shortfall of £12,000 and to provide a commentary on this statement;

 (b) comment on the practice of isolating material price variances at the time of the material's purchase;

 (c) comment on the transfer pricing method used by the Penbrock Division.

45.

Strider Limited budgets to make £20,000 profit during May when its fixed overheads are expected to be £80,000 based upon standard marginal costs as shown below:

Standard cost card

Raw material	10 kg @ 50p	£5·00
Labour	4 hours @ £1·50	6·00
		11·00
Factory variable		2·00
		13·00
Selling and distribution — variable		3·00
		£16·00
Standard selling price		£20·00

Actual results for May were:

Sales (20,000 units)	£408,000	
Production		22,000 units
Raw material — 250,000 kg (of which 20,000 kg have been put into stock)	130,000	
Labour — 95,000 hours (of which 5,000 were idle)	144,000	
Variable overhead —		
factory	43,000	
selling and distribution	62,000	
Fixed overhead	£78,000	

There were no opening stocks of raw materials or finished goods.

Your are required to calculate the actual result for the period and reconcile it with the budgeted contribution, identifying the appropriate variances.

46.

The Blendyarn Company Limited operate a number of overseas subsidiaries which spin a 50/50 blend of wool/synthetic hosiery yarn, supplying this to their respective local knitwear manufacturers.

One of these subsidiaries which operates in the Far East is called Blendyarn Berhad. Blendyarn Berhad produces a budget for a four-week operating period (during which 40-hour, five-day weeks are worked) as follows:

Blendyarn Berhad: budget for the four weeks ended 28 May

Sales		
(10,000 kg @ £10 per kg)		£100,000
Direct production costs		
Wool (5,000 kg @ £6)	£30,000	
Synthetics (5,000 kg @ £4)	20,000	
Oil, dyestuffs etc.	5,000	
Operatives (9,600 hours @ £1)	9,600	
Supervisors (320 hours @ £1·25)	400	
	65,000	
Fixed costs		
Administrative staff	1,000	
Sales staff	4,000	
Occupancy (rent, rates, power etc.)	10,000	
	15,000	
Total costs		80,000
Budgeted net profit		£20,000

Note: Occupancy costs are divided on the ratio of three to one between production and administration/ marketing.

Blendyarn Berhad only produces to order and into the foreseeable future it has full order books, so any lost production directly reduces sales.

In May this Far Eastern subsidiary faced operating difficulties ensuing from monsoon rains which flooded its factory during the second week of the operating period. Although no damage was caused to materials, the management incurred additional expenses by hiring contract cleaners for three days at £500 per day to clean up the mess. As the operatives could not work while the cleaning up was in progress, 60% of the week's production was lost. At the end of the three days' cleaning, management said that conditions within the factory had returned to normal, but on inspecting the factory themselves the operatives disagreed and walked out. Management brought the contract cleaners back for two more days and at the same time negotiated with the operatives to return to work. During the negotiations management offered to increase wages, although they refused to pay operatives for the period during which they had walked out. The operatives accepted the management's offer and at the commencement of the following week the factory was working normally. At the end of the four-week period during which the monsoon rains had caused the factory to be flooded, actual performance was as follows:

Blendyarn Berhad: actual performance for the four weeks ended 28 May

Sales			
2,500 kg @ £10			£25,000
5,000 kg @ £12			60,000
			85,000
Direct production costs			
Wool (3,750 kg @ £8)		£30,000	
Synthetics (3,750 kg @ £4)		15,000	
Oil, dyestuffs etc.		4,456	
Operatives: 3,840 hours @ £1	= £3,840		
4,800 hours £1·1	= £5,280		
		9,120	
Supervisors: 160 hours @ £1·25	= £200		
160 hours @ £1·40	= £224		
		424	
		59,000	
Fixed costs			
Administrative staff		1,250	
Sales staff		4,750	
Occupancy (rent, rates, power etc.)		10,000	
Contract cleaners (5 days @ £500)		2,500	
Total costs			77,500
Actual net profit			£7,500

You are required, as management accountant from the holding company who visited Blendyarn Berhad shortly after the monsoon, to write a report to the management of the subsidiary explaining the difference between the actual and the budgeted figures as you see them, in a way which will enable Blendyarn Berhad's management to trace and eliminate any inefficiency. Note that your report does not necessarily have to follow traditional variance analysis if you feel either that there is insufficient information for that approach or that it would be clearer and more helpful to present the information in a different way.

FURTHER VARIANCE ANALYSIS

47.

A chemical company has the following standards for manufacturing a machine lubricant:

5 gallons of material P @ £0·70 per gallon	£3·50
5 gallons of material Q @ £0·92 per gallon	4·60
10	£8·10*

*Cost of 10 gallons of standard mix which should produce 9 gallons of finished product at a standard cost of £0·90 (£8·10 ÷ 9) per gallon.

No stocks of raw materials are kept. Purchases are made as needed so that all price variances relate to materials used. Actual results showed that 100,000 gallons of material were used during a particular period as follows:

45,000 gallons of material P at an actual cost per gallon used of £0·80	36,000
55,000 gallons of material Q at an actual cost per gallon used of £0·97	53,350
100,000	89,350
Good output: 92,070 gallons at a standard cost of £0·90 per gallon produced	82,863
Total unfavourable material variance	£6,487

You are required to:

(a) analyse

    (i)   the total material variance in terms of price and usage variances,

    (ii) the usage variance in terms of mix and yield variance, and

(b) explain the circumstances under which a material mix variance is relevant to managerial control.

PROCESS COSTING

48.

Antimuk is a cleaning material which is formed by passing chemicals A, B and C in the proportion 3:2:1 respectively, through two successive processes, namely refining and blending. The acceptable output of the refining process is passed to the blending process into which additional chemicals D and E in the proportion 2:1 are introduced.

The following data apply to week ended 30 November:

Refining process:
   Materials introduced 4,500 kg: cost per kg: A 70p, B 60p, C 30p
   Labour 100 hours at £1·20 per hour
   Output 3,500 kg

Blending process:
   Additional materials introduced 2,100 kg: cost per kg: D 100p, E 120p
   Labour 40 hours at £1·60 per hour
   Analyst's test fee £74
   Output 5,100 kg

Overhead for the week of £840 is to be apportioned to the processes on a labour hour basis.

The normal output of the refining process is 80% of input and of the blending process 90% of input. Waste material from the refining process is sold for 20p per kg, and that from the blending process for 40p per kg.

It is the company's practice to complete each batch within the week and there is therefore no work-in-progress at either the beginning or the end of the week.

You are required to prepare the following accounts to record the production of Antimuk for the week in question:

   (a) Refining process account

   (b) Blending process account

   (c) Normal loss account

   (d) Abnormal losses and gains account

   (e) Finished stock account.

DECENTRALISATION AND PERFORMANCE EVALUATION

49.

Mr Lane, with his two sons, trades as Lanes Stores, a small family departmental store business with four major departments. Because of increased competition the business has not been doing very well during recent years. In fact, the last year's trading results show a loss of £750, the first time that the firm has not made a profit in its history.

Mr Lane calls a family meeting to discuss the following summarised trading and profit and loss account and departmental accounts:

Summary trading and profit and loss account for the year ended 31 March (all figures in thousands)

Sales		£397
Deduct: Cost of sales		308
Gross profit		89
Deduct: Expenses		
Direct departmental wages	£57	
departmental expenses	3	
advertising	7·75	
	67·75	
Indirect delivery expenses	5	
administrative expenses	6	
miscellaneous expenses	2	
finance charges	1	
management fees	8	
	£22·00	
		£89·75
Net loss		£(0·75)

Departmental accounts for the year ended 31 March (figures in thousands)

	Departments			
	Furniture	*Hardware*	*Drapery*	*Clothing*
	£	£	£	£
Sales	178	80	40	99
Purchases	160	60	30	60
Opening stock	30	30	30	42
Closing stock	34	30	34	36
Direct expenses:				
Wages	13	12	14	18
Expenses	1	0.5	0·5	1
Advertising	3	0.5	0·25	4
Selling:				
Floor space	35%	20%	15%	30%

At the meeting it was pointed out that the performance of some departments had been affected by the competition more adversely than others, so perhaps one such department could be closed to enable the others to be expanded.

It was also suggested that the firm had entered a situation where because margins were falling, these needed to be increased, yet the very effect of doing this would raise prices to make the firm even more uncompetitive with the various national group retailers who had recently opened up stores in the district.

You are required to:

(a) Prepare an operating report which includes pertinent ratios, to provide management with more helpful information in their decision-making than that shown above.

(b) Indicate matters which would justify further consideration and give your comments; refer specifically to any limitations in the form of the information which is available.

50.

The managing director of Worried Limited has been informed that last year the stock turnover ratio based on sales over average stock, for Similar Limited was 12 and for Different Limited 8, while this ratio for his own company was only 7.

Similar Limited is in the same industry as Worried Limited; Different Limited, however, is not. Furthermore, the managing director of Worried Limited understands that the stock turnover ratio for Similar Limited has improved from 9 for the year before last to the 12 of last year.

The managing director of Worried Limited expresses concern that his firm is inefficient in its stock control procedures.

You are required to assume that you have no other reasons to believe that Worried Limited is less efficient than either of the other two firms, and that the change in Similar's ratio is not due to any change in its level of efficiency during the years concerned.

Write a report to the managing director of Worried Limited, explaining in detail the full range of likely possibilities which could account for the differences in these ratios.

51.

(a) *You are required to:*

   (i)   define a profit centre
   (ii) list the management accountant's main difficulties in maintaining budgetary control over profit centre managers;
   (iii) explain briefly, the contribution a computer can make to resolving these difficulties.

(b) A large provincial garage is installing a responsibility accounting system. There will be three profit centres: parts and service; new cars, and used vehicles. Forecourt sales rights have been let to another company. The departmental manager of each profit centre has been told to run his activity as though he were in business on his own account.

However, there will be interdepartmental dealings. For example:

(i)   the parts and service department prepares new cars for final delivery, and repairs used vehicles prior to resale; and

(ii) the used vehicle department's major source of stock has been cars traded-in in part-payment for new cars.

The managing director asks his accountant to prepare a statement explaining the problems of transfer pricing and the principles to be followed. He says that clarity is of paramount importance because the statement will be relied on to settle disputes. He also wishes to be advised of any problems which might arise after the rules have been put into effect.

You are required to draft the statement requested. Specify and exemplify the rules to be used within the company for transfer prices in the case of the transfers cited.

TRANSFER PRICING

52.

B Limited, producing a range of minerals, is organised into two trading groups: one handles wholesale business and the other sales to retailers.

One of its products is a moulding clay. The wholesale group extracts the clay and sells it to external wholesale customers as well as to the retail group. The production capacity is 2,000 tonnes per month but at present sales are limited to 1,000 tonnes wholesale and 600 tonnes retail.

The transfer price was agreed at £200 per tonne in line with the external wholesale trade price at 1 July which was the beginning of the budget year. As from 1 December, however, competitive pressure has forced the wholesale trade price down to £180 per tonne. The members of the retail group contend that the transfer price to them should be the same as for outside customers. The wholesale group refute the argument on the basis that the original budget established the price for the whole budget year.

The retail group produces 100 bags of refined clay from each tonne of moulding clay which it sells at £4 a bag. It would sell a further 40,000 bags if the retail trade price were reduced to £3·20 a bag.

Other data relevant to the operation are:

	Wholesale group	Retail group
Variable cost per tonne	£70	£60
Fixed cost per month	£100,000	£40,000

You are required to:

(a) Prepare estimated profit statements for the month of December for each group and for B Limited as a whole based on transfer prices of £200 per tonne and of £180 per tonne when producing at:

   (i)   80% capacity; and

   (ii) 100% capacity utilising the extra sales to supply the retail trade.

(b) Comment on the results achieved under (a) and the effect of the change in the transfer price.

MANAGEMENT INFORMATION SYSTEMS AND COMMUNICATION

53.

In his reports, the management accountant may present quantitative information expressed in physical quantities, monetary values, or a combination of both.

You are required to:

(a) Give examples of reports showing how each of these measures may be used; discuss the advantages and disadvantages of drawing up reports in each of these different ways.

(b) Discuss situations where consideration should be given to qualitative information in decision-making and suggest ways in which details of such information may be brought into decision-analysis.

54.

(a) The information systems in many firms have grown in response to the needs of the individual departments within the organisations. Frequently no attempts have been made to integrate these systems within each firm. Discuss the advantages and disadvantages for a firm, of instituting a centralised data system.

(b) Discuss the validity of the arguments which support the view that the costs of service departments in a firm should be charged eventually to the production departments which use the services.

COST REDUCTION SCHEMES

55.

(a) Define "work study" and explain its primary objectives.

(b) Outline the two major techniques used by practitioners of work study.

Suggested Answers to Examination Questions

COST CLASSIFICATION

1.

(a)

Annual costs for	London lowest mileage 18,000 miles	Highlands highest mileage 40,000 miles
Fixed costs		
Road tax	£40	£40
Insurance (*note 1*)	160	160
Miscellaneous (*note 2*)	100	100
Depreciation (*note 3*)	1,000	1,000
	1,300	1,300
Variable costs		
Repairs @ 0·6p/mile (*note 4*)	108	240
Petrol and oil @ 4p/mile (*note 5*)	720	1,600
Semivariable costs		
Tyre replacement (*note 6*)	60	120
Total annual cost	£2,188	£3,260

In the above table costs have been classified into fixed, variable and semivariable. The following notes state the assumptions made in this classification.

Notes:

(1) The insurance costs are the same for each area. In reality this is unlikely because of different risk factors. (There is more traffic in London than in the Highlands and therefore there is a greater risk of an accident occurring in London. Insurance premiums should be higher.)

(2) Because of lack of information in the question, miscellaneous costs are assumed to be fixed. This is a valid assumption for motoring subscriptions and garaging allowances, but not necessarily correct for the other items. Parking fees should vary with number of calls made rather than mileage. More parking will occur in London where there is less distance betwen calls. Cleaning will be a function of both time and mileage.

(3) Annual depreciation charge $= \dfrac{£3,200 - £1,200}{2 \text{ years}} = £1,000$

The trade-in value appears to be based on time and unaffected by mileage, which is rather unrealistic.

(4)

		£
Annual repairs	=	80
Average annual additional repairs	=	$100 \nearrow \left(\dfrac{£200}{2 \text{ years}} \right)$

$£180 \div 30,000$ miles

$= \quad 0.6\text{p/ mile}$

Repairs are a function of use, and therefore treated as a variable cost.

(5) Petrol and oil are also based on usage and treated as a variable cost; 30,000 miles divided into £1,200 = 4p/mile. This ignores driving conditions, length of journeys, and the way an individual drives, all of which affect fuel consumption. It is assumed that the cost of petrol does not vary in different parts of the country.

(6) It is assumed that in the case of the lowest mileage only one replacement set of tyres will be required during the two-year cycle as a new set of tyres can be avoided at the end of the second year when the vehicle is traded in.

$\dfrac{£120}{2 \text{ years}} = \underline{£60}$

Tyres will move in a step function and are therefore classified as semivariable costs. (The way a person drives and road conditions have been ignored.)

(b) One possible way would be to charge a proportion of the total cost which reflects the mileage expected to be covered.

$$£2,188 \times \frac{1,800 \text{ miles}}{18,000 \text{ miles}} = \underline{\underline{£218.80}}$$

A more likely way is to ignore fixed costs and consider only the variable costs. Tyre costs for this purpose would be treated as variable costs.

$$\text{Tyre costs} = \frac{£120}{30,000 \text{ miles}} = 0.4\text{p/mile}$$

Repair costs $= 0.6\text{p/mile}$

$$\text{Petrol costs} = \frac{4\text{p/mile}}{5\text{p} \times 1,800 \text{ miles}} = \underline{\underline{£90}}$$

Perhaps a charge between £90 and £218·80 would be made depending on whether the firm wishes to use the availability of a car as a perk in order to motivate the salesman.

(c) If the car is used for the journey to Ireland, the relevant costs are the variable costs — petrol and oil 4p/mile and repairs 0·6p/mile, i.e. 4·6p/mile. The fixed costs and tyre replacement costs* are irrelevant as they will be unaffected by the 502 miles (return trip), and are therefore not incremental (additional) costs.

502 miles @ 4·6p/mile	=	£23
Ferry charge	=	£35
		£58

This is cheaper than the £60 air fare. However, qualitative benefits of air transport should be considered, and these include the speed, convenience and the prestige of flying.

Perhaps these benefits outweigh the small savings in travelling costs of £2 (£60 − £58).

2.

(a) *Diagram A* illustrates a variable cost, that is, one which varies with the level of activity. The variability here is directly proportional as shown by the linear relationship. Examples of variable costs include direct material, direct labour and direct expenses.

Diagram B could represent a firm's total costs, being the sum of its fixed and variable costs, or an individual cost which has a fixed and variable element. The latter is called a semivariable or mixed cost. Examples include maintenance costs and telephone costs consisting of a fixed rental and variable costs relating to the number of calls made.

Diagram C shows a decreasing variable cost. The straight lines could be smoothed out to produce a curvilinear relationship. An example is the purchase of raw materials where discounts are obtained on quantities in excess of a certain level of purchase, e.g. £10/kg for the first 2000 kg, £8/kg for the next 2000 kg and £7/kg for any further supplies.

---

*The additional 502 miles would not cause a second replacement set in the two-year period.

Diagram D illustrates a step-cost or (semi-fixed cost). It is a cost which is fixed over a certain level of activity, but increases by a fixed amount when activity rises above this level. Examples include most fixed costs — salaries, rent and depreciation. Some variable costs, such as raw materials, ordered in economic batch quantities, also fall into this category. However, the steps are too small to be significant:

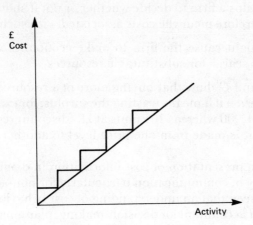

Diagram E shows a cost which is initially fixed, and then behaves in a variable fashion. An example could be the hiring of machine where a certain number of units can be made at no charge, that is, only the fixed charge is incurred. However, after this number has been exceeded, charges are incurred for additional units on a reducing scale.

Diagram F illustrates a variable cost which is incurred after a certain level of activity is achieved. Examples include overtime premiums or bonuses.

Diagram G shows a variable cost, whose straight lines could be smoothed out to produce a curvilinear function. This diagram is similar to that of *C*, except that in *G* discounts received in bulk purchases of raw materials are on every unit bought, including those in lower levels of units supplied.

Diagram H represents variable costs which are difficult to forecast, and therefore two cost functions have been drawn to show possible behaviour patterns.

Diagram I is an increasing variable cost, whose straight lines could be curvilinear. An example is where the purchase cost of a resource changes, as increases in activity, and therefore demand, for a limited supply increase the cost of the resource. Petrol requirements during an oil crisis would be characteristic of such a cost.

(b) A knowledge of major cost–volume relationships enables the management accountant to estimate budgeted costs of cost centres and thereby prepare budgets.

    Budgetary control and variance analysis are also facilitated, as by knowing cost behaviour the costs that should have been incurred, for a given actual level of activity, can be estimated. The diagrams in part (a) of the question provide the following assistance:

Diagram H is useful in a breakeven analysis situation, where uncertainty exists, and sensitivity analysis can be used to appraise the situation in the event of the higher and lower cost existing.

Diagram D helps a firm to decide whether or not it should increase its activity level and therefore incur the costs associated with such an increase.

Diagram I might cause the firm to make economies with respect to scarce resources, or search for substitutable resources.

Diagrams C and *G* show that buying more of a resource may be cheaper than buying less, even if it means wasting the surplus; for example, 100 units at £10 would cost £1,000 whereas 101 units at £8 (discount received) only cost £808. As movement is made from one price level to another, the average unit cost falls.

The above presentation of cost information in diagrammatical form is an excellent way of communication particularly for non-accountants.

It can be seen that an understanding of cost behaviour is invaluable to the management accountant for decision-making, planning and control purposes.

COST ESTIMATION

3.

Output (tonnes) = x Overheads (£) = y

Σx	Σy	Σx^2	Σy^2	xy
120	770	14,400	592,900	92,400
150	820	22,500	672,400	123,000
160	810	25,600	656,100	129,600
170	830	28,900	688,900	141,100
200	960	40,000	921,600	192,000
170	900	28,900	810,000	153,000
200	940	40,000	883,600	188,000
200	950	40,000	902,500	190,000
180	940	32,400	883,600	169,200
160	870	25,600	756,900	139,200
140	800	19,600	640,000	112,000
150	820	22,500	672,400	123,000
140	790	19,600	624,100	110,600
Σx 2,140	Σy 11,200	Σx^2 360,000	Σy^2 9,705,000	Σxy 1,863,100

Number of observations: $n = 13$

Using the normal equations:

(1) $\Sigma y = na + b\,(\Sigma x)$

(2) $\Sigma xy = a\,(\Sigma x) + (b\Sigma x^2)$

Substituting the above values:

(1) $11,200 = 13a + 2,140b$

(2) $1,863,100 = 2,140a \leqslant 360,000b$

Multiply equation (1) by 2,140 and equation (2) by 13:

(1) $23,968,000 = 27,820a + 4,579,600b$

(2) $24,220,300 = 27,820a + 4,680,000b$

Subtract (1) from (2):

$252,300 = 100,400b$

$b = 2\cdot513$

Substitute $2\cdot513$ for b in (1):

$11,200 = 13a + 2,140\,(2\cdot513)$

$\quad\quad\ = 13a + 5,377$

$a = 447\cdot9$

The estimated overhead costs are £447·9 + £2,513 per tonne.

OVERHEAD AND ABSORPTION COSTING PRINCIPLES

4.

(a) The most suitable procedure for apportioning overhead costs would be to distinguish machine costs from other costs:

		Departmental apportionment		
Expense	*Basis*	*Total*	*Department A*	*Department B*
Rent, heat, light	Floor area	£1,500	£750	£750
Supervision	Actual	600	250	350
Indirect labour	Actual	500	350	150
		£2,600	£1,350	£1,250
Depreciation	Plant values	500	400	100
Power	hp hours (see workings)	400	353	47
Repairs to machinery	Actual	175	122	53
		£1,075	£875	£200

In each department, machine costs can now be apportioned on the basis of a machine hour rate, and other costs on the basis of a direct labour/hour rate.

These rates would be:

	Department A		Department B
Machine hour rate	$\dfrac{£875}{25{,}000 \text{ hours}}$		$\dfrac{£200}{5{,}000 \text{ hours}}$
	= 3·5p	=	4p
Labour hour rate	= $\dfrac{£1{,}350}{30{,}000 \text{ hours}}$		$\dfrac{£1{,}250}{50{,}000 \text{ hours}}$
	= 4·5p	=	2·5p

Workings

Calculation of horsepower-hours	Department A		Department B
Total machine horsepower	300		100
Number of machines	2		1
Average machine horsepower	150		100
Machine hours worked	25,000		5,000
Total horsepower hours	3,750,000		500,000
Apportionment of costs	7·5	:	1
i.e.	$\dfrac{15}{17}$	:	$\dfrac{2}{17}$

(b) The apportionment of overheads in part (a) which was made on the basis of the information given can be criticised on the grounds that if the information is to be used for decision-making purposes, the whole procedure of overhead apportionment is inappropriate.

   If it is to be used for control information, then the bases chosen may be equally unsuitable, on the grounds that different bases of apportionment will give different absorption rates.

(i) The apportionment of rent, heat and light on the basis of floor area implies that each square foot gives service of the same value as every other.

(ii) The apportionment of depreciation on the basis of plant values disregards differences in the extent to which different pieces are subjected to wear and tear.

(iii) A basic machine hour rate for power costs within each department implies that the machines within a department consume equal quantities of power per hour.

No distinction is made between fixed and variable expenses. Avoidable costs will tend to be obscured by the calculations.

   A fall in the level of production would result in an increase in the overhead rate. If this cost were passed on to customers it might cause a further fall in production as a result of increased prices. This effect would be cumulative.

(c)

	Department A		Department B		Total	
	Total cost	Unit cost	Total cost	Unit cost	Total cost	Unit cost
Materials	£270	£0·27	£50	£0·05	£320	£0·32
Labour	2,500	2·50	4,000	4·00	6,500	6·50
Overhead	156·25	0·156	149	0·149	305·25	0·305
	£2,926·25	£2·926	£4,199	£4·199	£7,125·25	£7·125

Workings

Overheads apportioned to batch X 252

	Department A			Department B
	£			£
Labour hour rate: 1,250 × 3·5p	43·75	600 × 4p		24
Machine hours rate: 2,500 × 4·5p	112·5	5,000 × 2·5p		125
Total overheads	£156·25			£149

(d) The main argument in favour of such cost accounting statements is that overhead costs must be recovered if the firm is to make a profit and the best way of recovering overhead costs is to charge each department and, ultimately, each product or job with a share of them.

However, these statements must not be used for decision-making purposes, as the apportionment of overheads leads to a total cost figure which will be misleading if it is used as a basis for decision-making. Different methods of overhead apportionment and absorption give different results, and this technique fails to distinguish adequately between fixed and variable costs.

5.

(a)

	General factory overhead	Service cost centres		Production cost centres	
		1	2	A	B
Budgeted overhead	£210,000	£93,800	£38,600	£182,800	£124,800
Factory overhead apportioned	(210,000)	10,500	21,000	31,500	147,000
(By floor area)	—	104,300	59,600	214,300	271,800

Service centre 1 apportioned (by number of personnel)	(104,300)	—	91,262	13,038

$63:9$ i.e. $\dfrac{7}{8}:\dfrac{1}{8}$ —

Service centre 2, apportioned (by usage in hours)	59,600	305,562	284,838
$4:24$ i.e. $\dfrac{4}{29}:\dfrac{25}{29}$	(59,600)	8,221	51,379
	—	£313,783	£336,217
Budgeted direct labour hours		120,000	20,000
Revised overhead absorption rates		£2·61/hour	£16·81/hour

	A	B
Current overhead absorption rates	£3·10	£11·0
Revised overhead absorption rates	£2·61	£16·81
% change on current rates	(15·8%)	52%

(b) The large changes are owing to the following reasons:

(i) The basis for absorbing overhead is budgeted labour hours instead of normal activity for labour hours.

(ii) Fixed and variable overheads have not been distinguished.

(iii) There is a significant increase for A, and decrease for B, in the activity levels (in direct labour hours) used.

(c) *The algebraic approach*

Let a = Total overhead charge to department 1 after allotment from department 2

$$\therefore \quad a = £104,300 + \frac{1}{30}\,{}^{*}\,b \left[\begin{array}{l} {}^{*}Based\ on\ hours \\ 1,000\ \text{hours} : 4,000\ \text{hours} : 25,000\ \text{hours} \end{array} \right]$$

Let b = Total overhead charge to department 2 after allotment from department 1

$$\therefore \quad b = £59,600 + \frac{1}{5}\,{}^{*}\,a \left[\begin{array}{ccc} {}^{*}Based\ on\ personnel \\ 18 : 63 : \ \ 9\ or \\[4pt] \dfrac{2}{10} \quad \dfrac{7}{10} \quad \dfrac{1}{10} \end{array} \right]$$

$\therefore$ By substitution: $b = £59,600 + \dfrac{1}{5}\left(£104,300 + \dfrac{1}{30}b\right)$.

$$\therefore b = £59,600 + £20,860 + 0.0067b$$

$$\therefore 0.9933b = £80,460$$

$$\therefore b = \underline{£81,000}$$

$$\therefore a = £104,300 + \left(\frac{1}{30} \text{ of } £81,000\right) = \underline{£107,000}$$

	Service cost centres		Production cost centres	
	£ 1	£ 2	£ A	£ B
Charges by	104,300	59,600	214,300	271,800
Service 1	$(107,000) \rightarrow \frac{2}{10}$ 21,400	$\frac{7}{10}$ 74,900	$\frac{1}{10}$ 10,700	
Service 2	$\frac{1}{30}$ 2,700 $\leftarrow$	$(81,000) \rightarrow \frac{4}{30}$ 10,800	$\frac{25}{30}$ 67,500	
	—	—	£300,000	£350,000
Budgeted direct labour hours			120,000	20,000
Absorption rates			£2·50/hour	£17·50/hour

(d) *Note: The following points should be noted:*

For decision-making purposes a distinction should be made between fixed and variable overheads when allocated to cost centres, that is, fixed and variable absorption rates should be calculated.

Methods which recognise the existence of reciprocal services as in (c) should be used.

The use of a direct labour rate in production cost centre A is appropriate as it is labour-intensive, but centre B, which is highly mechanised, may require a machine hour rate.

Service cost centre 1 has low fixed costs and yet the basis for its cost apportionment is number of personnel. Direct labour hours would be a more appropriate basis.

Service cost centre 2 has high fixed costs and yet its costs are charged to other departments on the basis of services used, which seems more suitable for allocating variable costs. The main problem with the plant maintenance centre is that work undertaken by it may be attributable to past or future (preventive) operating activity.

The plant maintenance fixed costs may be apportioned on the basis of services made available as opposed to services used by other centres. Its variable costs could be charged out on a machine hour rate.

MARGINAL AND ABSORPTION COSTING

6.

Waverley Co. Ltd.

(a) *Absorption costing based on labour hours as absorption basis*

Year 1 (£000s)	A	B	C	Total
Sales	192	192	48	432
Costs	144	160	28	332
Profit	48	32	20	100
Year 2				
Sales	192	120	144	456
Costs	144	100	84	328
Profit	48	20	60	128

Absorption costing based on machine hours as absorption basis

Year 1 (000s)	A	B	C	Total
Sales	192	192	48	432
Costs	144	128	44	316
Profit	48	64	4	116
Year 2				
Sales	192	120	144	456
Costs	144	80	132	356
Profit	48	40	12	100

Direct costing

Year 1 (000s)	A	B	C	Total
Sales	192	192	48	432
Direct costs	48	64	12	124
Contribution	144	128	36	308
Total fixed costs				280
Profit				28
Year 2				
Sales	192	120	144	456
Direct costs	48	40	36	124
Contribution	144	80	108	332
Total fixed costs				280
Profit				52

(b) Summary of main points is:

   (i)   In direct costing fixed costs are regarded as *time* related and are therefore written-off in the period in which they are incurred irrespective of production or sales levels, whereas absorption costing attempts to match the fixed overhead with the actual production.

   (ii) Varying methods are available in absorption costing to apply fixed overhead to production, and where there is more than one product particular problems are caused. Considerations as to choice include:

   ease of application,
   cost benefit from using sophisticated methods,
   extent to which costs move in sympathy with absorption basis.

   (iii) Reasons in this example why the two absorption methods produce different results are:

   the different use that each product makes of labour and machine hours,
   the sales-mix changes between products.

   (iv) Only point of similarity is that product A produces the same profit under both absorption methods because both methods allocate the same fixed overhead per unit to A.

   (v)   Possible improvement: to break down the fixed overhead into that relating to manual operations and that relating to machine. Instead of a single fixed overhead recovery rate one would then have two.

(c) Additional expenditure = variable cost.

	A	B	C	Total
		Products		
Additional production (units)	6,000	4,000	2,000	
Variable costs per unit	£2	£4	£3	
Incremental cost	£12,000	£16,000	£6,000	£34,000

At a cost of 12% per annum, the cost of financing this would be:

$$\frac{12}{100} \times £34,000 = \underline{£4,080}$$

Workings to part (a)

(i) *Total labour and machine hours*

			A	*B*	*C*	*Total*
			Product			
Quantity			*30,000*	*20,000*	*10,000*	
Labour hours	— per unit		2	3	2	
	total		60,000	60,000	20,000	140,000
Machine hours	— per unit		1	1	2	
	total		30,000	20,000	20,000	70,000

(ii) *Recovery rates for fixed overhead*

$$\text{Labour hours} \quad : \quad \frac{£280,000}{140,000} \text{ hours} \; = £2 \text{ per hour}$$

$$\text{Machine hours} \quad : \quad \frac{£280,000}{70,000} \text{ hours} \; = £4 \text{ per hour}$$

(iii) *Cost per unit*

Product A	Variable cost £	Fixed cost £	Total cost £
Absorption (labour hours)	2	4	6
Absorption (machine hours)	2	4	6
Direct	2	—	—
Product B			
Absorption (labour hours)	4	6	10
Absorption (machine hours)	4	4	8
Direct	4	—	—
Product C			
Absorption (labour hours)	3	4	7
Absorption (machine hours)	3	8	11
Direct	3	—	—

7.

Preliminary workings

(a) In 19X0 and 19X1 the fixed overhead rate $= \dfrac{£600,000}{400,000}$ hours $= £1\!\cdot\!50/\text{hour.}$

Overall rate	=	£2·10
Fixed rate	=	£1·50
∴ Variable rate	=	£0·60

(b) In 19X2 and 19X3 the overhead absorption rate increased to £3·60.

$\therefore$ Overall rate   =   £3·60

     Variable rate   =   £0·60   (since efficiency levels are constant)

$\therefore$ Fixed rate   =   £3·0

$$\frac{\text{Budgeted fixed overhead}}{\text{New rate}} = \frac{£600{,}000}{£3} = 200{,}000 \text{ hours} - \text{output volume}$$

(c) Note that the above *fixed* rates apply in stock values at the following times: 19X1 and beginning of 19X2 (£1·50); end of 19X2 and all 19X3 (£3·0).

(d) Analysis of costs into fixed and variable costs.

	19X1		19X2 and 19X3	
	£		£	
*Variable cost/hour	3·5	$\frac{7}{10}$	3·5	$\frac{7}{13}$
Fixed cost/hour	1·5	$\frac{3}{10}$	3·0	$\frac{6}{13}$
Total cost/hour	5·0	100%	6·5	100%

*As the stock levels at 31 December 19X3 and 1 January 19X1 are the same, the difference in value must be owing to the increased fixed overhead rate.

Stock at end of 19X3	£130,000
Stock at beginning of 19X1	£100,000
Difference	£30,000 = 20,000 hours

Increase in fixed rate   £1·50 (£3 − £1·50)

	Hours of production	Total	Fixed	Variable
Therefore stock —				
beginning of 19X1	20,000 hours	£100,000	(20,000 × 1·5)	
			= £30,000	$\therefore$ £70,000
Therefore stock —				
end of 19X3	20,000 hours	£130,000	(20,000 × 3·0)	
			= £60,000	$\therefore$ £70,000

$$\text{Therefore } {}^{*}\text{variable overhead cost/hour} = \frac{£70{,}000}{20{,}000 \text{ hours}} = {}^{*}£3\text{·}50/\text{hour}$$

Production valuations for:

Opening stock	£ 19X1	£ 19X2	£ 19X3
Variable cost $\frac{7}{10}$	70,000 $\frac{7}{10}$	140,000 $\frac{7}{13}$	192,500
Fixed cost $\frac{3}{10}$	30,000 $\frac{3}{10}$	60,000 $\frac{6}{13}$	165,000
Total cost	100,000	200,000	357,500

Production			
Variable cost $\frac{7}{10}$	700,000 $\frac{7}{13}$	525,000 $\frac{7}{13}$	350,000
Fixed cost $\frac{3}{10}$	300,000 $\frac{6}{13}$	450,000 $\frac{6}{13}$	300,000
Total cost	1,000,000	975,000	650,000

Closing stock			
Variable stock $\frac{7}{10}$	140,000 $\frac{7}{13}$	192,500 $\frac{7}{13}$	70,000
Fixed cost $\frac{3}{10}$	60,000 $\frac{6}{13}$	165,000 $\frac{6}{13}$	60,000
Total cost	200,000	357,500	130,000

All workings have now been completed and a solution can be presented.

(a) Budgeted profit in 19X2   £128,750
      Budgeted loss in 19X3   (81,250)

                                        £210,000

Reasons are:

(i)   increase in overhead underabsorbed £(300,000 − 150,000)   = £150,000

(ii)   gain from low value of opening stock in 19X2 — based on rate
      of £1·50/hour instead of fixed rate of £3·0/hour.   = 60,000

                                        £210,000

(b) *Profit and loss accounts (on a marginal cost basis)*

	£ 19X1	£	£ 19X2	£	£ 19X3	£
Sales		1,350,000		1,316,250		1,316,250
Opening stock	70,000		140,000		192,500	
Factory cost	700,000		525,000		350,000	
	770,000		665,000		542,500	
Closing stock	(140,000)	(630,000)	(192,500)	(472,500)	(70,000)	(472,500)
		720,000		843,750		843,750
Fixed factory cost	600,000		600,000		600,000	
Administration						
and financial cost	220,000	(820,000)	220,000	(820,000)	220,000	(820,000)
Profit/(Loss)		£(100,000)		£23,750		£23,750

(c) When fixed overhead is underabsorbed the actual production volume is less than the budgeted production volume used to obtain the fixed overhead absorption rate. The advantage of increasing this rate will be to reduce the budgeted volume to a level similar to current actual volume.

  However, the danger of this approach is that because the company uses cost-plus pricing, the increase in fixed overhead absorbed will result in an increase in the full production cost per unit and hence in the sales price per unit.

  The increased selling price may cause a fall in demand, which could (i) reduce actual production volume to less than the new budgeted production volume, thereby still causing underabsorbed fixed overheads; (ii) reduce overall contribution earned (that is, drop in sales volume may outweigh increase in unit sales price).

  Perhaps if a cost-plus pricing method is to be used, Miozip should take into consideration the price elasticity of demand.

(d) The main reason why most management accountants favour marginal costing is that it emphasises differential costs, that is, those costs which change at the margin. This facilitates such decisions as whether or not to produce a product, or the product mix to choose.

  The majority of businesses will employ full costing systems because: (i) they fear that marginal costing will result in prices being set which are too low and will not cover fixed costs in the long-run; (ii) full costing complies with SSAP 9 regarding stock valuation.

  Some firms incorporate both techniques in their accounting systems using each method for different purposes. Other companies use a full costing system and adjust these figures for decision-making purposes.

COST–VOLUME–PROFIT ANALYSIS

8.

(a) Total profit made last year = Contribution − fixed costs

Contribution = (selling price − variable costs) = (10,000 units × £3)
                                                       − £20,000

$$= £15 − £12$$
$$= £3* \qquad = £10,000$$

New variable costs:			£		£
	material	= 5 × 1·2		=	6
	labour	= 6 × 1·1667		=	7
	other direct costs	= 0·6 × 1·67		=	1
	variable overhead	= 0·4 × 1·25		=	0·50
					£14·50

New contribution required = Profit + fixed costs
                          = £10,000 + (£20,000 × 1·05)
                          = £31,000
£31,000 ÷ 10,000 units   = £3·1/unit
∴ The selling price   = variable cost + contribution
                          = £14·50 + £3·10 = £17·60

This is an increase of £2·60 on the previous price of £15 — that is, a 17·33%
increase, which is below 17·5%, the threshold above which price elasticity of
demand becomes relevant.

(b) Number of units to be sold = $\dfrac{\text{Fixed costs} + \text{profit}}{\text{Contribution/unit}}$

$$= \frac{£21,000 + £10,000}{£15 − £14·50}$$

old selling   new variable cost
price

$$= 62,000 \text{ units}$$

(c) Price elasticity of demand is the responsiveness of quantity demanded of
goods or services to any change in price.

   When quantity demanded increases less than proportionately as price falls,
causing total revenue to decrease, the product is described as inelastic.

   However, when quantity demanded increases more than proportionately to
decreases in price, causing total revenue to increase, the product is called
elastic, for example:

A 17·5% price increase on £15 = £17·625.

$\therefore$ If the price charged is slightly below this figure, say £17·62, then there is no effect on demand and total revenue = 10,000 units at £17·62 = £176,200.

However, if the price charged is an 18·5% increase on £15 = £17·77, quantity demanded drops by 2% from 10,000 to 9,800 units. Total revenue = 9,800 units × £17·77 = £174,146, i.e. product is inelastic.

Price elasticity of demand is an integral part of a firm's pricing policy.

9.

A Merchant Esq.
Merchant Trading Ltd.
London W1

Keypon and Ticket
London N1
Date

Dear Sir,

Analysis of Trading Results for the last two years

We have now concluded our analysis of your trading results for the past two years with a view to determining why the 15% increase in turnover produced an 8% increase in net profit. Our investigation confirms your assurance that prices during the whole of the second year were 10% higher than those of the previous year and also that the mix of sales was not significantly different.

(1) *Reconciliation of net profit for the two years*

Increase in sales volume	(*note 1*)	£10,000	
Increase in sales price	(*note 1*)	21,000	
Increase in turnover			£31,000
Increase in cost volume	(*note 2*)	8,000	
Increase in cost price	(*note 2*)	£21,000	
Increase in cost of goods sold			(29,000)
Increase in gross profit			2,000
Add: Decrease in operating expenses			500
Increase in net profit			£2,500

Note 1 — *Increase in sales*
At year 1 prices, year 2 sales would have been:

$$\frac{100}{110} \times £231,000 = £210,000$$

an increase of £10,000 or 5% volume and an increase of £21,000 due to price increases.

Note 2 — *Increase in costs*

Cost of goods sold based on year 1 costs would have been:

$$\frac{105}{100} \times £160,000 = £168,000$$

an increase of £8,000.

The purchase price increase must account for the remaining £21,000.

(2) The 20% gross profit ratio (£40,000 : £200,000) earned in year 1 was not maintained in year 2. The chief reason for this was that the increased cost of £21,000 was "passed on" directly to the customer without being marked up. Had the £21,000 earned the appropriate gross profit the trading results for year 2 would have been as follows:

Sales	£236,250	(100%)
Cost of goods sold	(189,000)	(80%)
Gross profit	47,250	(20%)
Operating expenses	(9,500)	
Net profit	£37,750	

(3) The net profit as calculated above shows an increase of more than 25% over that of the previous year. Net profit would normally show a greater rate of increase than gross profit, due to the fact that included in the operating expenses are a number of items of a fixed nature which do not necessarily increase as output increases.

(4) In order to avoid erosion of gross profit, selling prices need to be under constant review and any significant increases in purchase price should be appropriately marked up.

(5) A system of budgetary control should be implemented on a monthly basis. A budgeted operation statement should be prepared, against which the actual results should be detailed. This would lead to greater control as variances could be investigated as they occur.

Yours faithfully,

Keypon and Ticket

10.

(a) Profitability statement

	Current year	Following year proposals (a)	(b)
Capacity utilised	80%	100%	88%
Sales	£800,000	£950,000	£880,000
Variable cost of sales			
Direct material	200,000	261,250	229,900
Direct labour	160,000	170,000	153,000
Variable overhead:			
Material	40,000	51,500	45,320
Labour	36,000	39,000	35,100
Other	24,000	30,900	27,192
Total variable cost	460,000	552,650	490,512
Contribution	340,000	397,350	389,488
Deduct: Fixed overhead	100,000	95,000	95,000
Profit	£240,000	£302,350	£294,488

(b) (i) Profit/volume ratios

	Current year	Following year proposals (a)	(b)
	$\dfrac{£340,000}{£800,000} \times 100$	$\dfrac{£397,350}{£950,000} \times 100$	$\dfrac{£389,488}{£880,000} \times 100$
	$= 42 \cdot 5\%$	$= 41 \cdot 8\%$	$= 44 \cdot 3\%$

(ii) Net profit/turnover

$\dfrac{£240,000}{£800,000} \times 100$	$\dfrac{£302,350}{£950,000} \times 100$	$\dfrac{£294,488}{£880,000} \times 100$
$= 30 \cdot 0\%$	$= 31 \cdot 8\%$	$= 33 \cdot 5\%$

(iii) Labour productivity indices

| | *Current year* | *Following year proposals* | |
		(a)	(b)
$\dfrac{\text{Capacity utilised}}{\text{Labour utilised}}$ $= \dfrac{80\%}{100}$		$\dfrac{100\%}{100\%}$	$\dfrac{88\%}{90\%}$

Indices			*Index*
Current year	$= \dfrac{80}{100}$ (base year)	$=$	100
Following year proposals (a)	$= \dfrac{100}{100} \times \dfrac{80}{100} \times 100$	$=$	125
(b)	$= \dfrac{88}{90} \times \dfrac{100}{80} \times 100$	$=$	122·2

(c) *Comments*

It can be seen from the profitability statement that the net profits forecast for both of the proposals are an improvement over the current position.
    This is attributable to three factors:

(i)   The increase in sales volume

(ii)   The reduction in fixed overhead

(iii) The improvement in labour productivity.

In terms of net profit, proposal (a) is more attractive than proposal (b). On the other hand, the *rate* at which profit is being made is greater in (b) than in (a) as can be seen from both the profit/volume ratios and the net profit/turnover ratios. This higher rate in the expansion of profit is due mainly to the fact that unit selling prices are higher under (b) than under (a). To achieve the higher sales volume, however, prices have to be reduced, and due to the elasticity of customer demand, the greater volume more than compensates for the reduction in selling price.
    This latter effect can be seen in the labour productivity indices, and explains why the index for proposal (b) is lower than the index for proposal (a). In other words, a reduction in volume of 12% is to be offset by a reduction of only 10% in the labour force.

Workings

(1) Sales:

(a)	£800,000 $\times \dfrac{95}{100} \times \dfrac{125}{100}$	$=$	£950,000
(b)	£800,000 $\times \dfrac{110}{100}$	$=$	£880,000

(2) Direct materials:

(a) $£200,000 \times \frac{3}{4} \times \frac{125}{100} \times \frac{105}{100}$ =   £196,875

         $£200,000 \times \frac{1}{4} \times \frac{125}{100} \times \frac{103}{100}$ =   £64,375

                                                    £261,250

(b) $£200,000 \times \frac{3}{4} \times \frac{110}{100} \times \frac{105}{100}$ =   £173,250

         $£200,000 \times \frac{1}{4} \times \frac{110}{100} \times \frac{103}{100}$ =   £56,650

                                                    £229,900

11.

Arithmetical Engineering Co. Ltd.

(a) Process	A	B	C
Contribution	20p	15p	10p
Breakeven point	$\frac{£95,000}{20p}$	$\frac{£60,000}{15p}$	$\frac{£37,500}{10p}$
	= 475,000 units	= 400,000 units	= 375,000 units
Loss if no production (equal to fixed cost)	£95,000	£60,00	£37,500

The profit graph given in Fig. 30 shows that:

(i)   A is most profitable at volumes in excess of 700,000 units

(ii)   B is most profitable in the volume range 440,000 – 700,000 units

(iii)   C is most profitable up to 440,000 units

(iv)   Losses are made at volumes below 375,000 units in even the most favourable low volume process.

The process to be chosen depends on the budgeted production quantity, and the margin of safety required.

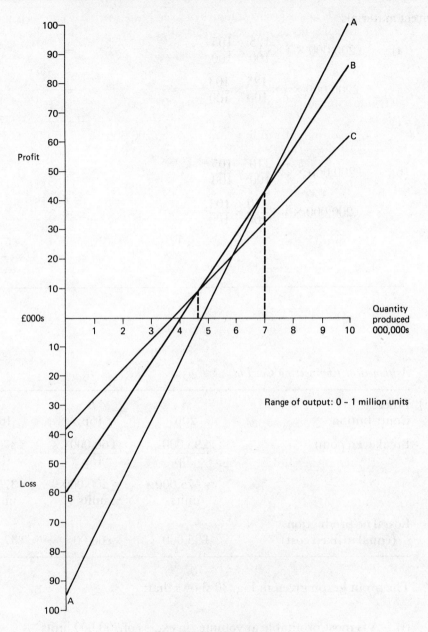

Fig. 30. *Profit graph.*

Tutorial note:

The following steps are necessary in constructing the profit graph (Fig. 30):

(i)   Determine maximum quantity to be shown on horizontal axis; this is one million razors.

(ii) Determine maximum values on vertical axis.

Maximum loss is greatest figure of fixed costs, which is £95,000. Maximum profit is found as follows:

	A	B	C
Contribution per unit	£0·20	£0·15	£0·10
Contribution at 1 million units	200,000	150,000	100,000
Deduct: Fixed costs	95,000	60,000	37,500
Profit	£105,000	£90,000	£62,500

Maximum value on vertical axis is therefore £105,000.

(iii) Mark both axes with suitable scales.

(iv) Draw profit/loss lines as follows:

    A loss £95,000 to profit £105,000
    B loss £60,000 to profit £90,000
    C loss £37,500 to profit £62,500

(b) *Other factors:*

  (i)   How reliable is the sales forecast?

  (ii) Do costs and revenues change as quantities change?

  (iii) How much capital employed is required for each process? Return on capital employed should be maximised.

  (iv) Do the volumes envisaged fit in with the other budgets (such as labour and material)?

  (v) Will sales of this product have any effect on other lines?

  (vi) What are the reliability, life and maintenance costs of machinery in each process?

(c) *See* Fig. 31.

Note: 1m units	Sales	£ 1,000,000
	Total costs — Variable	850,000
	Fixed	60,000
		£910,000

12.

(a) *Information provided by a breakeven chart*

A suitably drawn breakeven chart (an example is given in Fig. 31) will show:

(i)   profits and losses at various activity levels;

(ii) the breakeven point, that is, the activity level at which neither profit nor loss is made;

(iii) the contribution at various activity levels;

(iv) the margin of safety, that is, the sales volume between the breakeven point and the expected level of activity;

(v)   the sales volume necessary to yield a given profit;

(vi) the relationship between costs, sales and profits at various different levels of activity.

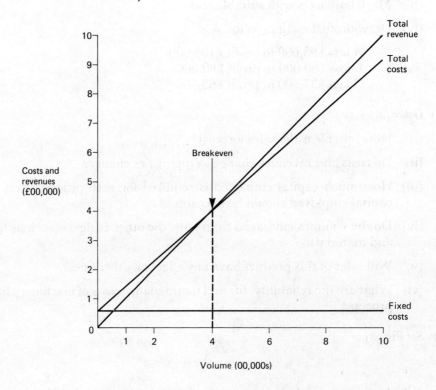

Fig. 31. *Breakeven graph for Process B.*

(b) *Assumptions underlying the construction of a breakeven chart*

(i)   fixed and variable costs can be accurately segregated;

(ii) cost behaviour and sales income have a linear relationship with the level of activity;

   (iii) semivariable costs can be reclassified into their fixed and variable elements;

   (iv) efficiency and productivity remain unchanged;

   (v) the analysis relates to one product only or to a constant mix of products;

   (iv) sales and production are equal;

   (vii) volume is the only factor which affects costs.

(c) *Usefulness of breakeven charts as an aid to planning*

As long as the assumptions referred to in part (d) below are borne in mind, the breakeven chart is a useful aid to planning. It has a number of specific uses, including:

   (i) showing the effect of suggested changes in selling prices by superimposing the appropriate sales lines;

   (ii) determining the effect of cost reduction programmes;

   (iii) assisting profit planning by determining the sales volume necessary to achieve a given profit;

   (iv) a pictorial or graphical representation often helps management's understanding of plans.

(d) *Usefulness in a multiproduct company*

The breakeven chart can be used in a multiproduct company if a constant product mix is assumed. An alternative graphical presentation is the profit–volume chart which shows the impact of changes in output on profit, and shows the information for each product separately.

13.

(a) The simple cost–volume–profit model assumes that stock levels are either nil or constant, and therefore profit is a function of sales.
       However, when a firm's sales volume differs from its production volume, and stocks are valued on a full cost basis then profit becomes a function of both sales and production, that is, two independent variables. Let us illustrate this point with an example; if sales are depressed, profit can be raised by increasing production and thereby stocks, which if valued on a full cost basis will inflate profits. Note that if stocks are valued at marginal cost then profit continues to be a linear function of sales.
       Because the conventional breakeven diagram is two-dimensional, it cannot cope with two independent variables, unless sales or production volume is held constant.

(b) It is unlikely that sales revenue function will be linear, because of the price elasticity of demand. Similarly, a total cost function will not be linear owing to economies and diseconomies of scale as output increases.
       Curvilinear sales and total cost functions can be plotted as in Fig. 32. This is often referred to as the economist's chart. Profit will be maximised when the

marginal revenue (the slope of the revenue curve) is equal to the marginal cost (the slope of the total cost curve). This can be determined by using the mathematical technique called calculus.

Although the above is a valid objection to the accountant's breakeven model, the latter will suffice over relevant ranges of output. It is difficult and time consuming to plot curvilinear functions accurately.

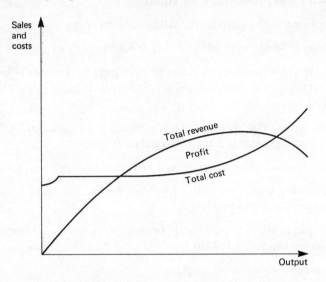

Fig. 32. *Sales and total costs functions.*

(c) It is assumed in the simple cost–volume–profit model that only one product is being sold, or if more than one then the sales mix is constant.

However, in reality, the sales mix will probably be continually changing owing to changes in demand.

A profit function will then take the following form:

$$P = (S_1 - V_1) X_1 + (S_2 - V_2) X_2 + (S_3 - V_3) X_3 \ldots (S_N - V_N) X_N - F$$

Where: P = profit, S = Selling price, V = variable cost, X = number and type of product, F = fixed costs, and N = number of product lines.

There are N independent variables, which the breakeven chart cannot cope with, but which a computer can.

(d) The conventional form of cost–volume–profit analysis does not incorporate the effects of uncertainty. However, sensitivity analysis can be applied to the variables in the breakeven model to ameliorate this situation.

Under this technique each variable in the model is manipulated, in turn, keeping all other variables constant. The effects of these movements on the final result (profit) are measured. If a small variation in a particular variable gives rise to a significant effect on the final result, then that variable is said to be sensitive and will warrant close observation.

Sensitivity analysis can be coupled with the probabilities for each variable, in order to provide a useful tool for decision-making under conditions of uncertainty.

DECISION-MAKING UNDER CONDITIONS OF CERTAINTY

14.

(a) (i)   *Absorption costing basis*

	Period 1		Period 2		Period 3	
Sales		£64,000		£72,000		£96,000
Opening stock		—	£12,000		£6,000	
Production costs:						
Materials, labour						
and variable						
overhead	£40,000		32,000		44,000	
Fixed overhead	20,000		16,000		22,000	
	60,000		60,000		72,000	
Less: Closing stock	12,000		6,000		—	
Cost of sales		48,000		54,000		72,000
Profit		£16,000		£18,000		£24,000

Note:
Over (under)absorption
of fixed overheads

		—		£(4,000)		£2,000

(ii)   *Marginal costing basis*

	Period 1		Period 2		Period 3	
Sales		£64,000		£72,000		£96,000
Opening stock		—	£8,000		£4,000	
Production costs:						
Materials, labour,						
and variable						
overhead	£40,000		32,000		44,000	
	40,000		40,000		48,000	
Less: Closing stock	8,000		4,000		—	
		32,000		36,000		48,000
Variable cost of sales						
contribution		32,000		36,000		48,000
Fixed overhead		20,000		20,000		20,000
Profit		£12,000		£16,000		£28,000

(b) The closing stock valuation under marginal costing will be lower than under absorption costing because of the method of dealing with the fixed overheads. In marginal costing the stock is valued on the basis of marginal costs only, in absorption costing an element of fixed overheads is included, resulting in a higher valuation. In the example in the question, in period 1 the closing stock valuation under absorption costing is £4,000 higher than under marginal costing. This represents 2,000 units at £2 — the fixed overhead element of £2 per unit.

The different in profit each period is directly related to the stock valuation, which in turn is directly related to the treatment of fixed overheads. A higher closing stock valuation has a direct effect on the period profit, in period 1, resulting in a difference of £4,000 between the two methods. The effect is that under marginal costing, fixed overheads are written-off in the period in which they arise, whereas underabsorption costing, a proportion of fixed overheads is included in the closing stock valuation and is therefore carried forward into the following period.

(c) SSAP 9 recommends that absorption costing, and not marginal costing, should be used in the preparation of financial accounts.

The introductory paragraph states:

> The applicable concept is the matching of cost and revenue in the year in which the revenue arises, rather than the year in which the cost is incurred.

This means that the stock valuation must include a proportion of the production overheads incurred which relate to that stock.

Paragraph 3 states that the "cost" of stock should comprise the expenditure which has been incurred in the normal course of business in bringing the product to its present location and condition. Such costs will include all related production overheads, even though they may accrue on a time basis.

In addition the overheads included will be based on the *normal level of activity*, taking one year with another.

15.

Easytune Radio Co. Ltd.

(a) *Operating statements*

   (i) *Absorption costing*

	Period 1	Period 2
Sales	£360,000	£420,000
Cost of goods sold:		
Variable costs of		
production	£288,000	£216,000
Fixed costs absorbed	72,000	54,000
	360,000	270,000
Add: Opening stock	—	90,000

	360,000	360,000
Deduct: Closing stock	90,000	45,000
	270,000	315,000
Gross profit	90,000	105,000
Deduct: Selling and distribution costs	20,000	20,000
Net profit	£70,000	£85,000
Note: Overhead over(under) absorbed	£12,000	(£6,000)

(ii) *Marginal costing*

Sales		£360,000		£420,000
Variable manufacturing cost of production	£288,000		£216,000	
Add: Opening stock	—		72,000	
	288,000		288,000	
Deduct: Closing stock	72,000		36,000	
Manufacturing cost of goods sold		216,000		252,000
Contribution		144,000		168,000
Deduct: Fixed costs:				
Manufacturing	60,000		60,000	
Selling and distribution	20,000		20,000	
		80,000		80,000
Net profit		£64,000		£88,000

Tutorial note: A more modern format for the operating statements is as follows:

	(i)		Period 1	Period 2
	Sales		£360,000	£420,000
	Deduct: Cost of sales		270,000	315,000
	Gross profit		90,000	105,000
	Deduct: Selling and			
	distribution costs		20,000	20,000
	Net profit		£70,000	£85,000
	Overhead over(under)-			
	absorbed		£12,000	(£6,000)

	(ii)			
	Sales		360,000	420,000
	Deduct: Cost of sales		216,000	252,000
	Contribution		144,000	168,000
	Deduct: Fixed costs:			
	Manufacturing	£60,000		£60,000
	Selling and			
	distribution	20,000		20,000
			80,000	80,000
	Net profit		£64,000	£88,000

Note: The full calculation of the cost of sales should be shown as workings.

(b) The difference between the two statements can be attributed to two factors:

(i)   The inclusion of fixed overheads in the valuation of stock in the absorption costing statement.

(ii) The fluctuation in the level of production away from the "normal" level.

If production has been at its "normal" level of 20,000 receivers in each period, there will have been no overabsorption or underabsorption of fixed production costs. In period 1 production was 4,000 receivers above the normal level, giving rise to an overabsorption of $4,000 \times £3 = £12,000$. In period 2 production was 2,000 receivers below the normal level, giving rise to an underabsorption of $2,000 \times £3 = £6,000$.

The inclusion of fixed production overheads in the stock valuation in the absorption costing statement effectively carries forward a proportion of the fixed production overheads from one period to the next. In period 1, the charge for fixed overheads for the period is £72,000, less the amount included in the valuation of stock — $6,000 \times £3$ (£18,000) — that is, £54,000, compared with the charge of £60,000 in the marginal costing statement.

The correct treatment of fixed production overheads in financial accounting is stated in SSAP 9 — *Stocks and Work-in-progress*. This states that:

(i) The applicable concept is the matching of cost and revenue in the year in which the revenue arises, rather than in the year in which the cost is incurred.

(ii) The "cost" should comprise that expenditure which has been incurred in the normal course of business in bringing the product or service to its present location and condition. Such costs will include all related production overheads, even though these may accrue on a time basis.

16.

Three assumptions about the machines used to manufacture Zippos must be stated before a definitive answer can be given:

(a) They would not be used for other work during the year.

(b) They would otherwise be used on their existing work and would be scrapped and replaced at the end of one year.

(c) They would have remained in service and would not have been sold.

These assumptions mean that there is no additional cost of using the machines to produce Zippos. In any case the machines will be used for one year and then replaced.

		£3·60		£3·10
Selling price of				
Sales revenue	15,000 @ £3·60	£54,000	22,000 @ £3·10	£68,200
	9,000 @ £1	9,000	2,000 @ £1	2,000
		63,000		70,200
Variable costs of manufacture (24,000 @ 70p)		16,800		16,800
Variable costs of assembly (15,000 @ 50p)		7,500	22,000 @ 50p	11,000
Opportunity cost from lost contribution (£ per unit)		15,000		22,000
Total variable costs		39,300		49,800
Contribution		23,700		20,400
Lease of factory		10,000		10,000
Other fixed overheads		1,000		1,000
Administration costs		5,000		5,000
Total fixed costs		16,000		16,000
Profit		£7,700		£4,400

Golden Ltd should manufacture 24,000 Zippos. If they are priced at £3·60, the market research study has suggested that 15,000 will be sold. The surplus of 9,000 sets of components can be sold to the supermarket at a price of £1 per set. The total additional contribution will then be £3,300.

Fixed overheads should not be included in the calculations unless they are affected by the decision — for example, the overheads which will be incurred in the new factory.

Tutorial note: If it is assumed that the fall in value of machinery is a relevant cost, both profit figures will be £4,000 lower.

17.

(a) The information shows that hiring the specialist machinery would be the most economical way of providing the machine capacity.

It may be possible to reduce the length of the period of hire, and therefore the cost, by one of the following methods:

(i)   Working overtime, and so completing the contract in three weeks instead of four, resulting in a saving of £300 in the hire costs. This may require payment of an overtime premium of, say, 50p per hour, or £80 over the total period of 160 hours. The net saving would be £220.

(ii) Introducing a second shift in order to produce the output in two weeks instead of four. In this case, the hire charge would be £800 (160 hours at £5 per hour). The cost of the shift premium would probably be 50p to £1 per hour, costing an additional £80 to £160. The net saving would therefore be £320 to £240.

The standard product has a 20% mark-up cost. This rate should be the company's minimum target for Wizard's modification.

Hire costs for machinery	£1,200
Labour costs (160 hours @ £1 per hour)	160
Cost of standard products	4,000
Total cost	5,360
Profit margin — 20%	1,072
Selling price suggested	£6,432
Minimum price per unit	£16·08

This price would allow for a normal profit for Witch Ltd. However, the management may decide that a higher price would be more appropriate to compensate for the disruption to normal production. On the other hand, as Wizard is a good customer a lower price may be quoted for a special job in order to retain the company's goodwill. The possibility of a regular order for the modification should be considered, along with the idea of putting the modification on general sale.

The Managing Director   Arthur, King & Co.
Witch Ltd.   Camelot Road
Merlin Road   London EC2
Tintagel   Date ....
Cornwall

Dear Sir,

Alternative sources of specialist machinery

The following information relates to the costs of the alternative methods of obtaining specialist machinery to enable you to modify your existing product to Wizard's specification. In the presentation of this information, labour costs have been omitted from the initial analysis as they are common to all alternatives.

(1)	*Adapting existing machinery*	
	Cost of adapting	£500
	Cost of reinstallation	600
	Maintenance (160 hours @ 50p per hour)	80
	Insurance (2% of £3,500)	70
		£1,250

Note: Insurance has been calculated assuming that the value of the machine is increased by the cost of adaptation.

(2)	*Hiring specialist machinery*	
	Hire charge — 4 weeks @ £300 per week	£1,200

Note: The variable charge of £5 per hour for 160 hours (£800) does not meet the minimum of £300 per week.

(3)	*Purchasing specialist machinery*	
	Loss in value from operation	
	(400 units @ £2 per unit)	£800
	Extra cost to cover transaction expenses —	
	10% of (£5,000 − £800)	420
	Maintenance (160 hours @ 50p per hour)	80
	Insurance (2% of £5,000)	100
		£1,400

In this case, the pricing policy should be examined carefully to determine whether economies of scale may result or whether the company can sustain its short-run pricing decision.

Yours faithfully,

Arthur, King & Co.

(b) If Wizard is likely to place a continuing order for the modified product, the costs of the three alternatives should be reappraised.

The cost of adapting existing machinery would be reduced by the £600 reinstalment cost. However, after three months it would be necessary to acquire an additional machine, which would probably cost about £10,000.

To hire the machine would cost a minimum of £300 per week and is not likely to be the most economical form of production in the long term.

The cost of purchasing specialist machinery will be proportionately the same, as the machine loses value at the rate of £2 per unit. The life of the machine should be considered in relation to the life of the project. The insurance costs per unit would be much lower, as the operating time is likely to be for a year.

18.

(a) (i)   The price to charge for material A for purposes of the special order must be the price that would otherwise have been received had the special order not been available, that is, the selling price prevailing at the time the order is executed. The current price is 6p per kg, but as the price is falling the company may find that when it is in a position to use the material, it is having to pay 5p per kg to have it removed. This negative price would then be the appropriate figure to use.

The price to charge for material A for the long-term manufacture of product 123 must depend upon future demand for the material and its availability, bearing in mind that it is a byproduct. If production of the new product is likely to absorb all the material normally available then adoption of a past weighted average price would be reasonable at the outset.

However, there may be insufficient material to meet future requirements, in which case suppliers' prices will need to be obtained.

(ii) As material B could be sold for 27p per kg this is the price to charge for the special order.

For further production the market price prevailing from time to time should be adopted. As this is currently 32p per kg this should be used in initial computations.

(iii) The current market price of material C is 51p per kg and as this is the nearest figure to a price which could be obtained if it were sold, the special order should be charged at this price. If known, the costs to be incurred in selling the material should be deducted.

The long-term price for material C needs to be estimated, since the figures quoted seem to suggest that the price is falling, that is, from a standard of 52p to an average of 50p. However, in the absence of additional information, the standard might be considered a reasonable assessment of the average of market price fluctuations.

(iv) The effect of using material D for the special order will be to incur costs of 72p per kg and therefore this is the price to charge.

The seasonal price variations will present difficulties in establishing a price to charge for future manufacture of product 123. It may be possible to plan production and purchasing arrangements so as to purchase when the price is low, and if necessary, maintain larger stocks. The cost of storage would then need to be taken into account in establishing an average price.

(b) When making a decision of this type you must distinguish between information which signifies a change in cash flows and that which does not.

(i) (1) *Conventional absorption cost statement*

Materials	"lush" (cost)		£1,000	
	"bulk"		1,000	
			——	£2,000
Labour	casual		600	
	supervision (100 hours @ £2)		200	
			——	800
Plant and machinery				
	depreciation $\dfrac{£5,000}{10}$			500
Overhead	100% casual labour costs			600
				——
		Total costs		£3,900

Conventional cost accounting may produce the above statement. On this basis the contract would not be entered into.

(2) *The relevant costs to consider in producing the cattle feed mix*

		Notes		
Materials	"lush"	1	£500	
	"bulk"	2	1,000	
			——	£1,500
Labour	casual	3	600	
	supervision	4	nil	
			——	600
Plant and machinery		5		nil
Overheads		6		nil
				——
				£2,100

The relevant costs are only £2,100, and the contract would, therefore, generate a surplus of £400.

Notes:

(1)   The opportunity cost of "lush" is that of its next best use — in this case, the realisable value. If the mix is not made the firm would be able to sell it for £500. This is the cost the firm is sacrificing if it produces the mix; the historical cost and replacement cost are irrelevant.

(2)   "Bulk" would have to be purchased for the contract at this price.

(3)   Casual labour would cost:

500 hours @ £1 per hour	£500
200 hours overtime @ 0·50p	£100
	£600

(4)   No additional cost will be incurred for quality control supervision as the supervisors are already paid a salary and able to cope with the additional work, so no extra cost is involved.

(5)   The machine has no scrap value and no other use. Thus is has no opportunity cost as its past costs are sunk costs; it does not increase the cost of producing the mix.

(6)   There are no overheads in producing the cattle mix; overheads remain unchanged whether the contract is accepted or not.

(ii)   The second approach only looks at those cash flows in and out of the firm which are changed by the decision to accept the contract. This is in contrast to the conventional approach.

The latter only considers marginal costs, so is essentially a forward-looking approach, whereas the use of the traditional approach is primarily a measure of historic costs so is unsuitable for decision-making, as this is a process concerned with the future rather than the past.

If, however, all contracts were entered into on the basis of a positive contribution, there is no guarantee that the aggregate contribution would cover the fixed overhead expenses of the business and give a satisfactory margin of profit.

19.

Rappup Ltd.

   (a) (i) *Price for new contract on absorption costing principles:*

Preservative — 1 can	$\frac{(£600,000)}{(50,000)}$	£12
Direct labour — 7 hours @ £1 per hour	$\frac{(£150,000)}{(150,000)}$	7
	Prime cost	19
Variable overhead — 7 hours @ £3 per hour	$\frac{£450,000)}{(150,000)}$	21
	Factory cost	40
Fixed overhead — $62\frac{1}{2}$% of factory cost		25
	Total cost	65
Profit 20% of total cost		13
	Price	£78

    (ii) and (iii)

In the budget for the six months ending 31 December, the contribution shown is as follows:

Fixed overhead	£750,000
Profit	390,000
Contribution	£1,140,000

This can be expressed as:

Contribution per can of material

$$\frac{£1,140,000}{50,000\ cans} = £22\cdot80\ per\ can$$

Contribution per direct labour hour

$$\frac{£1,140,000}{150,000} = £7\cdot60\ per\ hour$$

Prices for new contract assuming that major limiting factors are:

	(ii) Material	(iii) Direct labour
Factory cost as in (i) above	£40·00	£40·00
Contribution required:		
1 can @ £22·80 per can (see note)	22·80	—
7 hours @ £7·60 per hour (see note)	—	53·20
Price	£62·80	£93·20

Notes

(1) If direct material is the limiting factor, then minimum price is one which ensures that the same contribution will be obtained from material used for the new contract as would be obtained if the material had been used for orders in line with budget costs. It is assumed that it will not be possible to obtain additional material, and that fixed costs will not increase.

(2) If direct labour is the limiting factor, then the minimum price must ensure that each labour hour diverted to the new contract will provide the same contribution as per budget. This assumes that no additional labour will be available and that no increase will arise in fixed costs.

(b) *Price recommendations*

	Recommended price per fabrication (assuming no increase in fixed costs)
If delivery date for the new contact is:	
(i) 31 August	£94
(ii) 31 December	£63

The reasons supporting these recommendations (and reservations thereon) are set out in the notes below:

(i) Re: 31 August delivery date:

(1) The work involved in the new contract has a higher labour content than the production covered by the budget, that is, 7 hours to 1 can of preservative as opposed to the budget ratio of 3 : 1.

(2) If the new contract is to be completed by the 31 August the work will have to be done during the peak holiday months when it may be impossible to recruit additional labour. The price quoted should therefore provide at least the same contribution for every labour hour spent on the new work as would have been provided if the time had been spent on budgeted work.

(3) The price of £94 may not be competitive, although if Rappup Ltd. cannot obtain suitable labour in the summer months, then presumably neither can its competitors.

(4) The assumptions made in making this recommendation are:

(A) That the company will have no reserve labour capacity in the summer months, and additional labour cannot be obtained.

(B) That the proposed new contract is for a relatively large number of fabrications. If it is a small order only, then it might be possible to complete it without additional labour and, by working overtime, without diverting existing labour from other work. In this case, the price could be reduced.

(C) That the budget as prepared is in realistic terms in the sense that the company has firm orders or expectations which will utilise fully the labour hours available during the budget period. If this is not the case, then the company might welcome the new contract and might be willing to reduce the price and accept a lower contribution for the sake of securing a firm order.

(ii) Re: 31 December delivery date:

(1) If delivery date for the new customer is postponed to December, then the supply of labour will not be a limiting factor as there is no indication that it is scarce other than in the summer months.

(2) There is, however, consistent difficulty in obtaining regular supplies of material, regardless of the time of the year, and material therefore remains a major limiting factor. Assuming that it will be possible to provide additional labour for the new work, then the price must not be less than the figure of £63 calculated in (a) (ii) above on the basis of material as the limiting factor.

(3) The price of £63 does not, however, allow for any increase in fixed costs and it seems likely that additional labour will give rise to some additional fixed overheads, in which case an appropriate loading to the price should be made.

(4) Regard must be given to firm orders already received and to factory or workshop capacity. If the budget of 50,000 cans to be used during the budget period has been based on firm orders or on the known requirements of existing customers, then clearly it would not be possible to take on the new contract without the risk of not being able to satisfy existing customers. It is possible that despite difficulties in obtaining materials, production can be increased during the 6-month period to allow wholly or partly for the new contract. In this case the capacity of the workshop must be considered. No indication is given of this in the data. If additional capacity has to be taken on for the purpose of extra production, then consideration must be given to the effect on selling prices generally of the additional fixed costs arising.

If a large proportion of the budget relates to orders at an already fixed selling price, then it would be necessary to allow for the major proportion of the increased fixed costs in determining the price for the new work. This is, however, unlikely to give a price as high as the figure of £78 calculated in (a) (ii) above, where fixed costs have been added as a percentage (determined by the budget figures) of factory cost.

20.

(a) (i)   *KF Limited: Profit statement (in respect of budgeted production)*

	Product A	Product B	Product C	Total
Production (units)	10,000	5,000	6,000	21,000
Sales revenue	£500,000	£340,000	£540,000	£1,380,000
Deduct:				
Direct materials	100,000	150,000	120,000	370,000
Direct wages:				
Department 1	140,000	40,000	90,000	270,000
Department 2	50,000	30,000	60,000	140,000
Department 3	80,000	20,000	90,000	190,000
Variable overheads	30,000	10,000	30,000	70,000
Marginal costs	400,000	250,000	390,000	1,040,000
Contribution	100,000	90,000	150,000	340,000
Deduct:				
Total fixed overheads				200,000
Net profit				£140,000
Marginal cost per unit	£40	£50	£65	
Contribution per unit	£10	£18	£25	
Contribution per unit of limiting factor (1 hour of department 2 labour)	£4	£6	£5	

(ii)   The most profitable mixture should fully utilise the limiting factor, that
is, production would be related to the optimisation of the type of labour
required by department 2. Therefore the proposal should concentrate on
products B and C; any residue (up to maximum of 70,000 hours) being
made up by product A.

Product	Production in units	Department 2 Hours/product	Total hours
B	7,000	3	21,000
C	9,000	5	45,000
A	1,600	$2\frac{1}{2}$	4,000

(iii) *Profit statement (in respect of most profitable mixture)*

	Product A	Product B	Product C	Total
Production (units)	1,600	7,000	9,000	17,600
	£	£	£	£
Sales revenue	80,000	476,000	810,000	1,366,000
Deduct: Marginal costs	64,000	350,000	585,000	999,000
Contribution	16,000	126,000	225,000	367,000
Deduct: Fixed overheads				200,000
Net profit				£167,000

Tutorial note: The optimum level of production is calculated as follows:

Department 2 budgeted hours:

Product A	$10,000 \times 2\frac{1}{2}$	25,000
Product B	$5,000 \times 3$	15,000
Product C	$6,000 \times 5$	30,000
Total hours available		70,000

Maximising the contribution of the limiting factor:

Product B	$7,000 \times 3$	21,000 hours
Product C	$9,000 \times 5$	45,000 hours
Product A	$1,600 \times 2\frac{1}{2}$	4,000 hours
		70,000 hours

The number of units of product A to be produced is calculated as:

$$\frac{\text{Balance of hours of department 2}}{\text{Number of hours for each unit}} = \frac{4,000}{2\frac{1}{2}} = 1,600 \text{ units}$$

(b) Although the profit would increase by £27,000 if KF Ltd were able to produce *and sell* the alternative mixture of products, the attention of the directors should be drawn to the possibility of:

(i) the loss of customer goodwill in respect of (10,400) shortfall in production and sales of product A (that is, maximum level minus proposed level);

(ii) problems concerned with underutilisation of skilled labour and machine facilities associated with product A;

(iii) decrease in sales of product A may cause fall-off in sales of other products, particularly when customers buy combinations of two or three products.

21.

During two weeks of strike

Sales revenue lost (1,000 vehicles)		£500,000
Expenses avoided:		
Materials	£100,000	
Labour	50,000	
Fall in value of machinery	150,000	
Variable overheads	10,000	
Savings on overhaul	9,000	
		319,000
Contribution lost		£181,000

During week after strike

Additional sales revenue (500 vehicles)		£250,000
Expenses avoided:		
Materials	£50,000	
Labour (at time and a half)	37,500	
Fall in value of machinery	75,000	
Variable overheads	5,000	
		167,500
Contribution		£82,500

Summary

Contribution lost during strike period	£181,000
Increased contribution following strike	82,500
Total cost of the strike	£98,500

Tutorial notes:

(1) It is assumed that no payment is made to production labour during the period of the strike and that wage rates were not affected by the strike.

(2) The time depreciation of the machinery is unaffected by the strike. The only saving is in terms of user cost.

22.

(a) *Contribution by product* (£000s)

	V	W	Product X	Y	Z	Total
Sales revenue	4,400	4,900	6,500	5,100	9,100	30,000
Variable costs:						
Materials	(200)	(600)	(1,200)	(1,000)	(1,500)	(4,500)
Labour	(500)	(800)	(1,500)	(1,400)	(1,800)	(6,000)
Production variable overhead	(250)	(350)	(400)	(500)	(720)	(2,220)
Selling commission	(220)	(245)	(325)	(255)	(455)	(1,500)
Packaging	(200)	(100)	(200)	(100)	(300)	(900)
Transport	(100)	(300)	(600)	(500)	(500)	(2,000)
	1,470	2,395	4,225	3,755	5,275	17,120
Contribution	2,930	2,505	2,275	1,345	3,825	12,880
Allocated fixed costs:						
Production fixed costs	(100)	(200)	(350)	(300)	(50)	(1,000)
Advertising	(500)	(300)	(200)	(300)	(300)	(1,600)
	(600)	(500)	(550)	(600)	(350)	(2,600)
Net contribution to general overhead	2,330	2,005	1,755	745	3,475	10,280

General fixed (non-allocable) costs:

Production	(3,000)	
Stores	(450)	
Administration	(4,500)	
Transport	(450)	
		(8,400)
Profit		£1,880

Stopping the production of X and Y would cause the contributions from these products to be lost, namely:

X :	£1,725,000	
Y :	£745,000	
Reduction in profit	£2,470,000	

∴ Revised loss = £590,000.

(b) (i) *Effect on profit of advertising campaign* (£000s)

| | | | Product | | |
	V	W	X	Y	Z
40% of Contribution	1,172	1,002	910	538	1,530
Additional advertising	1,500	900	600	900	900
Change in profit	(328)	102	310	(362)	630

∴ Worthwhile to proceed with advertising campaign for products W, X and Z.

(ii) Incremental profit per £ of advertising:

	Rank	Funds
W : 102/900 = £0·113	3	—
X : 310/600 = £0·517	2	£300,000 (Bal.)
Z : 630/900 = £0·700	1	£900,000
		£1,200,000

∴ Increase in profit: Z : £630,000
X : £155,000

£785,000

(c)

| | Product (£000) | |
	V	W
Expected revenue	4,400	4,900
Contribution	2,930	2,505
Contribution per £	0·666	0·511
Increased sales	2,925	3,250
Increased contribution	1,948	1,661
Less: Contribution of X forgone	1,725	1,725
Benefit	223	(64)

∴ V should be substituted for X.

(d) An attributable fixed production cost is one that is "allocated" directly to a product/cost centre rather than having to resort to using arbitrary absorption basis, for example:

(i) wages of a supervisor specially employed on one product;

(ii) depreciation of specific machinery to one product.

23.

Intervero Ltd. — cost estimate

(a) *Material A*
2,000 units @ £20/unit £40,000
(this is a regular stock item which will necessitate
replacement)

Material B
200 units @ £20/unit 4,000
(this is the opportunity cost of not using B as a substitute
for another type of material and thereby saving £20/unit)

Other material and components 12,500
(incremental costs)

Direct labour
(Labour force are paid on a time basis regardless of whether
they are working. It is therefore not an incremental cost.)

Overhead departments
P — 200 hours @ £30 6,000
(£30 = £20 opportunity cost plus £10 incremental variable
cost)

Q — 400 hours @ £8 3,200
(incremental variable cost)

Estimating department .... —
(these sunk costs are irrelevant)

Planning department .... —
(these costs are not incremental)
$$\overline{\underline{£65,700}}$$

(b) The opportunity cost approach is relevant as the conventional pricing approach could overprice this contract by including costs which are unaffected by the decision at hand. This could result in the contract being lost and thereby the failure to utilise spare resources and make a contribution towards fixed costs.

   Problems associated with the use of the opportunity cost approach include the following:

(i) its misunderstanding by management;

(ii) its incompatibility with the company's conventional cost accounting system;

(iii) the difficulty in identifying all possible opportunitites and attributing values to these opportunities.

In practice traditional figures are used for control purposes, and the opportunity costs for setting the contract price.

24.

Styric plc

(a) *Y Division — profit and loss account for two years*

Sales revenue external		£440,000
internal		1,320,000
		1,760,000
Less: Costs:		
Direct material (80,000 units @ £15/unit)	£1,200,000	
Direct labour (£90,000 for 2 years = £180,000 + 10%)	198,000	
Variable overhead (80,000 units @ £3/unit)	240,000	
Fixed overhead (excluding depreciation)	570,000	
Depreciation	150,000	
		(2,358,000)
Loss		£(598,000)

(b) *Costs and benefits of closing down Y immediately*

	Costs	Benefits
Lost revenue from external sales	£440,000	
Lost revenue from internal sales	1,320,000	
Direct labour saved		£198,000
Variable overhead saved		240,000
Storage rental saved		20,000
Sale of equipment		50,000
Direct material saved (1,200,000 less 9/12 (450,000))		862,500
Revenue from sale of existing material (0·25 (9/12 (450,000)))		84,375
	1,760,000	
	(1,454,875)	1,454,875
Net cost if Y is shut down	£(305,125)	

Reconciliation of loss in part (a) with net cost in (b)

The net cost of shutting Y in part (b) is the estimated benefit if Y is kept open	+ £305,125
But in part (a) there is a projected loss if Y is kept open of	£598,000
The difference of	£903,125

can be explained as follows:

Relevant costs excluded from profit and loss:		
Lost proceeds from sale of machinery	£50,000	
Lost proceeds from sale of raw material held in stock	£84,375	
Warehouse rent of Z	£20,000	
		£154,375
Irrelevant costs included in the profit and loss:		
Cost of direct material in stock	£337,500	
Depreciation	£150,000	
Fixed overhead	£570,000	
		£1,057,500
		£903,125

DECISION-MAKING UNDER CONDITIONS OF UNCERTAINTY

25.

Allegro Finishes Ltd.

(a)			
Selling price	£70	£80	£90
Maximum demand (units)	75,000	60,000	40,000
Maximum revenue	£5,250,000	£4,800,000	£3,600,000
Variable costs	£3,750,000	£3,000,000	£2,000,000
Research and development (R & D) costs	250,000	250,000	250,000
Fixed costs	800,000	800,000	800,000
	£4,800,000	4,050,000	£3,050,000
Estimated profit	£450,000	£750,000	£550,000

The associated cost–volume–profit chart is given in Fig. 33.

The analysis assumes that the maximum demand can be obtained for each selling price. The best price is £80 and the optimum level of output is 60,000 units. It might be advisable to undertake sensitivity analysis in order to evaluate the effects of changes, for instance, in levels of demand.

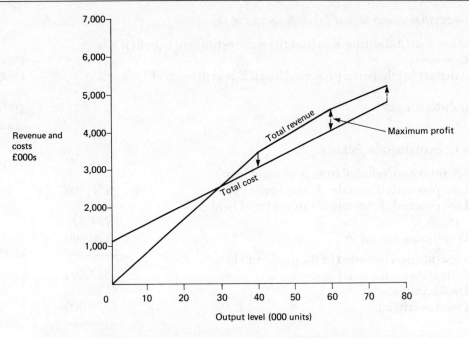

Fig. 33. *Cost–volume–profit chart for Allegro Finishes Ltd.*

(b)

	Annual demand	Probability		
Pessimistic	20,000	0·2	=	4,000
Most likely	35,000	0·7	=	24,500
Optimistic	40,000	0·1	=	4,000
		Expected demand	=	32,500 units

	Variable cost	Probability		
	£50	0·1	=	£5
	55	0·7	=	38·5
	60	0·2	=	12
	Expected variable cost		=	£55·5

Selling price	£90			
Variable cost	55·5			
Contribution	£34·5 × 32,500 units		=	1,121,250
Less: Fixed costs				1,050,000
Expected profit				£71,250

(c)

Demand 000s	Unit contribution	Total contribution £000s	Probability
20	£30	600	(0·2) (0·2) = 0·04
20	35	700	(0·2) (0·7) = 0·14
20	40	800	(0·2) (0·1) = 0·02
35	30	1,050	(0·7) (0·2) = 0·14
35	35	1,225	(0·7) (0·7) = 0·49
35	40	1,400	(0·7) (0·1) = 0·07
40	30	1,200	(0·1) (0·2) = 0.02
40	35	1,400	(0·1) (0·7) = 0·07
40	40	1,600	(0·1) (0·1) = 0·01

		Prices		
Probability of a loss		£70	£80	£90
Greater than or equal to	£500,000	0·02	0	0
	£300,000	0·07	0·05	0·18*
	£100,000	0·61	0·08	0·20
	0	0·61	0·10	0·34

		Prices		
Probability of a profit		£70	£80	£90
Greater than or equal to	0	0·39	0·91	0·80
	£100,000	0·33	0·52	0·66
	£300,000	0·03	0·04	0·15
	£500,000	0	0·01	0·01
Expected profit/(loss)		(£55,750)	£68,500	£71,250

*Workings *0·18*
If total contribution is £600,000 and fixed costs are £1,050,000 then loss = £450,000.

If total contribution is £700,000 and fixed costs are £1,050,000 then loss = £350,000.

Both losses are greater than £300,000, therefore probability = 0·04 + 0·14 = 0·18.

From the above it can be seen that although the selling price of £90 yields the highest profit, it carries a 0·34 probability of not making any profit. However, the selling price of £80 yields almost as much profit as the higher price, and has a probability of only 0·10 of not making any profit. It is therefore the best of the alternatives, that is, the price of £80 is recommended.

Subjective discrete probability distributions have two main disadvantages:

(i)   their subjectivity and bias;

(ii) it would appear that there are no probabilities of a profit or loss occurring for figures in between those given. For example, for the £90 price there is a 0·18 probability of a profit greater than or equal to £300,000 and a 0·20 probability of a profit greater than or equal to £100,000 but no probability of a profit between these two figures.

(d) Although these changes would affect reported profits, they would not alter the pricing decision, as they are irrelevant costs. The change in allocated fixed overhead is not an incremental cost, and the change in the research and development policy is irrelevant as such costs are sunk costs and will not affect the pricing decision.

26.

Central Co. Ltd.

(a) *Expected monetary value of each alternative* (£000s)

(i)   *SP of £15*

No contract

Quantity	Rev.	Variable cost	Materials	Fixed cost	Material sales	Profit	Probability	Estimated monetary value
20	300	100	160	50	—	− 10	0·1	− 1
30	450	150	240	50	—	10	0·6	6
40	600	200	320	50	—	30	0·3	9
								14

Contract for at least 40,000 kg

Quantity	Rev.	Variable cost	Materials	Fixed cost	Material sales	Profit	Probability	Estimated monetary value
20	300	100	150	50	—	0	0·1	0
30	450	150	225	50	—	25	0·6	15
40	600	200	300	50	—	50	0·3	15
								30

Contract for at least 60,000 kg

Quantity	Rev.	Variable cost	Materials	Fixed cost	Material sales	Profit	Probability	Estimated monetary value
20	300	100	210	50	40	− 20	0·1	− 2
30	450	150	210	50	—	40	0·6	24
40	600	200	280	50	—	70	0·3	21
								43

(ii)   *SP of £24*

No contract

8	192	40	64	160	—	− 72	0·1	− 7·2
16	384	80	128	160	—	16	0·3	4·8
20	480	100	160	160	—	60	0·3	18·0
24	576	120	192	160	—	104	0·3	31·2

46·8

Contract for at least 40,000 kg

8	192	40	150	160	48	− 110	0·1	− 11·0
16	384	80	150	160	12	6	0·3	1·8
20	480	100	150	160	—	70	0·3	21·0
24	576	120	180	160	—	116	0·3	34·8

£46·6

Note: It is not worth considering the final alternative (SP of £84, purchase at least 60,000 kg) as it is totally "dominated" by the last alternative above, that is, every profit figure is greater.

(b) *Summary of strategies*

SP	Purchase	*Estimated monetary value*	*Worst outcome*	*"Desirability"*
£15	None	£14,000	− £10,000	32
	40,000 kg	£30,000	0*	90
	60,000 kg	£43,000	− £20,000	109*
£24	None	£46,800*	− £72,000	68·4
	40,000 kg	£46,600	− £110,000	29·8

(c) (i)   Other factors might include:

risk levels of each alternative
risk attitudes of the company
availability of supplies
compatibility of the product with the company's existing products and marketing plans.

(ii)   The estimated monetary value ignores extreme values and does not take risk into account. The "best of the worst" outcome is very much a pessimistic view. The desirability test is an attempt to blend the features of each of these together to attempt to limit the requirements of the company. It must be, to a large extent, arbitrary but may well prove useful, not in isolation, but when compared with the other criteria.

Workings to part (a)

Realisable value of excess materials

	16,000 kg +		16,000 kg −
Sales price		£2·90	£2·40
Less: Packaging	£0·30		£0·30
Delivery	0·45		0·45
Insurance	0·15		0·15
		0·90	0·90
Realisable value		£2·00 per kg	£1·50 per kg

PRICING DECISIONS

27.

French Ltd.

(a) *Overhead recovery rates*

	Product			Rate
	X	Y	Total	per hour
Labour hours	40,000	80,000	120,000	£6
Machine hours	160,000	20,000	180,000	£4

(i) *Cost per unit*

Recovery based on labour hours £(000s)

	X	Y
Direct labour	200	280
Direct materials	240	160
Allocated overhead	120	280
General overhead	240	480
Total cost	800	1,200
Units produced	40,000	10,000
∴ Cost per unit	£20	£120
∴ Price (cost + 20%)	£24	£144

Recovery based on machine hours (£000s)

	X	Y
Direct labour	200	280
Direct materials	240	160
Allocated overhead	120	280
General overhead	640	80
Total cost	1,200	800
Units produced	40,000	10,000
∴ Cost per unit	£30	£80
∴ Price (cost + 20%)	£36	£96

(ii) *Profit and closing stock valuations*

(iii) *Labour hour recovery method (£000s)*

	X		Y		Total
Revenue		864		1,008	1,872
Opening stock	0		0		0
Production costs	800		1,200		2,000
	800		1,200		2,000
Less: Closing stock	80		360		440
		720		840	1,560
Profit		144		168	312

Machine hour recovery method (£000s)

	X		Y		Total
Revenue		648		960	1,608
Opening stock	0		0		0
Production costs	1,200		800		2,000
	1,200		800		2,000
Less: Closing stock	660		0		660
		540		800	1,340
Profit		108		160	268

(b) The variations above in prices and quantities from using varying cost allocation methods reflect the elasticity of demand for both products. Cost-plus pricing is therefore, in this case, *not* desirable because of the sensitivity of sales volumes to prices, and no guarantee of having reached an "optimum" price can be given.

(c) French Ltd. should maximise:

   (i) sales revenue for year 1, plus

   (ii) opportunity value of closing stock (based on revenue or savings to be realised in year 2), *less*

   (iii) total costs incurred.

Optimum prices for year 1 — Product X

			Closing stock	Case I		Case II	
Price	Quantity	Revenue	Quantity	Closing stock	Total	Closing stock	Total
£	000s	£000s	000s	£000s	£000s	£000s	£000s
24	36	864	4	44	908	120	984
30	32	960	8	88	1,048	240	1,200
36	18	648	22	242	890	660	1,308
42	8	336	32	352	688	960	1,296
Product Y							
96	10	960	0	0	960	0	960
108	10	1,080	0	0	1,080	0	1,080
120	9	1,080	1	44	1,124	130	1,210
132	8	1,056	2	88	1,144	260	1,316
144	7	1,008	3	132	1,140	390	1,398
156	5	780	5	220	1,000	650	1,430

Pricing strategy:

Case I   —   X £30 per unit   Case II   —   X £36 per unit
               Y £132 per unit   Y £156 per unit

28.

Exco

(a) The fixed overhead per unit of Exco $= \dfrac{£60,000}{15,000 \text{ units}} = £4/\text{unit}$

$\therefore$ the variable cost per unit $= £12 - £4 = £8$

$\therefore$ Contribution per unit $= £16 - £8 = £8$

and contribution per hour of finishing time $= \dfrac{£8}{1 \text{ hour}} = \underline{£8/\text{hour}}$

Wyeco

Fixed overhead per unit of Wyeco $= \dfrac{\text{£}300{,}000}{30{,}000 \text{ units}}$ $= \text{£}10/\text{unit}$

$\therefore$ variable cost per unit $= \text{£}24 - \text{£}10 = \text{£}14$

$\therefore$ Contribution per unit $= \text{£}32 - \text{£}14 = \text{£}18$

and contribution per hour of finishing time $= \dfrac{\text{£}18}{\frac{1}{2}\text{ hour}} = \underline{\text{£}36/\text{hour}}$

Available hours

15,000 for making (30,000 units) Wyeco
15,000 for making (15,000 units) Exco
_____

30,000 hours
_____

Recommended mix

$\therefore$ Make maximum of Wyeco — $\underline{40{,}000}$ units needing 20,000 hours
                Exco   — $\underline{10{,}000}$ units needing 10,000 hours
                                                        _____

                                            30,000 hours
                                            _____

(b) *Exco price/sales:*

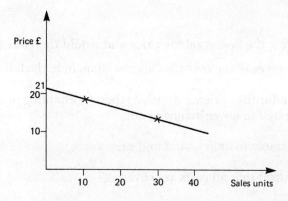

$P = 21 - 0.25x$, where $P =$ selling price of a unit of Exco
                      $x =$ demand for Exco

$\therefore TR = 21x - 0.25x^2$, where $TR =$ total revenue.

By using calculus $MR = 21 - 0.5x$, where $MR =$ marginal revenue.

The optimal level of output is where marginal cost equals marginal revenue,
i.e., $8 = 21 - 0.5x$.

$\therefore$ optimal output for Exco $= 26{,}000$ units
$\therefore$ optimal selling price $= \text{£}21 - (0.25 \times 26) = \text{£}14.50$

Wyeco price/sales

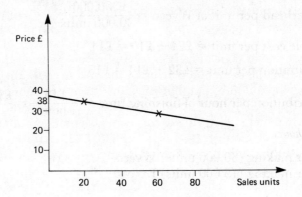

$P = 38 - 0.15y$, where P = selling price of a unit of Wyeco
y = demand for Wyeco

$\therefore TR = 38y - 0.15y^2$, where TR = total revenue.

By using calculus $MR = 38 - 0.3y$, where MR = marginal revenue.

The optimal level of output is where marginal cost equals marginal revenue,
i.e., $14 = 38 - 0.3y$

optimal output for Wyeco   = 80,000 units
optimal selling price   = £38 − (0.15 × 80) = £26·00
                                                 ===========

This is below the lowest selling price and would therefore be unacceptable.

(c) The advantages of the cost-plus approach include the following:

(i)   it standardises pricing decisions thereby enabling pricing decisions to be
      delegated to lower management;

(ii) it is simple to understand and easy to use;

(iii) it ensures that all costs are covered;

(iv) it justifies the selling price by clearly showing the firm's cost structure
      and profit margin — this is of particular importance when pricing for the
      public sector.

The "mark-up" element can be adjusted in order to reflect demand
considerations and competition. Also, overhead absorption rates used are
often derived from budgeted information (for example, direct labour hours)
which has estimated future demand.

   The theoretical approach assumes that profit maximisation is the firm's
overriding goal and that demand and cost functions can be easily found.

29.

Accountants and economists tend to start from different bases in their consideration of the price that should be charged for a product. The accountant places emphasis on cost whereas the economist mainly looks at demand. In their article, W. T. Baxter and A. R. Oxenfeldt state that one of their aims is to try and reconcile what they refer to as "the almost flatly contradictory views on pricing of the cost accountant and the economic theorist". However, it could be said that such an extreme opinion has become a non-issue for both the supply and the demand side must, even if only implicitly, be brought into the analysis when firms are trying to make an acceptable profit.

Writing in 1939, two economists, R. L. Hall and C. J. Hitch, brought to their readers' notice the fact that industrialists did not follow the economists' marginalist theory in their pricing policies. The industrialist was found to base his selling price on what Hall and Hitch termed "full cost". The aim of the industrialist in this was to cover the full production costs and add on some "fair profit" to produce a "just price".

Basically, this approach of full cost-plus pricing can be shown diagrammatically as follows:

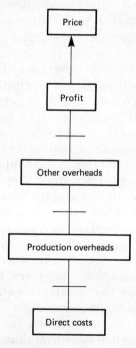

Here the direct costs have an addition which enables the absorption of production and other overheads to provide a "full cost" of the product. This full cost then has some profit "mark-up" applied to it to produce the selling price.

Obviously, because of the apparent simplicity of this method it has great appeal. For, apart from any simplicity, it enables a plausible selling price to be found very quickly without having to use up many additional resources in obtaining it, because standard accounting figures can be used in its computation. However, the method is deceptively simple and has the danger that in the use of *objective* historic costs to build up towards the final selling price it provides a figure that may appear to look exact.

Yet even if the fact that demand, especially as far as price elasticity is concerned, is seemingly ignored and the full cost-plus pricing approach is overlooked, a number of other criticisms can be levelled at it.

The first is to ask whether historic costs are relevant. If a factor of production still has to be purchased then its cost is relevant — but what if the factor is already owned? Then should not the replacement or some opportunity cost of the factor be brought into the analysis? Thus the producer's commitment as far as the resource is concerned becomes extremely important.

Going further, many resources will be used in the common production of a number of products or services which brings up the apportionment problem. When common costs are split between products some subjectivity must always enter into the apportionment.

There is also the fundamental problem that arises in setting price on a full cost-plus basis, that comes from the "gearing" effect of overhead absorption and mark-up which compound any initial direct cost classification errors in the final price, as explained in John Flower's description of the Bloodhound case.

So, all in all, full cost-plus pricing is neither as complete nor as logical as it appears on first sight. It could be suggested that in practice firms should strive towards some balance between consideration of the factors that affect price on both the supply side and the consumer demand side of the equation. Here perhaps it will be useful to discuss the extremes of the upper and lower limits between which the product could be sold.

No general statement on the determination of a price-floor can be made because a number of things need to be taken into consideration in the analysis of this. Yet commonly it is said that as long as the firm's variable costs are covered by the price set for the product, then the lower limit of the price for the product should be these variable costs. Usually a rider is added that in the long run if the firm is to survive it must also ensure that its fixed costs are covered. But it is not as simple as this as special situations need to be separated out for discussion. An example of such a special situation is where the product has already been made. In this case the firm should accept the best price that it can obtain even if this should fall below what the variable costs incurred in producing it were (subject to any goodwill considerations).

Another special situation arises when the firm hits any capacity constraints in its production. Then the firm should ensure that its product mix is such that it makes as much profit as possible from the items that it produces. In such a situation the price-floor for any product would not be that product's variable costs but rather these variable costs plus an addition equal to the contribution earned by the product earning the lowest profit for the firm. To give homogeneity, this addition would be made in proportion to the contribution per unit of the constraining factor involved.

The price-ceiling is a much more difficult problem to deal with and will depend to a large extent upon the skill, experience and judgement of the firm's marketing department. Here considerations of the prices charged by producers of fairly homogeneous products, and the competitive structure of the market, as far as price leadership and so on are concerned, will all have to be studied and taken into the analysis.

Even if a firm has the complete monopoly of a product, perhaps having developed a much wanted item which its innovator has patented to gain protection, contemplations of the relationship between quantity and price must be made. Once a final judgement is made as to what the relationship between the product's price and quantity is, it will enable the firm to know the output level that will produce the highest possible profit under the prevailing circumstances.

So if the firm has a monopoly in a product it may not, therefore, pay to produce it to full capacity but to use some of its production facilities to produce something else as well.

What a competitive firm really wants to do is to be able to just clear the output that it could produce when using full capacity, and to sell this at the highest possible prices obtainable for the quantity concerned.

A final point from Baxter and Oxenfeldt: they made a plea for "Cost statements with more precise words and less precise figures" and they say that as "Many cost figures must inevitably be guesswork, that this should be made plain; on occasion, they will be none the worse for being expressed as a range of probabilities, or for being sprinkled with question marks. Such vagueness accords with the facts of business life better than a facade of precision."

So all in all, it can be seen that it is important to get away from any rigid full cost-plus concept and to look at both sides of the pricing coin, supply costs and consumer demand.

JOINT PRODUCT AND BYPRODUCT COSTING

30.

(a) *Product profit statement*

	Total	Musk	Springtime	Joyeux
Sales	£650,000	£400,000	£200,000	£50,000
Operating costs:				
Joint process number 1 (*workings note (1)*)	300,000	300,000	—	—
Joint process number 2 (*workings note (2)*)	70,000	—	56,000	14,000
Separable costs	220,000	20,000	160,000	40,000
Total costs	590,000	320,000	216,000	54,000
Net profit (loss)	£60,000	£80,000	(£16,000)	(£4,000)

Unless the operation for Springtime and Joyeux can be improved it is apparent that both products should be discontinued as the total ultimate revenue of £250,000 is less than the separate costs of £270,000 (£70,000 + £160,000 + £40,000). Thus, if the flower oil were dumped in the river, overall company profits would be higher than at present.

Workings
Assignment of joint production costs

		Sales value
Further costs — Musk £20,000		£400,000

Joint costs

*Note 1

	Sales value
Additional costs Springtime £160,000	£200,000

Further costs — Springtime *and Joyeux £70,000*

*Note 2

Additional costs Joyeux £40,000	50,000
	£250,000

Note (1)   *Net relative sales value at split-off point — process No. 1*

Musk Final sales value		£400,000	
Less: Additional processing costs		20,000	
Notional sales value at split-off point			£380,000
Flower oil Final sales value — Springtime		200,000	
— Joyeux		50,000	
		250,000	
Less: Additional processing costs:	£		
Flower oil	70,000		
Springtime	160,000		
Joyeux	40,000		
		270,000	
Notional sales value at split-off point			(20,000)
			£360,000

Note that as Springtime and Joyeux show a net loss after the deduction of all further processing costs, *all the joint costs* of the first process are therefore assigned to Musk.

Note (2) *Net relative sales value at split-off point — process No. 2*

Product	Final sales value	Additional processing costs	Net relative sales value at split-off point	Weighting	Joint costs assigned
Springtime	£200,000	£160,000	£40,000	$\frac{4}{5} \times$ £70,000	£56,000
Joyeux	50,000	40,000	10,000	$\frac{1}{5} \times$ £70,000	14,000
	£250,000	£200,000	£50,000		£70,000

Assignment to Joint Costs

Musk	£300,000		
Springtime	—	$\frac{4}{5} \times$ (£70,000) =	£56,000
Joyeux	—	$\frac{1}{5} \times$ (£70,000) =	14,000
	£300,000		£70,000

(b)

	Old plan (per unit)		New plan (per unit)	
	Springtime	Joyeux	Springtime	Joyeux
Sales	£10·00	£1·00	£12·00	£1·00
Separable processing cost	8·00	0·80	10.00	0.80
Contribution (before joint costs)	£2·00	£0·20	£2·00	£0·20

Contribution per 10,000 lb of petals

Old plan:	Springtime	20,000 ounces × £2·00 =	£40,000		
	Joyeux	50,000 ounces × £0·20 =	10,000		
	Net contribution from old plan			£50,000	
New plan:	Springtime	18,000 ounces × £2·00 =	36,000		
	Joyeux	60,000 ounces × £0·20 =	12,000		
	Net contribution from new plan			48,000	
Overall disadvantage of new plan				£2,000	

The suggested changes would increase the losses on Springtime and Joyeux. They should not be undertaken.

Tutorial note: The apportionment of joint costs between the products is not relevant to a decision concerning further processing. In addition part (b) took no acount of the profit from Musk, as this will remain the same under both alternatives.

BUDGETARY CONTROL

31.

Aram company

   (a) (i)   *Profit and loss account for the year ended 31.12.X8*

	KL		JB		Total	
	M$	M$	M$	M$	M$	M$
Revenue		40,000		80,000		120,000
Less: Direct costs:						
Material	15,000		25,000		40,000	
Labour	20,000		30,000		50,000	
Variable overhead	10,000		10,000		20,000	
		45,000		65,000		110,000
Contribution		(5,000)		15,000		10,000
Less: Fixed overheads						6,000
Profit					M$	4,000

(ii) *Budgeted profit statement for year commencing 1.1.19X9*

	KL		JB		Total	
	M$	M$	M$	M$	M$	M$
Revenue		62,370		121,275		183,645
Less: Direct costs:						
Materials	21,773		35,280		57,053	
Labour	36,520		52,800		89,320	
Variable overhead	15,120		14,700		29,820	
		73,413		102,780		176,193
Contribution		(11,043)		18,495		7,452
Less: Fixed overheads						19,000
Profit (loss)						M$(11,548)

(b) The following points could be made:

(i) Analytical value important as providing a basis for requiring further more detailed information.

(ii) Comparison facilitated between past and expected future on a product basis.

(iii) Indicates KL's remaining unprofitability, and suggests contemplation of closure.

(iv) However, they do not give sufficient details of cost behaviour patterns resulting if KL were closed, namely:

> what costs would be avoided
> how would the "vacuum" be filled?
> how would JB's costs and revenues be affected if KL were closed?

Workings

(i) *Costs*

		M$
Materials — KL: $15,000 \times 1\cdot44 \times 1\cdot12 \times 0.90$	=	21,773
Materials — JB: $25,000 \times 1\cdot40 \times 1\cdot12 \times 0\cdot90$	=	35,280
Wages — KL: $(M\$20,000 \times 1\cdot44 \times 1\cdot10)$		
$+ (20,000 \times 0\cdot44 \times 1\cdot10 \times 0\cdot5)$	=	36,520
Wages — JB: $(M\$30,000 \times 1\cdot40 \times 1\cdot10)$		
$+ (30,000 \times 0\cdot4 \times 1\cdot10 \times 0\cdot5)$	=	52,800
Variable overheads — KL: $M\$10,000 \times 1\cdot44 \times 1\cdot05$	=	15,120
Variable overheads — JB: $M\$10,000 \times 1\cdot40 \times 1\cdot05$	=	14,700

Fixed overheads:	
Previous year	6,000
Rent increase	1,000
Advertising increase	12,000
M$	19,000

(ii) *Revenue*

		M$
Year ending 31.12.X8		
KL — 2,000 @ M\$25 less 10%	=	40,000
JB — 10,000 @ M\$10 less 20%	=	80,000
Year ending 31.12.X8		
KL — $1,000 \times 1\cdot44 \times 25 \times 1\cdot10$	=	39,600
plus $39,600 \times 1\cdot10$	=	43,560
		83,160
Less: 25% Discount		20,790
	M$	62,370
JB — $5,000 \times 1\cdot40 \times 10 \times 1\cdot10$	=	77,000
plus $77,000 \times 1\cdot10$	=	84,700
		161,700
Less: 25% Discount		40,425
	M$	121,275

32.

C and B Ltd.

(a) (i)   *Budgeted profit and loss account for six months ending 30 June 19X9*

Net sales (workings)		£87,188
Less: Cost of sales:		
Materials (workings)	£31,500	
Wages and salaries (workings)	20,672	
Overheads (workings)	20,700	
Bad debt provision	4,500	
	77,372	
Less: Discounts receivable (workings)	1,800	
		75,572
Budgeted net profit		£11,616

Workings to (a) (i)

1.	Net sales			
	Gross revenue			£90,000
	Less: Discounts: 5% × £45,000		£2,250	
	2½% × £22,500		562	
				2,812
				£87,188

2.	Materials	— 35% × £90,000	=	£31,500
	Wages and salaries	— 25% × (£87,188 − £4,500)	=	£20,672
	Overheads	— 23% × £90,000	=	£20,700
	Discounts receivable	— £36,000 × 5%	=	£1,800

(ii)   *Cash budget for six months ending 30 June 19X9* (£000s)

	January	February	March	April	May	June	Total
Balance b/d	(10,000)	(2,450)	(1,875)	(8,700)	(4,425)	1,975	(10,000)
Cash received							
October	8,000						8,000
November	9,750	8,000					17,750
December	9,500	4,875	4,000				18,375
January		1,900	975	800			3,675
February			1,900	975	800		3,675
March				15,200	7,800	6,400	29,400
April					9,500	4,875	14,375
May						4,750	4,750
Total	27,250	14,775	6,875	16,975	18,100	16,025	100,000

Less: Cash payments:

Materials	5,700	5,700	5,700	5,700	5,700	5,700	34,200
Wages and salaries	4,000	4,000	4,000	4,000	4,000	4,000	24,000
Overheads	10,000	2,000	4,000	3,000	2,000	3,000	24,000
Car		2,500					2,500
Total	19,700	14,200	13,700	12,700	11,700	12,700	84,700
Net cashflow	7,550	575	(6,825)	4,275	6,400	3,325	15,300
Balance c/f	(2,450)	(1,875)	(8,700)	(4,425)	1,975	5,300	5,300

(b) Reasons why profit will not equal cash include:

   (i)   deduction of non-cash items (that is, depreciation) in arriving at profit.

   (ii) capital expenditure is not charged against profit, but will be taken into account in cashflow statement.

   (iii) accruals and prepayments.

   (iv) stock valuation.

(c) It is necessary to show a cash budget not just in total, but for each month individually. This is because while the opening and closing balances may be acceptable, it is clearly possible for balances during the intervening period to be significantly adverse. This degree of elaboration may not be so necessary for the profit and loss account which is not used so much for *control* purposes (as is the cash budget), but more for forecasting and general information requirements.

33.

Earlham Ltd.

   (a) (i)   Additional cash = increase in working capital due to a scale expansion of 2.0 to 1.2

Additional working capital (£000s)

	Current	Revised	Increase
Debtors	210	350	140
Stocks RM	240	400	160
Work-in-progress	120	200	80
Finished goods	150	250	100
Creditors	(90)	(150)	(60)
	630	1,050	420

∴ additional cash requirement = £420,000.

   (ii) Additional cash = Increase in net working capital.

Additional working capital

Raw materials	£200,889
Work-in-progress	85,000
Finished goods	127,500
Debtors	206,667
Creditors	(2,500)
Increase	£617,556

Workings to (a) (ii)

1. *Materials:* Extra purchases $= 40\% \times £800,000$
                                                $= £320,000$

              Number of days in stock $= \dfrac{240}{420} \times 360 = 206$

                                    plus 10%   20

                                                  226 days

$\therefore$ Materials $= \dfrac{£320,000}{360} \times 226 = £200,889.$

2. *Work-in-progress:* Additional cost of sales $= 85\% \times £800,000 = £680,000$

Number of days in work-in-progress $= \dfrac{120}{960} \times 360 = 45$

$\therefore$ Work-in-progress $= \dfrac{£680,000}{360} \times 45 = £85,000.$

3. *Finished goods:* Number of days in stock $= \dfrac{150}{960} \times 360 = 56\cdot25$

                                           plus 20% $= 11\cdot25$

                                               67·50

$\therefore$ Finished goods $= \dfrac{680,000}{360} \times 67\cdot50 = £127,500.$

4. *Debtors:* Credit allowed (days) $= \dfrac{210}{1,200} \times 360 \qquad = 63$

$\qquad\qquad\qquad\qquad\qquad$ plus $\qquad\qquad\qquad$ 30

$\qquad\qquad\qquad\qquad\qquad\qquad\qquad\qquad\qquad$ 93 days

$\therefore$ Debtors $= \dfrac{£800,000}{360} \times 93 = £206,667$

5. *Creditors:* Purchases $= £420,000 + £320,000 = £740,000$

$\therefore$ Creditors $= \dfrac{£740,000}{360} \times 45 \qquad = £92,500.$

(b) Incremental contribution

£800,000 × 0·15	=	£120,000
Less: 14% of £617,556	=	86,458
Additional net profit	=	£33,542

34.

(a) *Sales budget for period 1*

Product	Quantity units	Unit price	Value
A	12,000	£20	£240,000
B	15,000	24	360,000
C	10,000	28	280,000
			£880,000

(b) *Production budget for period 1*

Product	Quantity per sales budget	Stock increase	Production required
A	12,000	200	12,200
B	15,000	220	15,220
C	10,000	180	10,180

(c) *Materials usage budget for period 1*

Product			Components			
	101 units	102 units	103 units	104 units	105 units	106 units
A	61,000	36,600	48,800	73,200	24,400	12,200
B	60,880	30,440	45,660	76,100	15,220	15,220
C	71,260	61,080	50,900	40,720	30,540	10,180
	193,140	128,120	145,360	190,020	70,160	37,600

(d) *Materials purchases budget for period 1*

			Components				Total value
	101 units	102 units	103 units	104 units	105 units	106 units	
Per materials usage budget	193,140	128,120	145,360	190,020	70,160	37,600	
Less: Stock decrease	5,000	3,000	3,500	4,500	1,700	900	
Purchases required	188,140	125,120	141,860	185,520	68,460	36,700	
Unit cost	40p	50p	35p	60p	75p	90p	
Value	£75,256	£62,560	£49,651	£111,312	£51,345	£33,030	£383,154

(e) *Direct labour utilisation budget for period 1*

Product	Per production Budget units	Assembly shop hours	Assembly shop cost £	Machine shop hours	Machine shop cost £	Total cost £
A	12,200	12,200	4,880	1,220	610	5,490
B	15,220	19,025	7,610	2,283	1,141·5	8,751·5
C	10,180	15,270	6,108	2,036	1,018	7,126
		46,495	£18,598	5,539	£2,769·5	£21,367·5

Labour hours available at normal working	44,800	5,120
Shortage of hours	1,695	419
Budgeted utilisation of existing capacity	104%	108%

(f) *Machine utilisation budget for period 1*

Hours required in machine shop per direct labour utilisation budget	5,539
Machine hours available at normal working (40 machines × 34 hours × 4 weeks)	5,440
Shortage of machine hours	99
Budgeted utilisation of existing machine capacity	102%

The shortage of labour hours as disclosed by the direct labour utilisation budget can be met by:

(i)   introducing overtime,

(ii) recruiting more employees,

(iii) subcontracting, or

(iv) increasing labour efficiency.

While overtime working would be a very quick solution, it is likely to increase the labour cost. The recruitment of additional employees (11 in the assembly shop and three in the machine shop) may be costly and take some considerable time. Subcontracting would probably be expensive, perhaps also presenting additional administrative problems, while the control of quality would be very important. Increasing labour efficiency would be a useful long-term aid if there has, as yet, been no attempt to study working methods. A great deal depends upon the company's estimate of future trends in sales. If the high level of sales is likely to continue then the company should adopt long-term solutions, such as the recruitment of additional employees. If, however, sales are likely to fluctuate, then it would be better not to increase the labour force, and cope with periodic rises in sales by overtime working and/or subcontracting.

The shortage of machine time as disclosed by the machine utilisation budget could be met by:

(i) reducing setting time,

(ii) maintaining machines outside normal working time,

(iii)   obtaining more machines and employees,

(iv)   introducing overtime,

(v)   subcontracting, or

(vi)   increasing efficiency.

The reduction in setting times could be achieved by producing in longer runs which may require changes in production scheduling arrangements. The introduction of a separate maintenance shift to maintain machines after hours would be more expensive, and here again the company needs to forecast future sales carefully before committing itself to a particular policy.

35.
Processors Ltd

(a) *Calculation of initial selling price at 1 January:*

(i)   Budgeted output and sales 20,000 kg

(ii)   Variable costs

			per kg
Materials	23,000 kg @ £10 per kg (11·5 kg usage per kg)	£230,000	£11·50
Labour	360,000 hours @ £0·80 per hour (18 hours per kg)	288,000	14·40
Overhead power	2,400,000 units @ £0·01 per unit	24,000	1·20
	Distribution — 20,000 kg @ £2·40 per kg	48,000	2·40
		£590,000	£29·50

(iii)   Fixed costs per month

Works overhead	£20,000		
Administration	14,000		
Distribution	1,000		
Selling	7,500		
	42,500 × 12		
		510,000	25·50

(iv) Total costs		1,100,000	55·00
(v) Profit margin – 20%		220,000	11·00
(vi) Sales and selling price		£1,320,000	£66·00

(b) *Statement showing revised budgeted profit for the year:*

| | | Half-year ended | |
		30 June	31 December
Contribution			
Contribution per kg shown by original budget:			
Selling price	£66		
Variable costs	£29·50	£36·50	£36·50
Adjustments arising from decisions taken and events occurring:			
(i) Increase in selling price		—	2·40
			38·90
(ii) Increase in variable costs 5% × £29·50		—	1·475
		£36·50	£37·425
Output and sales		kg	kg
Total per original budget		10,000	10,000
Estimated increase 2·5%		250	250
		10,250	10,250
Anticipated decrease due to higher selling price		—	246
		10,250	10,004
Budgeted profit			
Contribution: 10,250 × £36·50		£374,125	
10,004 × £37·425			£374,400
	£000		
Less: Fixed cost per original budget	510		
half-year		255,000	
half-year + 1%			257,550
Revised budgeted profit		£119,125	£116,850

36.

(a) *Finished goods production:*

	October kg	November kg	December kg
Budgeted sales (units)	120,000	90,000	120,000
Closing stocks required	18,000	24,000	24,000
Total monthly requirement	138,000	114,000	144,000
Deduct: Opening stocks	24,000	18,000	24,000
Budgeted production	114,000 kg	96,000 kg	120,000 kg

Raw materials purchases:

	October kg	November kg
Budgeted production ($\frac{1}{2}$ kg per unit)	57,000	48,000
Closing stocks required	19,200	24,000
Total monthly requirement	76,200	72,000
Deduct: Opening stocks	22,800	40,800*
Minimum purchase	53,400 kg	31,200 kg
Budgeted purchases: (Minimum lot 25,000 kg)	75,000 kg	50,000 kg

*Opening stocks + budgeted purchases − budgeted production = expected stocks in October. The materials can only be purchased in lot sizes of 25,000 kg.

$$22,800 + 75,000 - 57,000 = 40,800 \text{ kg}$$

(b) *Meadow Plastics Ltd: Projected profit statement (November)*

Sales (90,000 units @ £2)		£180,000
Deduct: Cash discounts (2% × $\frac{1}{2}$ sales)	£1,800	
Bad debts ($\frac{1}{2}$% of sales)	900	
		2,700
		177,300

Net sales

Cost of goods sold:

Standard cost (90,000 @ £1·20)	108,000	
Add: Unfavourable volume variance	400*	
		108,400

Gross profit	68,900

Expenses:

Selling (10% of sales)	18,000	
Administrative	33,000	
Interest	1,250	
		52,250

Net profit	£16,650

*(Expected production *less* budget production) × £0·10

= (100,000 − 96,000) × £0·10 = £400(U)

Note: The standard cost of sales is based on budgeted sales of 90,000 units, whereas the volume variance is based on budgeted production of 96,000 units. This assumes that the company is using absorption costing as a measurement of income.

Cash forecast for November

Opening balance					£10,000
Receipts from sales:					
Date of invoice	*Amount invoiced*	*Proportion received*	*Date received*		
15 October	£120,000	50% *Less:* ½% Bad debts (*note 1*)	15 November	£59,400	
31 October	120,000	50% *Less:* 2% Discount (*note 2*)	10 November	58,800	
31 October	120,000	50% *Less:* ½% Bad debts	30 November	59,400	
15 November	90,000	50% *Less:* 2% Discount	25 November	44,100	
				221,700	
Bank loan				100,000	
					321,700
					331,700

Cash available
Payments:

October purchases (75,000 kg)	£75,000
November labour (96,000 units @ 40p)	38,400
October variable overhead (114,000 units @ 20p)	22,800
October fixed overhead (10,000 *Less:* £4,000 depreciation)	6,000
October selling expenses	24,000
October administrative expenses (£33,000 *Less:* £500 depreciation)	32,500
Interest on loan	1,250
	199,950
Closing balance	£131,750

Notes:
(1) The ½% bad debts is based on gross sales invoiced.
(2) The 2% discount is based on cash received within the discount period, that is, 2% of sales value of receipts.

37.

Manning Wholesale Ltd
Cash forecast statement for the period 1 July 19X7 to 30 September 19X7

Receipts	Workings note	July	August	September
Sales	1	£510,000	£432,000	£518,400
Obsolete stock	2	25,000		
		535,000	432,000	518,400
Payments				
Suppliers	3	370,000	342,000	288,000
Fixed and variable expenses		160,620	118,800	158,400
Dividend				40,000
Advertising			10,000	15,000
Equipment replacement		3,000	3,000	3,000
Corporation tax				60,000
Bank loan, including interest	4			288,400
		533,620	473,800	852,800

Surplus (deficit) for month	1,380	(41,800)	(334,400)
Balance at beginning of month	100,000	101,380	59,580
Balance at end of month	£101,380	£59,580	£(274,820)

Workings

1. *Cash receipts from debtors*

		Collected in:					
			July		*August*		*September*
Sales							
May	£60,000*	(9%)	£54,000				
June	320,000**	(30%)	240,000	(9%)	£72,000		
July	360,000	(60%)	216,000	(30%)	108,000	(9%)	32,400
August	420,000			(60%)	252,000	(30%)	126,000
September	600,000					(60%)	360,000
			£510,000		£432,000		£518,400

* May balance outstanding at 30 June — 10% of May sales.
**June balance outstanding at 30 June — 40% of June sales.

2. *Sales of obsolete stock*

Cost of stock	60%	£30,000
Gross profit	40%	20,000
Normal selling price	100%	50,000
Sales proceeds (half normal selling price)		£25,000

3. *Purchases from suppliers*		*August–October*	*September–November*
Sales forecast	100%	£1,560,000	£1,620,000
Cost of sales	60%	936,000	972,000
Stock held at		1 August	1 September
Purchase requirements		*July*	*August*
Sales (100%)		£360,000	£420,000

Cost of sales (60%)	216,000	252,000
Closing stock required	936,000	972,000
	1,152,000	1,224,000
Opening stock available	810,000	936,000
Purchases	£342,000	£288,000
Paid	10 August	10 September

4. *Bank loan and interest*

Balance at 1 July	£280,000
Add: Interest @% 12/ for 3 months	8,400
	£288,400

38.

(a) *Wellpland Ltd.: Cash budget for July, August and September*

	July £000	August £000	September £000
Cash outflow			
Creditors (see workings)	65	75	117
Wages (one-eighth previous month)	5	$5\frac{1}{2}$	$4\frac{1}{2}$
(seven-eighths current month)	$38\frac{1}{2}$	$31\frac{1}{2}$	$31\frac{1}{2}$
Factory expenses	7	7	7
Rent	—	—	15
Salaries and expenses	35	42	47
Advertising	14	10	16
Sales commission	10	11	13
Dividend, tax and retention money	—	25	30
	$174\frac{1}{2}$	207	281
Cash inflow	£000		
Loan repaid	8		
Debtors	220 228	230	210
Net inflow/(outflow)	$53\frac{1}{2}$	23	(71)
Opening balance	$(21\frac{1}{2})$	32	55
Closing balance	32	55	(16)

Workings Materials purchased	*May*	*June*	*July*	*August*
Closing stock	64	56	82	47
Add: Usage	76	83	91	53
	140	139	173	100
Deduct: Opening stock	75	64	56	82
Purchased	65	75	117	18

(b) When wishing to control the cash flow of a company, management will investigate the position of:

(i)   *The control over debtors* to ensure that a correct credit control system is in operation and the overdue debts are collected efficiently. A check will be made to ensure that all appropriate facilities such as those available from ECGD and debt collection agencies are being used.

(ii) *The payment of creditors* will be investigated to ensure that all available "free" credit is being taken and that creditors are not being paid before the contractual date.

(iii) *The levels of stocks and work-in-progress* will be investigated as cash can be generated by running down unnecessary stock holdings. Production schedules will be investigated so that stock purchases can be matched to production requirements in an attempt to minimise inefficient stock holdings.

(iv) *The use of land and buildings* will be investigated to see if any unused space can be rented out, or unused assets sold. The raising of funds by way of mortgage may provide funds to pay off "more expensive" loans.

(v)   *Any capital projects* will be reappraised to see if there are cheaper means available for financing the operation.

(vi) *The position of current cash holdings* if held in separate accounts will be investigated to see if any possible consolidation will eliminate overdraft charges.

(vii) Linked with this area of investigation *temporary idle balances* if identified can be placed on short-term lending.

(viii)Having carried out these investigations, management should carry out a detailed *cost reduction* enquiry. It will be necessary to identify uneconomic products and carry out a "value analysis" into all procedures.

(c) In the particular circumstances of Wellpland Ltd, a combination of the following tactics will improve the cash flow:

(i)   Put off the payment of the dividend or make a part payment only of this dividend.

(ii)   Take longer credit on the payment of advertising expenses.

(iii) Try to encourage earlier payment from the debtors. The offering of discounts for earlier payment may facilitate this.

39.

(a) Variances occur when there is a difference between actual costs and expected or budgeted costs. For cost control purposes, the expected costs are adjusted or "fixed" at the actual level of output.

Ultimately, a budgetary control system is the responsibility of top management although for administration purposes this responsibility is normally delegated to a budget officer, who is in charge of the routine running of the system.

Variances reported because of defects of management are those concerned with inefficiency in the running of the business, and can be controlled, whereas those because of defects in the design of a budgetary control system can only be attributed to the person responsible for the design of the system.

(i)   It is a defect of management. It seems unusual that the foreman is prepared to wait seven months for this bonus. Even so, this should have been charged to overhead during the budget period in which it was incurred, so that it can be promptly controlled. However, if this is the normal treatment of a bonus, this would be a defect of the budgetary control system.

(ii) It is a defect of the budgetary control system. If consumable stores are charged to overhead as they are purchased, there will be no control over the issue of these items to production and the overheads incurred each month will depend partly on the purchasing policy of the company. In addition, there will be no accounting control over the storage of the consumable stores, as all purchases are assumed to be issued to production.

(iii) It depends on how the iron founder's pattern-making costs are estimated. If these are the responsibility of the founder, it could be that he understimates these costs in his own self-interest, that is, in order to ensure that he has a constant supply of work. In this case, the defect is the responsibility of management and his estimates should be scrutinised before job quotations are prepared. Conversely, the iron founder may be preparing his costs on the basis of information supplied to him by another department in which case this is more likely to be a defect of the system.

(iv) It depends on the procedures for forecasting the value of scrap from production, and the value of scrap depends on two factors, the quantity and the prevailing price. The quantity of scrap from production should be forecast with a reasonable degree of precision based on past results, but the price at which this can be sold will depend on market conditions. Any inaccuracies in the salvage value of scrap are basically due to defects of management.

(v)   It is normal spoilage and therefore can be attributed neither to a defect of management nor to a defect of the budgetary control system. If management wishes to reduce the amount of normal spoilage, the procedures within the fruit packing station should be reviewed.

(vi) It is a defect of the system, although as the system was undoubtedly designed by management, they can also be held responsible. If the salvage value of scrap is in any way material and can be forecast with any degree of accuracy, it should be included in the budget.

(vii) If a worker is inefficient because he is new to a job this is basically the fault of the system. Normally a system of budgetary control allows a worker a specific time to complete a given task and this is based on the time taken by a normal efficient worker, allowing for various factors. A new worker cannot be expected to complete the task in the same amount of time, as he will still be learning the skills required. Scientific attempts have been made to measure the learning process by means of "learning curves", but these are too complex to be incorporated into a system of budgetary control.

(viii) If a worker is inefficient because he is not concentrating the system does not normally allow for such factors and it is the responsibility of his foreman, supervisor, or higher management to ensure that workers are sufficiently well motivated to carry out the task efficiently.

(b) (i) The bonus should be charged to overhead when it is incurred; provided the bonus can be calculated promptly, no difficulties should arise.

(ii) Consumable stores should be charged to overhead when they are issued to production, not when they are purchased. It will not be possible to achieve a high level of accuracy in this case, as consumable stores cannot be issued with particular jobs due to the nature of the items. In this case it would be better for items to be issued on a regular basis, such as weekly, when they are requested by the production foreman.

(iii) The reasons underlying this defect should be examined. It may be necessary to update the standards which are used as a basis for the estimates, or it may be necessary to ensure that the estimates are thoroughly checked before a quotation is made. This may cause opposition from the iron founder and should therefore be handled with tact.

(iv) The quantity of normal scrap and the forecast price of scrap should be reviewed for inaccuracies. As the latter cannot be predicted with total accuracy, very little action can be taken in this case.

(v)   No action would be taken as the loss of fruit is considered to be normal. If 5% is considered an excessive normal loss, the fruit packing procedures should be reviewed to see if a reduction in the normal loss is considered possible.

(vi) The quantity of scrap should be estimated and the selling price predicted in order to forecast the salvage value. As the salvage value has been ignored completely so far, it seems possible that the physical existence of the scrap has also been ignored, which in turn means that there has been no control of the disposal of the scrap. This is likely to result in considerable opposition from the workers who may have, in the past, disposed of the scrap.

(vii) Initially no action would be taken where a new worker is inefficient. If his inefficiency continues after the normal period of training, his suitability for the job should be considered.

(viii) If a worker is not concentrating then he should be carefully watched by the foreman or supervisor to make him concentrate on his work. If necessary he should be warned of the possible dangers to fellow workers and to the quality of the product, and his continued employment by the company should be kept under review.

40.

(a) The factors to be taken into consideration in establishing the length of the proposed budget periods are:

(i) the type of budget, for example, sales, capital expenditure, cash, production;

(ii) the economic situation in general;

(iii) the stability of the market for the product;

(iv) probability of changes in products and/or product mix.

The usual period for manufacturing budgets is a year ahead. Sales may be established as a trend over, say, the next three years, but this forecast will be limited for budget purposes to the next year.

Cash budgets may be made for a year in order to complete the master budget, but shorter, more detailed budgets of three months' duration in advance are usually made as well.

Capital expenditure has to be planned well in advance, so that it is common to have budgets for the next five years, and in some concerns, such as airlines, shipping, etc., for much longer. This enables fixed assets to be ordered in time and finance and government grants to be organised.

(b) (i) A budgeted system for a year is operated in the following manner:

(1) the production and sales plans will have been formulated for each month or four-weekly period of the year;

(2) production cost budgets will have been prepared for each product, so that the applicable budget figures can be compared with actual figures;

(3) the budget comparison statements will therefore show:

Flexible budget   Actual   Variance

for the month, and cumulatively. The corresponding figures for last year may be valuable, provided that the manufacturing pattern was the same. In the case of overhead statements, they would certainly be required;

(4)   the variances must be carefully calculated and explained;

(5)   corrective action must be taken where necessary, by line management;

(6)   with regard to overhead, the budgeted annual expenditure will be divided into 12 or 13 periods. Actual results will be compared with the budget and variances calculated and explained;

(7)   budgeted sales will be compared with actual sales, and the variances as to price and volume will be shown and explained. The effect on profits will also be demonstrated;

(8)   a comparison of budgeted results with actual will be made for all the budgets produced and any necessary action as a result of divergences, taken; for example,

the budgeted figure for average collection period for debtors will be compared with actual,

the cash budget will be compared with actual results to enable either action to be taken over unplanned cash shortages or excess unplanned surpluses to be invested.

(ii) A continuous budgeting system, sometimes known as a rolling budget, is normally for a total period of 12 months.

At the end of every month the 12-month figures are revised by omitting the past month's figures and adding on an extra month's figures. Thus, at 1 June 1977 the budget would be for the 12 months from June 1977 to May 1978 inclusive. One month later, on 1 July 1977 the budget would be updated and would then cover the period from July 1977 to June 1978 inclusive.

The advantage of this method is that at all times figures for the next 12 months are available and management is made continually aware of the budgeting process.

The disadvantage of this type of budgeting stems from the fact that each and every month the whole procedure of preparing budgets has to be undertaken, whereas with the periodic system the preparation is only required once a year. It would be expected that the company's objectives and limiting factors would be more critically assessed on an annual basis than when the assessment is required 12 times a year.

(c) The level of attainment to be adopted in budgeting is that of normal capacity allied to good management and satisfactory employee cooperation.

Setting targets too high means that the levels will not be achieved, and constantly adverse results will be discouraging and bring the system into disrepute.

Setting targets too low means that there is no challenge, and production will tend to drop to the low level sufficient to meet the budget requirements.

Targets must therefore be set which are attainable with reasonable endeavour.

41.

(a) (i) Controllable costs are those costs which may be directly regulated at a given level of managerial authority within a given time period. The two major factors which are useful to evaluate whether a given cost is controllable or not are the managerial area of responsibility and the time period in question.

   (ii) Responsibility accounting uses budgets, variances and reports which are tailored to areas of responsibility, called cost centres, profit centres or investment centres, and which provide managers with the information necessary for planning and control. So that this system can work well, a company must be organised with clearly defined lines of authority, ensuring that each manager knows exactly what is expected of him.

   (iii) The following guidelines are useful in deciding what costs may be appropriately charged to a person:

   (1) If the person has authority over both the acquisition and use of the services, he should be charged with the cost of such services.

   (2) If the person can significantly influence the amount of cost through his own action, he may be charged with such costs.

   (3) Even if the person cannot significantly influence the amount of cost through his own direct action, he may be charged with certain elements so that he will help to influence those who are responsible.

(b) Budgets and responsibility accounting will naturally tend to encourage a narrow orientation, as they tend to draw management's attention inwards towards the department rather than outwards towards the firm as a whole. However, it is unlikely that the lack of a budget will improve matters and broaden the supervisor's horizons, and make him conscious of the organisation as a whole instead of his own departmental sphere of influence. The administration of budgetary techniques should be distinguished from the techniques themselves.

The plant manager probably took the best action under the circumstances, but he should not have waited two months before doing so. The decision should have been made two months ago when the defective goods were returned, so that the supervisors could at least remain on speaking terms. It appears that the lines of authority in this firm are not clearly defined, otherwise the problem would not have arisen in the first place.

The budget and the departmental accounting system cannot be blamed for the problem. The weakness is the failure of either the production or the accounting system to isolate responsibility. In a few cases it is not possible to define responsibility but in most cases there is one person who is primarily responsible.

BEHAVIOURAL ASPECTS OF BUDGETING

42.

Up to half the marks for this answer could be obtained by giving a thorough exposition of the straightforward organisational steps of budgetary control. However, a good answer would need to demonstrate a grasp of the behavioural aspects of budgeting.

The organisation and operation of budgetary control

(a) *The budget committee:* comprising the budget officer, and its permanent members and those coopted for particular aspects of the budget where their expertise is required; the responsibilities of this committee for coordinating and communicating the budgets, and its other duties should be discussed; in particular the need to establish objectives and communicate these to operational managers in meaningful terms.

(b) *The budget manual:* to chart the organisation, and detail the budget procedures including account codes, and the budgeting timetable.

(c) *The budget period:* planning the budget period(s) including the capital expenditure budget, and control procedures.

(d) *The principal budget factor:* the factor which limits the expansion of the firm's activities, and thus determines the overall limits of the budget for profit maximisation. The firm's sub-budgets will be derived from this.

(e) *Accounting records:* budget cost centres should align with management control and responsibility for performance; accounting records must therefore provide adequate and prompt information in relation to these cost centres.

(f) *Budget review:* the comparison of the actual performance with the budget targets must be promptly performed if there is to be effective control; when reporting to higher management, "management by exception" techniques should be used so that only important deviations are raised for consideration. Uninformed criticism of adverse variances should be avoided: "The investigation of budget deviations is the line-manager's responsibility" (C. T. Horngren).

Follow-up

If top management is not seen to identify itself with the budget objectives by following up to see that deviations are corrected then the budget system will come to be ignored. "Budgets should not be prepared in the first place if they are ignored, buried in files or improperly interpreted" (C. T. Horngren).

In some research carried out by Dew and Gee, it was found that for a number of small firms once the budgets had been prepared they were pushed away in a drawer and ignored in three-quarters of the cases examined.

In the article, "Why budgets go wrong", in Solomon's *Studies in Cost Analysis*, Charles Hughes cites the case of an oil company, where budgeting was referred to by managers as the "silly season", and forecasting was called "playing Monopoly". Their subordinates took their cue from the managers, and record keeping in the department became a numbers game, with funds shifted from one account to another, and expenses charged where it seemed most convenient. Budgets were obviously considered a formality and there was no top management follow-up or support.

Motivation

A number of writers have suggested that budgets can be used to motivate. Andrew Stedry, one of the first to consider this, said that motivation could be achieved by harnessing people's aspiration levels, and that if there could be congruence between a person's aspiration level and the budget drawn up for him then the budget would become a motivational device.

Although beset by many behavioural problems, one of the ways in which such congruence can be achieved is to allow people to participate in the setting of their own budgets. However, there is the danger that they may try to rig these. Hughes referred to this idea as the "fudge factor", whereby each level of management may secretly add an "allowance" to the original budget in order to ensure that their actual results will appear favourable in a comparison with the budget. Yet when an accountant draws up a budget in isolation from the operating people concerned and they do not keep to it, they can easily justify deviations, saying that it was an impossible budget in the first place! Once participation takes place, such arguments cannot be used. However, some writers, for example, Chris Argyris, point out the difficulties of obtaining real participation, and say that some participation, referred to as pseudo-participation, is more apparent than real. Pseudo-participation will occur where a supervisor is asked to sign a budget as evidence that he is in agreement with it. In practice, this may be his first chance to actually see the budget, and he is unlikely to have been consulted at the earlier stage of preparation. The fact that the supervisor has signed the budget can be used later as evidence of his agreement. Argyris suggests that this is worse than no participation at all, as his signature implies an element of responsibility for carrying out the budget.

INTRODUCTION TO STANDARD COSTING AND BASIC VARIANCE ANALYSIS

43.

Mingus Ltd

(a) *Standard costs for actual output of 50,000 granoids:*

Direct materials	250,000 kg @ £10	£2,500,000
Direct labour	100,000 kg @ £5	500,000
Variable overhead	250,000 kg @ £1	250,000
Standard direct cost		3,250,000
Fixed overhead	100,000 hours @ £5	500,000
		£3,750,000
Actual costs of production:		
Actual costs (total)		4,080,000
Actual fixed overheads		380,000
Actual direct cost		£3,700,000

Inventory = 20% of output

(i)	Actual absorption costing		
	20% × £4,080,000	=	£816,000
(ii)	Standard absorption costing — variances written-off		
	20% × £3,750,000	=	£750,000
(iii)	Standard absorption costing — variances		
	prorated as (i)	=	£816,000
(iv)	Actual direct costing		
	20% × £3,700,000	=	£740,000
(v)	Standard direct costing — variances written-off		
	20% × £3,250,000	=	£650,000
(vi)	Standard direct costing — variances		
	prorated as (iv)	=	£740,000

(b) (i) *Actual absorption costing*

This system values inventory as a proportion of the actual total cost incurred to produce the output in the period. Fixed overhead is carried forward as part of product cost. It would thus appear both to follow the principle of matching costs with revenue, as well as valuing stocks at "cost". However, two points can be made:

1. The element of direct cost in inventory does not reflect the valuation if production were carried out at the expected level of efficiency.

2.   The amount of fixed overhead carried forward is dependent on the activity level achieved. Thus the increase in activity above the normal level of 40,000 units results in a lower fixed overhead cost per unit than would normally be expected.

Unit inventory values will fluctuate according to efficiency and production levels.

(ii)   *Standard absorption costing with variances written-off*
This system values inventory at the standard total cost. It is thus carrying forward fixed costs based on the normal activity level of 40,000. However, it implicitly assumes that all variances are avoidable and that standard cost and activity reflect current attainable targets. Since the total variances are £330,000 adverse, it gives a lower inventory valuation than (i), and hence a lower reported profit.

Since the standards were set one year ago, it would seem reasonable that some, especially relating to resource costs, are out of date. Inventory would thus be undervalued.

Similarly, the activity level of 50,000 units is a 25% increase on normal, and it would appear that a revised standard fixed overhead cost per unit would be appropriate, that is, inventory is overvalued for fixed overheads.

Under this costing system, unit inventory values will be stable until standards are revised.

(iii) *Standard absorption costing with variances prorated*
This method identifies the variances from standard, but adds a proportion back to inventory. It thus gives the same inventory valuation and reported profit as (i), and the same comments apply. An improvement could be made by considering whether each variance is controllable or uncontrollable and only prorating the uncontrollable variances, thus writing off variances due to operating inefficiency in the year.

Unit inventory values will fluctuate as in (i).

(iv)   *Actual direct costing*
This is similar to (i) except that fixed overhead cost is not carried forward in inventory. It thus gives a lower valuation by £76,000, which is 20% of the actual fixed overhead cost.

It can be argued that fixed costs are not inventory costs, but time costs of the period, and should be written off; however, SSAP 9 recommends that fixed cost should be carried forward, using normal activity levels.

Unit inventory values will fluctuate according to efficiency but not production levels.

(v)   *Standard direct costing with variances written-off*
This is similar to (ii) except that fixed overhead cost is again written-off. Thus the extent of "normality" of the actual output level does not affect inventory values, but if the standards are out of date, inventory will be undervalued and profit understated.

Unit inventory values will be stable until standards are revised.

(vi) *Standard direct costing with variances prorated*
As in (iii), this method identifies the variances for control purposes but then adds the appropriate proportion back to inventory. It thus gives the same inventory value as (iv). The same comment as to whether variances are controllable or uncontrollable as was made in (iii) applies. Unit inventory values will fluctuate as in (iv).

44.

Amalgamated Processors plc: Analysis of profit shortfall

(a)

Budgeted profit		£45,000
Less: Sales variances:		
External sales		
(2,000 units @ (£10 − £5·20))	£9,600 Adverse	
Internal sales		
(1,000 units @ (£9 − £5))	£4,000 Favourable	(5,600)
		39,400
Less: Cost variances		
Direct material usage:		
Material A (34,000 − 32,000) 0·20p =	£400 Adverse	
Material B (80,000 − 78,500) 0·37p =	£555 Favourable	
Direct material price:		
Material A — 30,000 @ 0·01 =	£300 Favourable	
Material B — 90,000 @ 0·03 =	£2,700 Adverse	
Labour efficiency (4,250 − 4,000) £2 =	£500 Adverse	
Labour rate 4,250 hours @ 0·10 =	£425 Adverse	
Variable manufacturing overhead:		
Efficiency variance — 250 hours @ £3 =	£750 Adverse	
(150% of £2)		
Variable manufacturing overhead:		
Spending variance (4,250 × £3)		
− £12,325 =	£425 Favourable	
Fixed spending variance (15,000 × £1·50)		
− £25,505 =	£3,005 Adverse	
Fixed manufacturing overhead:		
Volume variance 1,000 units @ £1·50 =	£1,500 Favourable	
Selling overhead spending variance:		
£(13,000 − (9,600 + 10,000 (0·20)) =	£1,400 Adverse	
		(6,400)
	Actual profit =	£33,000

Sales volume variance: failure to achieve the planned volume of external sales will reduce the month's profit by £9,600. However, this is partly offset by £4,000, obtained from making more internal sales than planned.

Direct material price variances: although there is a favourable price variance for material A, there are adverse variances for material usage, labour efficiency and variable manufacturing overhead. This could be a result of the poor quality of A, which should be investigated.

Labour variances: the substandard quality of material A may have caused the adverse labour efficiency variance.

Variable manufacturing overhead variances: the adverse efficiency variance of £750 is caused by the excessive time taken on manufacturing.

Fixed overhead manufacturing variances: the adverse spending variance is partly offset by a favourable volume variance. This volume variance is achieved by producing more than the normal budgeted level.

(b) The isolation of material price variances at the time of the material's purchase facilitates stock control. An accounting problem is that variances relate to purchases rather than usage and this breaks the accrual concept used in measuring profits. This problem can be overcome by making appropriate year-end adjustments.

(c) Using a market price as a transfer price (a) puts the buying and selling divisions on the same footing as independent contractors, and (b) should lead managers to make decisions which are in the best interests of the organisation as a whole. It does not appear that the market is perfectly competitive and an adjustment has been made to the external selling price to give a transfer price of £9 per unit.

45.

Strider Ltd.: Profit and loss statement for May

		Favourable	Unfavourable	
Budgeted contribution				£100,000
Variances				
Sales price		£8,000		
Sales volume			£20,000	
Materials	price		5,000	
	usage		5,000	
Labour	rate		1,500	
	efficiency		3,000	
	idle time		7,500	
Factory variable	expenditure	2,000		
	efficiency		1,000	
Selling and distribution			2,000	
		£10,000	45,000	35,000 (U)
				65,000

Actual contribution		
Budgeted fixed overhead	80,000	
Deduct: Expenditure variance	2,000 (F)	
		78,000
Actual loss		£13,000

Tutorial note: The sales and selling and distribution variances are based on actual sales of 20,000 units. The production cost variances are based on actual production of 22,000 units.

Workings

(a) Budgeted output was 25,000 units, i.e. $\dfrac{£20,000 + £80,000}{£4}$

(b) *Sales variances*

	Units	Contri-bution per unit	Contri-bution		Units	Contri-bution per unit	Contri-bution
Budgeted sales and profit	25,000	£4·00	£100,000	Profit from actual sales,			
Price variance (F)	—		8,000	assuming all costs are standard	20,000	£4·40	£88,000
				Volume variance (U)	5,000	4·00	20,000
	25,000		£108,000		25,000		£108,000

(c) *Materials variances*

Actual cost of purchases	250,000 kg	£130,000	Standard cost of output	220,000 kg	£110,000
			Price variance (U)	—	5,000
			Usage variance (U)	10,000 kg	5,000
			Closing stock	20,000 kg	10,000
	250,000 kg	£130,000		250,000 kg	£130,000

(d) *Labour variances*

Actual cost	95,000 hours	£144,000	Standard cost of output	88,000 hours	£132,000
			Rate variance (U)	—	1,500
			Idle time variance (U)	5,000 hours	7,500
			Efficiency variance (U)	2,000 hours	3,000
	95,000 hours	£144,000		95,000 hours	£144,000

(e) *Factory variable variances*

Actual cost	90,000 hours	£43,000	Standard cost of output	88,000 hours	£44,000
Expenditure variance (F)	—	2,000	*Efficiency variance (U)*	2,000 hours	1,000
	90,000 hours	£45,000		90,000 hours	£45,000

(f) *The actual loss can be verified as follows:*

Actual sales			£408,000
Variable production costs:			
Materials		£130,000	
Labour		144,000	
Factory variable overhead		43,000	
	c/f	317,000	£408,000
	b/f	£317,000	£408,000
Less: Stocks (at standard marginal cost)			
2,000 units finished goods at £13	£26,000		
20,000 kg raw material at £0·50	10,000		
		36,000	
Variable production cost of sales		281,000	
Add: Variable selling and distribution costs		62,000	

Total variable cost of sales	343,000
Actual contribution	65,000
Less: Actual fixed overhead	78,000
Loss	£13,000

46.

Blendyarn Co. Ltd.
Bradford
Yorks
12 June 198X

To:
The Managing Director
Blendyarn Berhad
Kuala Lumpur
Malaysia

Dear Mr Lee

Performance report for KL factory for four weeks ending 28 May

The following statement of performance of the KL factory for the four weeks ending 28 May has not followed the conventions of traditional variance analysis. The statement compares the factory's actual performance with the budget in a way which highlights the reasons for major differences between the two sets of figures. This provides management with useful information for interpreting the variances and considering what control measures may be necessary.

If the statement is to be useful, it must be prepared immediately after the end of the control period. If there is any delay in the preparation of the statement then there will be an equal delay in the corrective action to be taken.

The statement of performance reconciles the actual profit for the period with the budgeted profit. The variances have been classified according to the information obtained, so that an appraisal of performance can take place of the planning of the original budget and an appraisal of operations, by attributing variances to those who have control over them, on the basis of responsibility accounting.

The main conclusion to be drawn from the statement is that the company is not well equipped to deal with such a crisis and that management's relations with operatives are inadequate.

Yours sincerely,

P. T. Perkins
Management Accountant

Blendyarn Berhad: Analysis of actual performance for the four weeks ending 28 May

Budgeted profit (on 10,000 kg)			£20,000
Add: Fixed overheads			
Administrative staff wages		£1,000	
Marketing staff wages		4,000	
Occupancy costs		10,000	
			15,000
Budgeted contribution			£35,000

Notes:	*Variances*	*Favourable*	*Unfavourable*
1	Gain in contribution due to increase in selling price	£10,000	
2	Loss in contribution due to monsoon		£5,250
3	Costs still paid during period cleaning up after monsoon:		
	Wages to operators		1,440
	Wages to supervisors		60
4	Loss in contribution due to walkout		3,500
5	Costs still paid during walkout		
	Wages to supervisors		40
6	Increase in material prices:		
	Wool		7,500
	Oil, dyestuffs etc (usage/price)		706
7	Increase in labour costs:		
	Operators		480
	Supervisors		24
	Total variances	£10,000	£19,000

		9,000
Actual contribution towards fixed overheads and profit		26,000

Deduct: Budget fixed overheads:			
Administrative		5,000	
Occupancy		10,000	
		15,000	
Variances:			
Administrative staff	250		
Sales staff	750		
Additional expenditure due to monsoon (contractors' costs)	2,500	3,500	18,500
Actual net profit for period			£7,500

Workings

Sales

	Notes	kg	£ contribution		Notes	kg	£ contribution
Budgeted sales		10,000	35,000	Actual			
Price (F)	(1)	—	10,000	sales		7,500	36,250
				Volume (U)			
				monsoon	(2)	1,500	5,250
				walkout	(4)	1,000	3,500
		10,000	£45,000			10,000	£45,000

Materials — wool

	kg	£			kg	£
Actual cost	3,750	30,000	Standard cost			
			of output		3,750	22,500
			Price (U)	(6)	—	7,500
	3,750	£30,000			3,750	£30,000

Materials — oil, dyestuffs

	£			£
Actual cost	4,456	Standard cost		3,750
		of output		
		Total variance		
		(U)	(6)	706
	£4,456			£4,456

Operatives

	hours	£			hours	£
Actual cost	8,640	9,120	Standard cost			
			of output		7,200	7,200
			Rate (U) — due			
			to walkout	(7)	—	480
			Idle time (U)			
			during cleaning	(3)	1,440	1,440
	8,640	£9,120			8,640	£9,120

	hours	£	*Supervisors*		hours	£
Actual cost	320	424	Standard cost of output		240	300
			Rate (U) — due to walkout by operatives	(7)	—	24
			Idle time (U) — during cleaning	(3)	48	60
			Idle time (U) — during walkout	(5)	32	40
	320	£424			320	£424

Notes:

(1) In the sales variance account the actual sales are always stated at the *actual contribution* assuming that costs are at *standard*.

In this example:

2,500 kg @ £10	£25,000
5,000 kg @ £12	60,000
Total revenue	85,000
Deduct: Standard variable cost 7,500 kg @ £6·50	48,750
	£36,250

Alternatively, the normal selling price is £10 per kg, giving the contribution of £3·50 per unit. As 5,000 kg were sold at £2 more than the usual selling price this brought in an additional £10,000 contribution:

Normal contribution — 7,500 kg @ £3·50	£26,250
Additional contribution due to increase in price	10,000
	£36,250

(2) Budgeted production was 10,000 kg for May, whereas actual production was 7,500 kg. One week's production was lost — three days while the contract cleaners were in the factory and a further two days when the operatives refused to work until further cleaning had been carried out.

The volume variance can be attributed to these two factors:

60% of lost production, i.e. 1,500 kg to the monsoon
40% of lost production, i.e. 1,000 kg to the walkout.

(3) The idle time in the operatives' variance account represents the three days when the contract cleaners were working in the factory. The original budget called for 9,600 hours of operatives' time for four weeks (20 working days); 1,440 hours would therefore be lost during three working days.

Note: There is no efficiency variance as the time allowed is 7,200 hours and the time worked is (8,640 − 1,440) = 7,200 hours.

(4) The idle time in the supervisors' variance account is equivalent to five working days, that is, 80 hours. This can be analysed between the two causes:

60% of 80 hours for cleaning operation   =   48 hours
40% of 80 hours during the operatives' walkout   =   32 hours

FURTHER VARIANCE ANALYSIS
47.

(a)

	Material P gallons	Material P £	Material Q gallons	Material Q £	Total gallons	Total £
(1) Actual price, actual mix, actual quantity	45,000	36,000	55,00	53,350	100,000	89,350
(2) *Price variance*	— (U)	4,500	— (U)	2,750	— (U)	7,250
(3) Standard price, actual mix, actual quantity	45,000	31,500	55,000	50,600	100,000	82,100
(4) *Mix variance*	5,000 (F)	3,500	5,000 (U)	4,600	— (U)	1,100
(5) Standard price, standard mix, actual quantity	50,000	£35,000	50,000	£46,000	100,000	81,000
(6) Normal loss 10%					10,000	—
(7) Standard yield					90,000	81,000
(8) *Yield variance*					2,070 (F)	1,863
(9) Standard cost of actual output					92,070	£82,863

Summary

		£		£
(i)	Material price variance			7,250 (U)
(ii)	Material usage variance:	Mix 1,100 (U)		
		Yield 1,863 (F)		
				763 (F)
	Total material variance			£6,487 (U)

(b) *Relevance to management control*

Calculation of a material mix variance implies that the input ingredients are interchangeable. In the above example, an assumption exists that a product of acceptable quality can be manufactured most economically by using materials P and Q in equal proportions; consequently, when the standard proportions are varied, and the prices of individual materials are different, a variance will arise which represents the cost effect of deviating from the manufacturing specification.

For management control purposes, the material mix variance will have relevance by indicating an area of inefficiency for further investigation and remedial action. If the variance is unfavourable, management will need to know why the standard has not been complied with: if favourable, management will be concerned with the possible adverse effect on yield and/ or product quality.

PROCESS COSTING

48.

(a) *Refining process account*

	kg	£		kg	£
Materials					
A (3/6)	2,250 70p	1,575	Blending process		
B (2/6)	1,500 60p	900	account	3,500 90p	3,150
C (1/6)	750 30p	225	(working 2)		
Labour		120	Normal loss a/c		
Overhead		600	(20% of 4,500)	900 20p	180
(working 1)			Abnormal loss		
			a/c (working 2)	100 90p	90
	4,500	£3,420		4,500	£3,420

(b) *Blending process account*

	kg		£		kg		£
Refining process				Finished stock			
account	3,500	90p	3,150	account			
D (2/3)	1,400	100p	1,400	(working) 3)	5,100	110p	5,610
E (1/3)	700	120p	840	Normal loss a/c			
Labour			64	(10% of 5,600)	560	40p	224
Overhead							
(working 1)			240				
Analyst's fee			74				
Abnormal gain							
account							
(working 3)	60	110p	66				
	5,660		£5,834		5,660		£5,834

(c) *Normal loss account*

	kg		£		kg		£
Refining process							
account							
(20% of 4,500)	900	20p	180	Blending process			
				account			
				(sacrifice of			
Blending				normal loss,			
process account				being abnormal			
(10% of 5,600)	560	40p	224	gain)	60	40p	24
				Cash (sale			
				proceeds)			
				refining	900	20p	180
				blending	500	40p	200
	1,460		£404		1,460		£404

(d) *Abnormal losses and gains account*

	kg	£		kg	£
Refining process a/c (abnormal loss)	100 90p	90	Blending process account (abnormal gain)	60 110p	66
Normal loss a/c (sacrifice of normal loss, being abnormal gain)	60 40p	24	(Sale proceeds) — refining	100 20p	20
			Profit & loss a/c (net abnormal loss)		28
	160	£114		160	£114

(e) *Finished stock account*

	kg	£		kg	£
Blending process a/c	5,100 110p	5,610			

Workings

(1) *Apportionment of overheads*

Total overhead	£840
Basis of apportionment	Labour hours
Labour hours refining	100
blending	40
	140

Refining process overhead $= £840 \times \dfrac{100}{140} = \underline{\underline{£600}}$

Blending process overhead $= £840 \times \dfrac{40}{140} = \underline{\underline{£240}}$

(2) *Refining process account — valuation of output and abnormal loss:*

$$\text{Cost per kg} = \frac{\text{Materials} + \text{Labour} + \text{Overhead} - \text{Proceeds from normal loss}}{\text{Expected output}}$$

$$= \frac{£2,700 + £120 + £600 - £(900 \times 20p)}{3,600\,\text{kg}}$$

$$= \frac{£3,240}{3,600 \text{ kg}}$$

$$= \underline{90\text{p per kg}}$$

(3) *Blending process account — valuation of output and abnormal loss*

$$\text{Cost per kg} = \frac{\substack{\text{Transfer from refining} + \text{Materials} + \text{Labour} + \text{Overhead} \\ - \text{Proceeds from normal loss}}}{\text{Expected output}}$$

$$= \frac{£3,150 + £2,240 + £64 + £240 + £74 - (560 \times 40\text{p})}{5,040 \text{ kg}}$$

$$= \frac{£5,544}{5,040 \text{ kg}}$$

$$= \underline{\underline{£1 \cdot 10 \text{ per kg}}}$$

(4) *Charge to the profit and loss account*

The amount debited to the profit and loss account from the abnormal loss and gains account can be checked as follows:

Refining process Abnormal loss of 100 kg @ 90p − 20p = 70p, that is,	£70
Blending process Abnormal gain of 60 kg @ 110p − 40p = 70p, that is,	£42
Net loss	£28

Tutorial note: The normal losses are shown at their sales value (if any). It is a basic principle of management accounting that abnormal losses are separated and shown at cost.

DECENTRALISATION AND PERFORMANCE EVALUATION

49.

(a) *Lanes stores: Operating report for the year ended 31 March £(figures in thousands)*

	Furniture £	Furniture £	Furniture %	Hardware £	Hardware £	Hardware %	Drapery £	Drapery £	Drapery %	Clothing £	Clothing £	Clothing %	Total £	Total £	Total %
Sales		178	100		80	100		40	100		99	100		397	100
Cost of sales		156			60			26			66			308	
Gross profit		22	12		20	25		14	35		33	33		89	22
Direct expenses															
Wages	13			12			14			18			57		
Expenses	1			0·5			0·5			1			3		
Advertising	3			0·5			0·25			4			7·75		
Total		17			13			14·75			23			67·75	
Departmental contribution		5	3		7	9		(0·75)	(2)		10	10		21·25	5

Indirect costs	
Delivery expenses	5
Administrative expenses	6
Miscellaneous expenses	2
Finance charges	1
Management fees	8
Total	22·00
Net loss	(£0·75)

	Furniture	Hardware	Drapery	Clothing
Ratios Percentage selling floor space	35%	20%	15%	30%
Percentage total contribution	23·5%	33%	(3·5%)	47%
Average stock (£000)	32	30	32	39
Stock turnover ratio $\left(\dfrac{\text{Cost of sales}}{\text{Average stock}}\right)$	4·9	2	0·8	1·7

(b) The summary trading and profit and loss account and additional departmental information illustrate a conventional way of classifying costs and revenues into direct and indirect categories. In this case, it is apparent that "direct" items are those that can be accurately associated with and allocated to the four major departments. For decision-making purposes regarding pricing/output policies of the various departments, information is required in the form which would enable comparisons of marginal cost and revenues to be made for the various alternatives.

Using the information provided requires an understanding of its limitations for this purpose, and an awareness where further investigation would be necessary. "Direct" is not synonymous with variable, and fixed cost items may be included. Similarly, the "indirect" expenses are likely to include items which do not vary with the level of activity achieved, not only of the firm as a whole, but of that of individual marketing departments. For example, the indirect delivery expense level of expenditure is likely to be related in large part to the volume of sales of the furniture department.

Departmental closures

From the above operating statement it can be seen that the drapery department is making a negative contribution to the firm's fixed overheads and profit, therefore, on the basis of these figures, this department should be closed down. This would have the effect of releasing 15% of the firm's selling floor space, which could then be utilised by the departments making positive contributions to the firm's fixed costs and profits. The floor space should be allocated to the departments offering the most contribution potential.

However, it may be that a drapery department attracts customer traffic to other departments within the store. It may be that other stores do not place much emphasis on the sale of drapery items, so that the negative contribution may be acceptable because of the service value of this department. So, before any final decision is made, the firm should try and ascertain the impact of closing this department in the form of the business other departments would lose.

The positive contribution attributed to the furniture department should be interpreted with care, in view of the earlier reference to the incidence of indirect delivery expenses. Information would be required of the effect on total delivery expense if the furniture department were closed, to enable the marginal cost to be measured and related to the apparent contribution of £5,000.

Pricing policies

Tables should be prepared showing the effect of reducing prices on the same volume of sales as presented in the operating statement. With this information, the management must then assess the effect of price elasticity of demand on sales of the departments. For example, what will be the effect in sales volume terms of a 3% increase (or decrease) in prices? This could be tabulated in flexible budget form, which would show, in the case of a price reduction, by how much sales must be increased to ensure that the same contribution is made, and, if prices are increased, by how much sales could fall before contributions were reduced.

It may be that selective price changes for different departments, or within different departments, would be a better approach. The main point is that information showing the effect of price changes, for a range of changes in sales volume at these possible prices, must be prepared and presented to management to enable them to decide whether they are prepared to face the risks and probabilities involved.

Stocks, gross profit margins, contribution ratios etc.

The stock turnover and other ratios should be examined on an interfirm basis, and also over time. From national statistics, it will be found whether ratios are favourable or not. For example, the stock turnover ratio for furniture would come out as very favourable, while those of the hardware, drapery and clothing departments are poor. This may point to an inefficient use of resources in the latter department. The firm should examine ways in which these ratios can be improved, bearing in mind the relationship between asset turnover ratios and margins.

Tutorial note: other acceptable ratios for discussion include: contribution to floor space, and expenses to sales, etc.

50.

Reporting Accountants
Middle Street
DOWNTOWN
1 November 19X5

To:
The Managing Director
Worried Limited

Dear Sir

Re: Stock turnover ratios

There are a number of reasons which make it impossible to draw conclusions on relative efficiency from the comparison of firms' stock turnover ratios. Similarly, an improvement of a firm's stock turnover ratio over time does not necessarily indicate that it is becoming more efficient in its stock control procedures.

The most obvious reasons relate to how the ratios have been calculated. Before any useful comparison can be undertaken it is necessary to be sure that the variables used in the calculation of the ratios have been valued on a standard basis. Although it is stated that the ratios have been calculated on sales over average stock, no indication is given as to whether the average stock values are calculated at cost or selling prices, and if at cost whether or not overheads are included (*see note 1*).

If it is assumed that the ratios have been calculated in the same way, many problems are still left, the major of which can be summarised as follows:

(1)   As Managing Director of Worried Ltd you are making the assumption that the higher the turnover rate the more efficient the firm, yet a higher turnover rate may not minimise stock costs. Consideration must also be given to the organisation's procurement costs if buying in, or set-up costs if manufacturing your own production. If these are high it may be that the optimum stock control policy will be to buy, or make a few very large batches each period. Although this would give a higher average stock, and thus a lower stock turnover ratio, the company's policy may minimise total cost.

(2)   One of the costs of a low stock turnover ratio are stock-out costs. Lost sales through being out of stock are not directly measurable by the stock turnover ratio, and if there are frequent stock-outs a high ratio may indicate inefficient stock control.

(3)   We are not told anything about the size of the organisations concerned. It may be that Similar Ltd is a much larger organisation than Worried Ltd and thus can gain economies of scale from lower stock holdings relative to the size of its sales. Or it may be, if Worried and Similar are in the distribution industry (either as wholesalers or retailers), where one operates a single premises, while the other has a number of premises, that the one with many outlets could gain economies of stock holding by having limited stock at each branch outlet and a centrally held "back-up" stock, thus gaining from reduced total stock holdings.

(4) Even if the companies are of the same size we are told nothing of the number of products handled. Obviously if Similar has a single product while Worried has a number of products, Similar will have advantages as far as stock holdings are concerned. In the case of Different Ltd, as far as this point is concerned, different firms in different industries can be expected to have different stock turnovers — for example, a greengrocer would be expected to have a higher stock turnover ratio than a furniture dealer.

(5) There is also the point that stock holdings are but one of the current assets a firm can have. Thus a firm may be able to "move" stock to debtors by having a special sales campaign to encourage people to buy on special credit terms. This would then reduce stock holdings and so improve the ratio. This point may also come into inter-temporal comparisons, for firms' credit policies may change (*see Note 2*).

(6) There may be problems associated with the different classes of stock, such as raw materials, work-in-progress, and finished goods. The relationship between these, their valuation methods (for example, are they valued by direct costs only or are all costs absorbed?) and so on, will affect the ratios.

(7) Different pricing policies are likely to affect turnover ratios. Various combinations of turnover ratios and gross margin will produce the same ratio of return on capital employed.

It is generally the case that when ratios are used in the comparison of different organisations, or comparisons of the same organisation on an interdepartmental or inter-temporal basis, that there are many difficulties. Without going behind the ratios and the figures used to compile them and considering the characteristics of the industry and organisation concerned, it is inadvisable to draw conclusions about comparative efficiency.

Yours faithfully

....
for Reporting Accountants

Notes:
(1) Both the numerator and the demonimator *must* be in terms of either cost or selling prices (and mathematically you will see that whichever base is used the ratio must come out at the same value).

(2) Over time, firms change the bases of stock valuation. Any such changes affect inter-temporal comparisons of stock turnover ratio between different years for that firm.

51.

(a) (i) A profit centre is a division of a business organisation which is responsible for both revenue and expenditure, that is, a division whose manager's objective can be expressed in terms of profit.

(ii) The major problem in maintaining effective budgetary control in a decentralised company is the need to reconcile the individual objectives of profit centre managers with overall company objectives. The management accountant, therefore, will aim at constructing a budgetary control system which will enable top management to plan and control activities in accordance with corporate objectives without detracting from the motivational force of profit centre goals. His main difficulties are likely to be:

(1) Definition of profit centre responsibility; activities and authorities may overlap and if it is difficult to pinpoint responsibility, the effectiveness of profit centre targets is impaired.

(2) Determination of realistic targets; as stated above, individual profit centre targets can only be set after consideration of the overall business objectives. If the profit centre manager's profit achievement requires considerable adjustment before it can be compared with the target, budgetary control procedures are cumbersome and lose impact.

(3) Short-term profit goals may conflict with longer-term objectives, even within individual profit centres. It will be difficult to allow for this factor when formulating budgets or when measuring performance.

(4) Intra-company transactions; where one profit centre purchases goods or services from another centre, problems will arise in pricing such transactions.
    The management accountant will be actively concerned in ensuring that transfer prices are fair to both parties, that the pricing system does not act to the detriment of the company's interests and that negotiation and administration involved in transfer pricing are not disproportionate to the benefit derived from maintaining autonomous profit centres.

(5) Apportionments; establishment of profit centres usually involves apportionment of common costs and/or assets. The management accountant will aim at making such apportionments as equitable as possible.

(6) Uncontrollable costs; profit centre results may be materially affected by costs which are outside the responsibility of the profit centre manager. Such costs need to be identified for meaningful performance reports.

(iii) A computer can contribute in resolving the management accountant's difficulties by improving the quality and availability of information at his disposal. The establishment of profit centres generates a large amount of analysis work in preparing budgets and operating reports. The ability of a computer to store a mass of data and its facilities for speedy calculation and analysis will reduce the constraints which face the management accountant when he determines the information requirements of the budgetary system. In addition, the following facilities available in a computer-based system can enable information to be presented in ways which will meet the needs of different management levels:

(1) Consolidation of information to reflect organisational responsibilities.

(2) Suppression of selected data.

(3) Automatic identification of exceptions.

(4) Calculation of performance indicators.

Availability of computer facilities will also increase the scope for use of management techniques, such as simulation, probability/sensitivity analysis and linear programming. Use of these techniques will aid the assessment of how individual profit centre objectives affect corporate goals.

(b) To: The Managing Director
From: The Accountant   5th June 19X5

Problems of transfer pricing

The main problem with transfer pricing is to determine a suitable price at which the goods and services may be transferred between profit centres. In this case the manager of each profit centre has been told to run his activity as if he were in business on his own account. Each manager is therefore responsible for the level of profits in his department and his performance will also be evaluated on the basis of the profit level in that department.

The basic concept underlying a profit centre is that the profit centre manager must be able to act with complete freedom and independence, and still be able to act in the overall interests of the company. The method of transfer pricing must satisfy three criteria:

(i)   it must ensure that the manager is able to achieve goal congruence without explicitly considering the actions of the managers of other profit centres;

(ii) it must be a fair system so that a manager's performance can be evaluated on the basis of the profits of his profit centre;

(ii) it must also give the manager the freedom to deal outside the company if he is able to obtain better terms.

In this case, the parts and service department should charge a normal commercial rate for the preparation of new cars for final delivery and for repairing used vehicles prior to delivery. If this method is not acceptable to the profit centre managers, an alternative method would be for the two managers to negotiate a price at something below the normal market rate, so that the new cars and used vehicles departments are encouraged to use the parts and service department which in turn is assured of a customer who may be willing to wait while more urgent repairs are carried out, so enabling facilities to be used which may otherwise be idle and bringing in an income which is comparable to the normal commercial rate. It is essential in this case that the departmental managers have the full support of company management to negotiate a market-based transfer price.

The company's second problem is the transfer of used cars (which have been traded-in for new cars) between the new cars and used cars departments. The company's commission policy should be examined, as salesmen usually have a limited authority to adjust prices for new and used cars and to quote a price for a trade-in car, knowing that by doing so their level of commission will be affected. Guidelines should be established for a transfer price for used cars, perhaps based on *Glass's Guide*, and provided that trade-in cars are purchased at these prices, the used car department will be happy to accept the cars. If special terms are given to a customer who is buying a new car and trading-in a used car, this is the responsibility of the new cars department and is a cost which should be charged to that department.

TRANSFER PRICING

52.

(a) (i) *Producing at 80% capacity: transfer price £200/tonne*

	Wholesale customers 1,000 tonnes £/tonne	Retail group 600 tonnes £/tonne			Retail group B Ltd 600 tonnes £/tonne
Selling price	180	200			400
			T'fer price	£/t 200	
Variable cost	70	70			60 260
Contribution	110	130			140
Total contribution	£110,000	£78,000			£84,000
		188,000			
Fixed costs		100,000			40,000
Profit		£88,000	+		£44,000 = £132,000

Wholesale group 1,600 tonnes

Producing at 80% capacity: transfer price £180/tonne

	Wholesale group		Retail group	B Ltd
Profit as above	£88,000		£44,000	£132,000
Transfer price adjustment				
600 tonnes × £20 =	− 12,000		+ 12,000	—
	£76,000		£56,000	£132,000

(ii) *Producing at 100% capacity: transfer price £200/tonne*

	Wholesale group 2,000 tonnes		Retail group	B Ltd
	Wholesale customers 1,000 tonnes £/tonne	Retail group 1,000 tonnes £/tonne	1,000 tonnes £/tonne	
Selling price	180	200	320	
		T'fr price £/t 200		
Variable cost	70	70	60 260	
Contribution	110	130	60	
Total contribution	£110,000	£130,000		
		240,000	60,000	
Fixed costs		100,000	40,000	
Profit		£140,000 +	£20,000 = £160,000	

Producing at 100% capacity: transfer price £180/tonne

	Wholesale group		Retail group	B Ltd
Profit as above	£144,000		£20,000	£160,000
Transfer price adjustment				
1,000 tonnes × £20	− 20,000		+ 20,000	—
Profit	£120,000		£40,000	£160,000

(b) The following points should be noted:

(i) A change in the transfer price has no effect on the group's profit, but only on the distribution of this profit between the two divisions.

(ii) An expansion of volume to the 100% capacity level is beneficial to the wholesale group and the whole group — B Ltd — but not the retail group, irrespective of the transfer price used.

MANAGEMENT INFORMATION SYSTEMS AND COMMUNICATION

53.

(a) The first questions that the management accountant should ask before drawing up a report are "What is the purpose" of the report and "Who is going to use it?" His answers to these questions will have a bearing upon how he will deal with any quantitative information in it.

His reports may express the quantitative information in physical or money terms or a combination of both. Reports on the number of employees cannot easily have a value placed upon them so will be expressed in physical terms. Reports on the liquidity situation will be in money terms. Other reports, such as those concerning sales, purchases or stock may be in a combination of both. For example, a report on stock may have stock levels reported in physical terms, showing details of maximum and minimum stock holding quantities and reorder quantities. Stock currently held could be expressed in both physical and money terms. The former is useful when prices are changing, as once the price is known the total value of the stock can easily be calculated.

When the reporting accountant has a choice he will consider the level of the management to whom he is reporting. For example, management at lower levels may be disinterested in accounting jargon and prefer reports in terms of physical items. Top management, who are concerned with profit, want information in money terms. Money terms enable heterogeneous physical items to be converted for reporting purposes into a common base. At lower levels within a firm there tends to be more homogeneity, which is perhaps one factor which influences the generalisation that reports at lower levels are easier to express in physical terms.

With the problem of inflation it is becoming increasingly prevalent to express things in "real terms". Physical units are already in real terms, and expressing them this way avoids the necessity of any conversion into terms of money in current purchasing power.

(b) Most decisions are made using information about factors which are quantifiable — that is information for which the costs of alternative courses of action are easy to state and verify in money terms. However, qualitative factors may raise important considerations, although if an attempt is made to measure them in money terms this will be imprecise or impossible.

Yet if the qualitative factors are taken into consideration, frequently a different decision may result. For example, in make-or-buy decisions using the contribution approach, qualitative factors are left out of the calculations. Rarely is it suggested that, when there is short-run spare capacity available, the cost of returning to an original supplier after having made a "make" decision may be difficult and should be allowed for in the appraisal exercise. Thus any qualitative costs associated with becoming self-reliant must be added to the other, easily verifiable, costs of making the product yourself.

Simple examples of this approach of quantifying qualitative factors can be seen by looking at examples from manpower and materials.

It may cost a firm less to employ an inexperienced production controller, but the work of such a man will be inferior to that of his experienced counterpart. On the factory floor a firm may be able to replace certain types of skilled labour with semi-skilled. However, a greater wastage of material may result.

In both these cases the organisational decision-maker should try to allow for the effect of these decisions on output in terms of losses in production or wastage of materials.

The cheaper materials or components used in making a product will reduce its quality as well as its cost. The effect of this may show up in terms of lost custom, a larger number of rejects, more complaints or greater servicing costs at a later date. Thus the firm should try to quantify the qualitative effects of a decision to use cheaper materials.

Although it may be that the qualitative factors are implicitly weighed by the decision-maker, the more he tries to put a value on them in money terms, the better. Even if this cannot be done precisely, the fact that an effort has been made to do it will lead towards better decisions.

Qualitative factors can also be brought into decision-making by the use of some points-rating system, in which points on a scale are allocated to the factor concerned as far as each decision-pathway is concerned. If a number of qualitative factors are being considered this way, then their relative importance can also be weighted.

Thus, qualitative factors can be brought into decision-making situations (i) by trying to place a money cost or value on them, (ii) by rating them, or (iii) at least listing them for formal consideration in some intuitive way.

54.

(a) There are a number of disadvantages to a firm when each of its information systems is considered in isolation. These disadvantages concern both the type and amount of information generated for use by the organisation, which includes both internal and external information, and problems of access to, and duplication of, information.

As far as the management accountant is concerned, if he looks at the information of a single area for decision-making and uses this, and only this information, it may lead to suboptimal decisions being made. For example, a department may be making an unprofitable product and decide to discontinue it — a decision which in respect of the department concerned may be correct. However, it may be that this product is part of a range which helps to make the other products the firm produces more marketable.

As far as external information is concerned, as with all information, there are certain costs associated with collecting it. It may be that, by using economies of scale and collecting all the external information required by the firm's subinformation system, this can be done more efficiently and more cheaply on a centralised basis. To take an example from market research: in a survey, questions required to be answered by a number of departments could be included on the same questionnaire.

Perhaps it was the coming of the computer, together with IDP (integrated data processing) that highlighted the need for a firm's information systems to be integrated into a coherent whole. For example, labour cost information from the same source can be used for costing purposes, payroll applications, and by the personnel department. Through the central storage of such information in the computer, wasteful duplication is reduced and access of all departments within an organisation to this information is facilitated. It also has the advantage of meaning that all decision-makers within the organisation can make their decisions using identical information, which reduces the likelihood of incompatible decisions being made.

(b) Many organisations in manufacturing industries do try to make sure that all costs are eventually charged on some basis, to production departments.

The major argument generally given for doing this is based upon the idea that all costs must be met by the firm, and to ensure that this is done these costs must be passed down through all levels of the organisation. Furthermore, it is suggested that if overheads were not absorbed at lower levels, such as departmental or product level, then there would be the danger that even if all departments and products seemed to be profitable, the firm as a whole might be incurring a loss. So as well as allocating those direct costs which are controllable by departmental managers, the firm's marketing, administration, and other general overheads, which are not controllable by departmental managers at those levels, are also apportioned to departments. (Horngren has attributed the practice to the powerful influence that product costing has on information presentation.)

It is the validity of an argument such as this that can be questioned, and there are three important points which arise:

(i)   Should uncontrollable costs be apportioned to departments, and can departmental managers really be responsible for them?

(ii)   The departmental manager may realise that the apportionment of such costs is arbitrary. Today most production engineers in charge of departments have either been taught, or picked up, many of the ideas in cost and management accounting applicable to decision-making and control. Thus they may be led to think that all the cost data produced for their department is just as arbitrary, and so ignore it all when making decisions.

(iii) There is a danger of departmental managers thinking that the firm's common costs apportioned to their department are, in fact, relevant, and so make decisions about departmental activity based on these and vary activity accordingly.

The departmental manager should be made to focus his attention on the costs which he can control and which are his direct responsibility. If an apportionment of other costs is to be made to a department, then it should be clearly separated out, so as not to become confused with direct costs when decisions are being made. The costs that a departmental manager should be concerned with are the direct costs of the products that his department makes, the direct expenses of the department itself, and also information on the shadow prices of resources from other areas within the firm necessary to enable him to achieve the level of activity that will move the firm into a profit-maximising situation.

COST REDUCTION SCHEMES

55.

(a) Work study is also called time and motion study in the United States, and is defined in the *British Standard Glossary of Terms* (3138) as follows:

> A generic term for those techniques, particularly method study and work measurement, which are used in the examination of human work in all its contexts, and which lead systematically to the investigation of all the factors which affect the efficiency and economy of the situation being reviewed in order to effect improvement.

Basically, this definition is stating that work study is the systematic investigation of human work in order to find more efficient methods of carrying it out, and it can be seen that the techniques of work study can be used to examine either existing or proposed work. It should be noted that, as with the majority of management techniques, it can only help and guide management and does not in itself replace good management.

The major objectives of work study can be classified as:

(i) The development of optimum work methods which provide for the optimum use of factors of production available to an organisation, including money, materials, machines, men and management, with the emphasis on the human input into the work involved.

(ii) The establishment of standards against which performance can be measured.

(iii) The installation of the optimal work methods developed, and work measurement systems established.

The objectives are most likely to be achieved if it is appreciated that work frequently becomes carried out in a routine manner by habit, and that even if local management have the time to examine work which is their responsibility they are not likely to do this as objectively, nor appreciate possible improvements, as well as a group of specialists carrying out the investigations. The work study people will be able to examine problem areas, such as where there are bottlenecks, too much rejected work, or poor morale, as well as considering incentive schemes to improve productivity. They should focus their efforts on those areas which will have the greater significance on the organisation's profitability.

(b) The two major techniques used in work study are:

(i)   method study, and

(ii) work measurement.

Method study

This is the critical study of the ways of doing work. The steps in method study are to:

(1) *Select an area of study* which will frequently be done by the management of the organisation or a work study committee. This will be done taking cognisance of the fact that any such study will have costs associated with it, so there must be the prospect of gains which are greater than the costs concerned. Thus, the ranking of possible areas of study, taking a cost-benefit approach, is useful.

(2) *Collecting the facts.* The work study personnel will collect and record the facts about the area of study being undertaken. This will be done by observation rather than by asking people what tasks they do. Data for analysis can be recorded using films, charts, diagrams etc., and in the latter two cases, standardised symbols have been developed to enable the succinct recording of operations, transporting, storage etc.

(3) *Consider alternative methods.* As well as analysing the current methods used, in the case of the study of existing work, alternative approaches will be considered as to how to carry out this, or new, assignments. This is the stage where it becomes important to have people who are objective in dealing with the study, who have no self-interest to preserve and can have an open mind about improvements. It is also at this stage that the purpose of what is being (or required to be) done, will have to be carefully questioned. Consideration will be given to changes in the location of the work, the type of personnel carrying it out, and other factors which affect cost and efficiency.

(4) *Develop and install.* Once the best alternative has been decided upon it may be that changes in the technology used or operations carried out will require the development of new methods, tools, etc. Developments will have to be carefully considered in the light of such factors as costs, safety, possibility of acceptance etc. These will then be installed after careful planning for their introduction, in order to minimise interruptions to production flows. Frequently, a network analysis approach will be taken in the installation of new methods.

(5) *Reappraise.* Once any new system has been installed this is not the end of the Work Study department's involvement. There must be follow-up to ensure that the system is installed and maintained as envisaged, and also to check whether the benefits expected to be gained from the new approach do, in fact, accrue.

Work measurement

This is the assessment of the time that the job or operation should take to be carried out. It should follow the method study of a particular area. For, if the method of carrying out the job is not the optimal one, then there is little sense in trying to time and set standards for doing it.

The approach of work measurement is to examine the human work content of a job, and measure the various aspects of this with the aim of producing standard units of measurement for it in time terms. When obtaining the standard time for jobs, a number of things have to be taken into consideration. These include information on the *standard performance* of a job, based on the time that an average qualified worker should take to do it. This is done by timing such an average worker by observation of his/her performance of the job. Timings will be adjusted for such things as relaxation allowances (official breaks), and contingency allowances (which will cover any difficulties envisaged concerning carrying out the work).

Work measurement is usually carried out either by time study or motion study. In the former, the worker is directly observed, timed and rated for carrying out the job. In this it is important that the timing of the natural rhythm of the worker is obtained and that the worker is working as normally as possible. In the case of the latter, due consideration is given to the efficiency and placement of tools and equipment and the movements of the operatives.

Because of the cost of doing this, the use of statistical methods has been developed in the form of activity sampling to help reduce the costs associated with work study surveys. The biggest problems associated with time and motion study come from the behavioural area. To help overcome these it is important that the study is not carried out in secret and that the people being studied are kept informed about its purpose. There should be emphasis on the fact that the objective of such studies is not to cause redundancies within the organisation, although it may lead to some transfers.

In conclusion, work study is one of the ways in which the management can try and reduce the costs, or achieve greater production from the same costs. The standards produced by work study form the basis of many of the management accountant's control systems, and although he/she cannot be expected to be an expert in this area, he/she should be familiar with the advantages that it offers, and be aware of its limitations.

APPENDIX FOUR

Glossary of Financial Terms

Note: The chapter and paragraph numbers indicated in brackets show where a full explanation is given in the text.

Absorption costing. Each unit of output is charged with both variable and fixed production costs. The fixed production costs are treated as *part of* actual production. Closing stock is therefore valued on a full production cost basis, and when sold in the next period these costs are released and matched with the revenue of that period. (5, 1.0)

Attributable cost. The cost per unit that could be avoided if a product or function were discontinued without changing the supporting organisation structure. (7, 5.0)

Breakeven point. The point at which sales equal total costs, and there is no profit or loss. (6, 2.0)

Budget. A financial and/or quantitative plan for a defined period of time. (11, 1.0)

Budgetary control. A control technique whereby actual results are compared with budgets, and any differences arising are made the responsibility of key individuals who can either exercise control action or revise the original budgets. (11, 1.0)

Byproduct. A product which is incidental to the main product(s) and of lower sales value. (10, 1.0)

Cost. The value attributed to a resource. (2, 1.0)

Cost centre. Any area of activity which attracts costs. (4, 2.0(a))

Cost reduction techniques. These enable costs to be reduced from some predetermined norm, while maintaining the functional value of the product or service. (22, 1.0)

Decentralisation. The freedom to make decisions. (18, 1.0)

Dysfunctional decision. A decision made by a manager which is beneficial to his own division, but suboptimal to the organisation as a whole. (18, 4.0)

Expected value. A weighted average representing the most likely future average outcome on the assumption that the activity is repeated a large number of times. (8, 2.0)

Fixed cost. A cost which is unaffected by changes in activity levels. (2, 2.0(g))

Flexible budgets. These are prepared for a range of activity levels in order to provide a basis for comparison with actual. (11, 7.0)

Investment centre. Where responsibility lies for costs, revenue, and investments. (18, 5.0)

Joint products. These are simultaneously produced from a common set of inputs via a single process. (10, 1.0)

Management accounting. The application of accounting techniques to the provision of information designed to assist all levels of management in *planning* and *controlling* the activities of the firm, and in *decision-making*. (1, 1.0)

Management information system (MIS). A system which enables management to provide the appropriate information at optimal cost so that managers can manage. (21, 1.0)

Marginal costing. Each unit of output is charged with variable production costs. Fixed production costs are not considered as actual costs of production, but rather as those costs which provide for a period the capacity to allow production to take place. They are therefore treated as costs of the period and charged to the period. They are not carried forward in closing stock, which is valued on a variable production cost basis. (5, 1.0)

Opportunity cost. The greatest benefit foregone or sacrifice made by choosing a particular course of action or using a particular resource. (7, 3.0)

Probability. Expresses the likelihood of an event occurring. (8, 2.0(e))

Profit centre. Where responsibility lies for costs and revenue. (18, 5.0)

Relevant cost. Any cost which is effected by the decision at hand. (7, 2.0)

Sensitivity analysis. A control technique whereby the effects of changes in the variables on the final result are gauged. (8, 2.0(d))

Split-off point. The point at which joint products become separately identifiable. (10, 1.0)

Standard costing. The setting of predetermined cost estimates in order to provide a basis for comparison with actual. (13, 2.0)

Standard hour. A measure of work content that should be achieved in one hour. (13, 3.0)

Transfer price. Where notional value placed on goods and services is transferred from one division to another within a business organisation. (19, 1.0)

Value analysis. A technique which examines all aspects of an existing product or component in order to reduce costs whilst maintaining or improving its quality. (22, 2.0)

Variable cost. A cost which varies directly with changes in the level of activity. (2, 2.0(g)(ii))

Work study. A technique which investigates work, existing or proposed, in order to find more efficient ways of performing tasks. (22, 2.0)

Zero base budgeting. A technique whereby every item of expenditure in the budget is fully justified — that is, one starts from zero. (11, 8.0)

Index